PADRE PIO
AND AMERICA

*"He shall feed his flock like a shepherd:
he shall gather together the lambs with his
arm, and shall take them up in his bosom,
and he himself shall carry them that are
with young."* —Isaias 40:11

D0725615

Our Lady of Grace Friary

Padre Pio distributing medals to American GIs.

PADRE PIO AND AMERICA

(Formerly *The Holy Man on the Mountain*)

Frank M. Rega

"And I will give you pastors according to my own heart, and they shall feed you with knowledge and doctrine."
—Jeremias 3:15

TAN BOOKS AND PUBLISHERS, INC.
Rockford, Illinois 61105

Copyright © 2004, 2005 by Frank M. Rega

First edition published in 2004 by Aventine Press, Chula Vista, CA, under the title *The Holy Man on the Mountain.*

ISBN 0-89555-820-3

Cover photo of Padre Pio and many other photos courtesy of Our Lady of Grace Capuchin Friary, San Giovanni Rotondo, Italy.

All rights reserved. Brief selections of text from this book may be quoted or copied for non-profit use without permission, and brief selections may be quoted by a reviewer in a review without permission. Otherwise, no part of this book may be reproduced or transmitted in any form or by any means, electronic or mechanical, including photocopying, recording, or by any information storage or retrieval system, without permission in writing from the Publisher.

Printed and bound in the United States of America.

TAN BOOKS AND PUBLISHERS, INC.
P.O. Box 424
Rockford, Illinois 61105

2005

Dedication

This book is dedicated to the American GIs who met
Padre Pio during World War II,
and to their families and friends, whose co-operation,
sharing and enthusiasm
have made this book possible.

Table of Contents

Acknowledgments

Although many people have co-operated and helped with this book, it would never have gotten off the ground were it not for two Padre Pio devotees, Jeanette and Joan Salerno of Brooklyn. It was the Salerno sisters, along with Buck Fleming from Colorado (CEO of Admin Force), who first suggested that I pursue my interest in writing, after my early retirement from the computer field. When I emailed Jeanette and Joan, asking them what they thought of a book about Padre Pio and America, Joan replied, "As soon as I read your idea, it was, WHAM!"

Thanks go to Alice Coble for allowing me to include her husband Bob's manuscript in the book, and to the Salernos for introducing me to Alice. Special thanks to the late Charles Mandina for providing the contact information for a critically important core group of American GIs who had met Padre Pio during World War II. In addition, Julie Fitts-Ritter, of the Padre Pio Foundation of America, provided the names of a number of persons who were interviewed for this book, including Mrs. Rita Peluso. Julie also arranged to have the chapter on Padre Pio's father, Grazio Forgione, published in the Foundation's newsletter. The efforts of Ray Waychunas, who gives talks about Padre Pio in the Pennsylvania area, are especially appreciated. Ray read and commented on every chapter during the course of the writing of the book. Also, I want to recognize the kind assistance of Maria Calandra of the National Centre for Padre Pio. I am grateful to Mario Avignone for granting permission to reproduce parts of his unpublished manuscript, which describes his encounters with Padre Pio during the war years. Also, thanks to C. Bernard Ruffin for sharing documents he received from the late Fr. John Schug, related to the "Flying Monk" episodes.

There are so many World War II veterans and their spouses who eagerly shared their stories and photos, that I don't want to single out any in particular, since it would be unfair to the others. Their names appear together in the "oral history" section of the references, as well as in the text itself. I would like to thank them for giving me a sense of the great affection they felt for Padre Pio, and of how important it was for them to be able to share their memories of him. They made me realize that it was both a privilege and a responsibility to be able to gather their testimonies for this book.

At the Friary in San Giovanni Rotondo, I would like to thank Charles Abercrombie, Antonio Siena and Julie Cifaldi for their help in resolving many issues. I am also grateful to the Capuchins of Our Lady of Grace Friary for permission to quote extensively from their many books and periodicals, as well as to use a number of their photos.

Preface

I came to know of Padre Pio only gradually, discovering him just a few years after his death in 1968. Perhaps a friend had told me about him, or I might have heard of him through my interest in St. Francis of Assisi. As a Capuchin friar, Padre Pio was himself a Franciscan. I cannot recall any particular book or article I read about him; instead, it seems that this friar from Southern Italy, well, just crept up on me.

As I learned more about him, and saw the photos of his friary, of Our Lady of Grace Church and of the adjacent hospital he built, called the House for the Relief of Suffering, an attraction for this distant realm began to grow. Soon the very words themselves, such as "Gargano" mountain and the nearby shrine to St. Michael, "Monte Sant'Angelo," and the Italian name for his hospital, *Casa Sollievo della Sofferenza*, began to take on a fairy-tale quality. Even the names of the towns associated with him, "San Giovanni Rotondo" and "Pietrelcina," conjured up some magical sunshiny world. Included in this world was "Foggia," the provincial capital which played an important part in Padre Pio's life and turns up in so many stories about the American soldiers who visited him during the War. Foggia was the closest rail terminal to the Friary, where the trains from Rome and Naples dropped off their pilgrims and visitors, and to me it seemed to be the imaginary gateway to this mystical land.

But most of all, it was the sense of the spiritual and of the peaceful awareness of God that one associates with Padre Pio and the places where he lived that continued to attract me. Finally, in the early 1990's, with the approach of the 25th anniversary of his death, I began to read about a spate of

"Padre Pio Pilgrimages" leaving from the United States for San Giovanni Rotondo, Rome, Assisi and other Italian shrines. The lure could no longer be resisted. Although I had never been out of the U.S.A. and was about 50 years old, I obtained my passport, signed up for an anniversary trip and began to learn the Italian language during Monday evening adult education classes. Even though my heritage is from the "Old Country" via my grandparents, I had never learned the language. My parents, who were born in America, only spoke Italian when they didn't want us children to know what they were talking about!

On the 1993 pilgrimage that I had ultimately chosen, our group's anticipation grew as the bus made its way into Southern Italy. As we climbed the slopes of the Gargano, my eyes were taking in everything, hoping to catch that first glimpse of a building or landscape that I could recognize from the pictures I had seen. We reached the outskirts of San Giovanni Rotondo while it was still daylight, and then suddenly I spotted it, jutting out from the side of the mountain, extending along the hillside, solid looking, like a golden granite monument. It was Padre Pio's great legacy, his majestic hospital, the House for the Relief of Suffering. I had seen so many photos of it in books, and now it seemed that one of these photographs had just come to life, moving in three dimensions as the bus slowly rolled along. Soon the Friary and its churches, the original and the newer one, came into view. I had entered another world, not just geographically, but spiritually and with my whole being.

Here was a world where the only regret is that one has to leave it behind—but always with the hope of returning soon. Hence, it was not long before I began planning my second trip, and a year later I joined Jeanette and Joan Salerno's "Pilgrimage to Padre Pio—1994." We were fortunate to have as our spiritual director the late Fr. John Schug, author of

two of my favorite books about Padre Pio. It was on this pilgrimage that I heard the story of the "Flying Monk." During
the Second World War, not a bomb fell on San Giovanni
Rotondo, although nearby cities such as Foggia lay in ruins.
Reportedly, Allied pilots did not drop their deadly cargo over
Padre Pio's town because the apparition of a bearded monk
in the skies waved them away. Coincidentally, at the very
time of our visit, one of the leading Italian weekly magazines
ran a feature story on the "Flying Monk," which had most of
us on the trip buzzing, especially Fr. Schug. Tales such as
this only enhanced my interest in learning more about this
saintly "miracle man."

There were two more visits to San Giovanni Rotondo during the nineties. During this time I continued progressing
little by little in my Italian, to the point where I subscribed
to the Italian language edition of the monthly magazine, *The
Voice of Padre Pio*, published at Padre Pio's friary by the
Capuchins. I also kept up my interest in him by building an
extensive web site, www.sanpadrepio.com and by starting an
internet-based Padre Pio discussion and prayer group.

In the fall of 2003, I took an early retirement from my
career as a software engineer. Two of my friends, who do not
know each other and who live on opposite sides of the country, suggested, almost simultaneously, that I pursue my
interest in writing. It seemed the natural choice to write
about Padre Pio. The idea for this particular book about his
connections with America and Americans . . . well . . . just
crept up on me.

Introduction

Rome, June 16, 2002. Pope John Paul II canonized a new Saint, an Italian known and loved throughout the world and especially in the United States of America, Padre Pio of Pietrelcina. The Pope announced that he is to be officially designated in the registry of the Church's Saints as "St. Pio of Pietrelcina." But to millions around the world he remains simply . . . Padre Pio.

Padre Pio was one of the spiritual giants of the 20th century, and among contemporary Catholics, he ranks with Mother Teresa in fame and following. Born in 1887, he lived until shortly after Vatican Council II, passing away in 1968. He belonged to the Capuchin Order, a branch of the Franciscans, and was the first Catholic priest in history to receive the stigmata, the wounds of Christ. (St. Francis, the first known stigmatist, was a deacon.) His popularity continues to grow in the United States, where numerous organizations, foundations and individual ministries are dedicated to propagating his memory and teachings.

Americans familiar with Padre Pio view him from a host of perspectives. Some see him as a great thaumaturge, the miracle worker of the age, who effected innumerable cures of both body and soul. Many are fascinated by tales of his gift of bilocation, when reliable witnesses saw him in faraway places and countries, while at the same time he was ensconced in a little friary in Italy. He was a priest who heard Confessions like no other priests of his day, revealing to people the secret sins they had neglected to confess. He communicated with the souls of the deceased in Purgatory and with his Guardian Angel. Many consider his Mass to have been our most perfect living image of Christ's own suffering and death. Theologians see him as one of the most important mystics in the history of the Church. But to himself, he was merely a "simple friar who prays."

The life of this 20th-century Saint, who never left Italy, is interwoven with America to a surprising extent. It was his father's emigration to the United States in order to find employment that earned the money that enabled him to study for the priesthood. Although basically a cloistered monk, he built one of the greatest hospitals in Europe, largely through generous contributions from American citizens. Like St. Francis of Assisi, who had his counterpart in St. Clare, or like St. John of the Cross and his contemporary, St. Teresa of Avila, St. Padre Pio had a counterpart in Mary Pyle. She was a wealthy Manhattan heiress who renounced an aristocratic lifestyle in order to live near his friary for the last 45 years of her life. Her home in San Giovanni Rotondo came to be considered "an extension of the monastery." It was Mary Pyle who once said, "The world will some day be surprised to find out who Padre Pio really was."[1]

Padre Pio owed much of his international fame to the American and other Allied soldiers who visited him during World War II and returned home to tell friends, relatives and others about him. The eyewitness accounts of the American GIs, many presented here for the first time, reflect the deep affection they felt for Padre Pio. In addition to their obvious admiration and reverence for him, their stories often convey the strong personal bond they developed with the Saint, sometimes even after the briefest of visits. The portrait of Padre Pio that is revealed from their observations is that of a likeable, warm and friendly man, filled with Franciscan joy and cheer. This is in contrast to a false impression of him that has occasionally surfaced, that of a gruff, ill-mannered and even testy ascetic. This unjust conclusion arose primarily because he was sometimes forced to be harsh with fanatical visitors, and on occasion he refused absolution in Confession to insincere penitents.

In order to understand the interaction between Padre Pio and the Americans, it is necessary to do so against the backdrop of an overview of his life; thus, a comprehensive biography of the Saint is presented within these pages. However, much of the book is comprised of the testimonies and impressions of those fortunate GIs who met him during the War years. Whenever possible, these stories are told in the soldiers' own words. Their narratives also include some of the supernatural occurrences that were almost a normal part of the everyday events that encompassed the Saint's life. What emerges is a valuable historical record of that important period when America, in the person of hundreds of GIs in uniform, met Padre Pio for the first time.

The book also discusses people who popularized Padre Pio in this country, both during and after his lifetime, such as William Carrigan and Mario Bruschi. In addition, Americans who chose to live and work beside the Saint are given special focus, including Mary Pyle and Joe Peterson. Mary's observation that "There is a living Saint in this world, and it saddens me not to be near him,"[2] amply explains why many Americans took up residence in San Giovanni Rotondo for varying lengths of time.

Some would volunteer to aid the friars in handling the enormous English-language correspondence. Others acted as interpreters, assisted pilgrims, or helped out in the monastery. They would return to the United States as changed persons, often inspired by Padre Pio to enter the priesthood or religious life. One American from Brooklyn initially came to see him out of curiosity and ended up becoming an ordained Capuchin priest assigned to Padre Pio's friary. He was Fr. Joseph Pius, known and loved by hundreds of

American pilgrims who were fortunate to have met him
before he passed away unexpectedly in May, 2000. In 1985,
while he was editor of *The Voice of Padre Pio* magazine, Fr.
Joseph wrote,

> You would need a book to tell the complete story of
> Padre and "the good America." Maybe that will be
> completed in Heaven, for there are many signs show-
> ing that Padre Pio is still keeping up the friendship.
> And so are the Yanks.[3]

Padre Pio often told the GIs that he wanted all Americans
to be his spiritual children. In fact, in the United States, and
indeed throughout the world, devotion to him continues to
grow, as ever greater numbers of Catholics and non-
Catholics become aware of his greatness. Since it has been
primarily the sanctity and personal qualities of Padre Pio
that have drawn Americans toward him, this book will
emphasize the spirituality and humanity of the Saint. Yet,
stories of signs and wonders are also recounted in this volume, as they invariably are when telling of Padre Pio. The
book attempts to illustrate the remarkable connection
between the Saint and Americans, and hopefully it will shed
some light on the mystery of Padre Pio's affection for us and
how it has been reciprocated. Of course, the complete story
of Padre Pio and America will only be told in Heaven.

PADRE PIO
AND AMERICA

I now "rejoice in my sufferings for you, and fill up those things that are wanting of the sufferings of Christ, in my flesh, for his body, which is the church."
—Colossians 1:24

Chapter 1

Pietrelcina

SO many Americans have demonstrated a special affinity for Padre Pio, that they seem to have adopted him as one of their own. One reason for this special attraction stems from the story of his humble beginnings. Born in a virtually unknown hill town in the south of Italy called Pietrelcina, the circumstances of his early life are similar to those of millions of Americans who came from obscure villages in their own particular "Old Country" of Europe or elsewhere. His origins in a poor farming village perhaps strike a sympathetic chord with many who live in the United States, settled primarily by European immigrants who sought relief from poverty and oppression by coming to the New World.

Pietrelcina at the end of the 19th century was an isolated, sparsely populated hamlet composed primarily of farmers and peasants. They were basically simple people who lived off the land, taking advantage of the fertile fields that surrounded the town. Perhaps between three and four thousand lived in the village at the time of the birth of Francesco Forgione, the future Saint. The closest available data to the 1887 birth of Francesco is a census of 1901 which gave a count of 4,258 people.[1]

Geographically, Pietrelcina is located in the Italian region of Campania in Southern Italy, and is situated in the province of Benevento, which is also the nearest large city. Campania is one of the twenty official regions of Italy, and its capital is Naples. Pietrelcina is located in the interior, a

1

section not so familiar to Americans as the coastal areas of the Campania region, such as Sorrento, Pompeii, the Amalfi coast, and Capri.

The name Pietrelcina is of ancient, uncertain origin. In the old local dialect, the city was known as Pretapucina, and there have been many explanations proposed for its meaning. One of the more colorful stories is that an old foundation stone (*pietra*) was once found in the ancient castle district of the town, and on it were carved a hen (*pucina*) and a brood of chicks, hence Pretapucina.[3] Another is that the word *pucina* is a derivative of *piccina* (small), and the name was intended to distinguish the town from *Petra Maiore* (major), a neighboring city that was eventually destroyed by an earthquake.[2] At any rate, to this day the locals refer to themselves as *Pucinari*.

Today, one can still travel the quaint winding streets, bordered by small stone homes that are laid out one after the other, each one connected to its neighbor. Francesco was born in a tiny house on one of these twisted ancient roads, *Vico Storto Valle*, which in fact means Twisted (or Crooked) Valley Lane. We could truly say that Padre Pio was born in a one-room house, since actually his birthplace was a separate building in a household that consisted of two buildings, one having only one room and the other having two rooms. There was an intervening building between the two houses, and one had to exit by the street from one house to enter the other house two doors away! The second house consisted of only a kitchen and a dining area which doubled as a bedroom, with a small window that offered a magnificent view of the grand Italian countryside.[4]

Francesco Forgione was born May 25, 1887, to two devout Catholic parents, Grazio Maria Forgione and Giuseppa De Nunzio. He was their fourth child, but two had previously died in their infancy, leaving only his 5-year-old brother,

Michele. Eventually there were three more additions to the
family, all girls. His mother, known to all as Mamma Peppa,
was humble, hospitable and gentle. Very religious, she
abstained from meat three days a week instead of just
abstaining on Fridays. Francesco's father Grazio, also serious about his religion, was a bright and cheerful person, with
a good sense of humor, but he had a more complex character
than his wife. He prayed the Rosary and was described by a
neighbor as being "holy";[5] however, another friend characterized him as "a good man but not a saint."[6] On rare occasions
he was heard to use that colorful language "which darkens
the faces of good Christians."[7] Although he was baptized as
Grazio, he is often referred to as Orazio, or Zi'Orazio. (*Zi*
means "Uncle" in Italian.)

The Forgiones were hard-working country folk, the salt of
the earth, and well liked by their neighbors. As farmers, they
tilled a small plot of land consisting of a few acres that was
about a thirty minute walk from the town, in an area called
Piana Romana (the Roman plane). They used an old stone
farmhouse to store their goods, and to sleep in overnight during the busy periods.

As a child, Francesco was quiet and unassuming, yet still
sociable with the boys his age. It is said that by the time he
was five, he was already having mystical experiences, including ecstasies, visions of the Madonna and occasional harassment from diabolic forces. Interestingly enough, it was only
in his late twenties that he told anyone about them, because
he thought they were just ordinary occurrences that everyone had. His earnest and life-long devotion to the Blessed
Virgin was fostered in part by the Rosary, which was faithfully recited together by the family every evening.[8]

Although he was attracted to the spiritual life even as a
young child, he did not openly display this side of himself,
and on the surface seemed like everyone else his age. But as

he grew older, he began attending Holy Mass every morning, and he often spent much time praying alone in the church. In his modesty, he asked the parish priest and his assistants not to tell anyone. Once he was so rapt in prayer that the church assistant who found him on the floor was sure he was dead. He ran to the priest and told him as much; but the priest, knowing of the boy's ecstasies, calmly replied, "Don't worry. He will rise again!"[9]

Although named after St. Francis of Assisi, to whom his mother was devoted, his definite vocation to the branch of Franciscans known as the Capuchins developed under such interesting circumstances that it is almost the stuff of legend.

The Capuchins are called such because of the hood (*cappuccio*) that they wear, after the custom of St. Francis. They are a strict branch of the Franciscans and actually were founded hundreds of years after the death of the Saint. In addition to their hood, they wear a plain brown habit, girded by a white cord, with sandals and bare feet, and in imitation of Christ and St. Francis, they wear beards. Though they generally live a monastic life, they prefer to be called friars and not monks. Friar in the Italian is *frate*, meaning brother. Since St. Francis wished to found a brotherhood, his followers are properly known as friars, although Padre Pio is also commonly referred to as a monk.

About fifteen miles from Pietrelcina is the Franciscan Capuchin friary of the town of Morcone. It was the custom at that time for a friary to send one of its own to the neighboring villages to ask for alms and provisions, in order to help support the friars and the novices—those studying to be friars. The begging friar was known as the questor, and at Morcone the questor was Brother Camillo of Sant'Elia a Pianisi. He often visited Pietrelcina carrying his questing sack. He was greeted warmly, especially by the children, because of his kind words and the little gifts he gave them, such as medals, holy cards or chestnuts. But what made Brother Camillo even more special to the children was his long dark beard, the mark of the Capuchin.

When the boy Francesco Forgione first met this friar—he might have been about age ten at the time—he was deeply impressed by the large flowing beard worn by Brother Camillo. Francesco made up his mind that he too wanted to enter the religious life, and be a friar with a beard. In later life, Padre Pio would say, "I had gotten the idea of Brother Camillo's beard into my head, and no one could take away my desire to be a bearded friar."[10]

Chapter 2

"Emigrate or steal . . ."

ALTHOUGH young Francesco was supported by his parents in his desire to enter the religious life, there was a major problem to be overcome. At that time in Italy, public education only lasted three years, and the Forgiones would have to make arrangements to complete his education before Francesco could be accepted in a friary as a candidate for the priesthood. Therefore, he would have to be tutored privately, at an expense his parents could not readily afford. This was a big step for a family with limited material means. What little the family eked out from their farm was barely enough to provide for their day-to-day survival.

While his parents were deliberating on what to do, Francesco's father Grazio received a letter from a friend who had emigrated to Brazil to find work. Anxious to make an impression, the friend painted a rosy picture of life in "Big America," as the Italians called South America. The story goes that in this letter, his friend bragged about all the riches he was acquiring and described how he could see the golden tiles on the roofs of the palatial homes there. The letter apparently helped Grazio make up his mind to travel to America. There he could try to earn enough money to enable Francesco to continue his studies and become a priest some day, as well as to meet his own pressing financial obligations.

Grazio was often heard to say *"emigrare o rubare"* ("emigrate or steal").[1] But for the pious Forgione family, there could be only one choice. Thus, sometime in early 1898

Grazio sailed from Naples to Brazil, becoming part of the great Southern Italian movement of men looking for work overseas. In most cases, they had the intention of returning home to their native land with something to show for their labors, rather than permanently residing in the Americas. At times, almost one third of the men in Pietrelcina were working abroad.

Unfortunately for Grazio, the roofs in Brazil were not tiled with gold. Some of his fellow emigrants from Pietrelcina located the man who had written the glowing letter about life in America. He was found slaving away in a restaurant kitchen as a dishwasher. He was so downcast and embarrassed at being found out, that his townsmen did not have the heart to rebuke him. Unable to make a go of it, some say it was because he became ill, Grazio had to borrow money to make the return trip home after only a few months. Similar disappointments befell many of the other *Pucinari* who had made the trip to South America, only to return home as poor as when they had left.

With the need to bring in additional earnings still pressing, Grazio made a second effort to find work in America. However, this time he left for "Little America," that is, the United States. In March of 1899, after long weeks of silence, his family finally heard from him. In a letter that someone else wrote for him, since he could neither read nor write, Grazio had good news to share. He was staying with some cousins, and was working with them on a farm in Mahoningtown, Pennsylvania, owned by a family named Myers.[2] He and his relatives were living in a frame house on Montgomery Street. His extensive knowledge of farming, combined with hard work, had caught the attention of his employer, and he was put in charge of the other farmhands.

Each week Grazio sent money back home to the family in

Pietrelcina. It was Francesco who was entrusted with the task of retrieving the mail at the post office and then having the check cashed. Similarly, it was Francesco who wrote to his father, since he was the only family member who knew how to write. By means of these letters back and forth, Grazio was able to exercise from afar his influence on family matters, as well as on the activities of the farm in Piana Romana.

He also kept an eye on how Francesco's studies were progressing. The boy had enrolled in a private school run by a married ex-priest* named Tizzani, in order to finish his primary schooling. Francesco's studies were not going well, and one day his mother Giuseppa spoke to Tizzani, who reported that Francesco spent so much time in church, both in the morning and in the afternoon, that he was neglecting his schoolwork. That evening his mother reproached Francesco: "What am I going to write to your father, who emigrated to America to pay for your studies to become a monk?" Her son replied that his poor performance was due to the distracting and nagging thought that Tizzani had been a bad priest.[3] At the same time, Grazio in America was having doubts about the wisdom of having Francesco study under a defrocked priest. So he wrote home and asked Mamma Peppa to find a better teacher for their son.

Francesco did finish his primary education with Tizzani, but subsequently was enrolled under a new teacher for the secondary level, a strict schoolmaster named Angelo Caccavo. Francesco mentioned this in a letter of October 5, 1901, to his father:

---

*The term "ex-priest" is used to refer to a man who is no longer exercising his priesthood—but strictly speaking, the Sacrament of Holy Orders elevates a man to the Priesthood *forever*, placing an indelible "mark" or *character* upon his soul.—*Publisher*, 2005.

Now that I find myself under the guidance of a new teacher, I see myself showing improvement from day to day, for which Mamma and myself are most content. I continue to pray to our beautiful Virgin that everything will go well and that you will return to our family safe and sound.[4]

Also in the same letter, Francesco apologized to his father. A short time before, he had gone on a pilgrimage with some of his classmates to the shrine of Our Lady of Pompeii. However, he had left without asking his mother's permission, and also he had to spend some of his savings for the trip. Grazio had apparently shown his disapproval in one of his letters home, so Francesco wrote back:

Regarding the complaint made to Mamma about my going to Pompeii, you are right a thousand times over . . . True, I did spend some money, but now I promise you I will make up for it by my studies. However, you should consider that, the Lord willing, next year will mark the end of diversions and festivities for me, because I will abandon this life in favor of a better one.[5]

In 1903 Grazio returned to his family in Pietrelcina, but this time it was with some hard-earned currency. Besides paying for Francesco's education, he was able to purchase two additional land holdings and some livestock. Later, he emigrated back to the United States to continue working, but returned to Pietrelcina intermittently to be with his family for short periods. Following his stay at the farm in Pennsylvania, Grazio moved north to New York in 1907 and worked on a farm in Queens, which was a rural suburb of Manhattan at that time.[6] Then on to Jamaica, Long Island, where he worked on the Erie railroad and where his oldest son Michele joined him.

The only Ellis Island record for Grazio shows that he arrived in America again on April 12, 1910, at age 49, on the ship *Berlin*, which had sailed from Naples. Michele has two Ellis Island entries. The first shows he arrived on March 2, 1906, at age 23 and single, on the ship *Italia*, from Naples. Then he arrived on May 12, 1909, at age 26, now married, on the *Madonna*, also sailing from Naples. Both men probably continued to travel back and forth, but Grazio was unable to return from his final trip until 1919, because of the First World War (1914-1918).[7]

Grazio's willingness to make the sacrifice of crossing the ocean so that his son could become a priest gave the world St. Padre Pio. In later years Padre Pio often remarked with some emotion: "My father crossed the ocean twice so that I could become a monk." The "twice" probably referred to Grazio's travels to both "Big" and "Little" America. For his part, young Francesco's early impression of America had to have been a favorable one, and we can safely surmise that he was grateful, not only to his father, but also to that faraway land for providing the means for his priestly education.

Chapter 3

Road to the Priesthood

AFTER completing his preliminary studies, Francesco Forgione prepared to leave home for the Capuchin Friary at Morcone in January, 1903. His father was still abroad, and Francesco wrote to reassure him about the family:

> Don't worry about my brother, he does his duty and is always kind to Mother. The same is true of my sisters. My mother and brother always look after them.[1]

Young Francesco's strong family ties and his closeness to the good earth of Pietrelcina and Piana Romana caused him great anguish at the time of his departure for the Friary. In later years he said it felt like his very bones were crushed. It was worse for his mother, who said to him, "My son, do not think of your mother's sadness at this moment. My heart is bleeding, but St. Francis has called you and you must go." Years later Padre Pio wrote:

> It was then that I felt the two forces within me, who were struggling amongst themselves and lacerating my heart. The world that wanted me for itself, and God who was calling me to a new life. Dear God! Who could explain that interior martyrdom that was taking place within me?[2]

When the door of the Morcone Friary was opened for him at the age of 15, the first person he saw was the bearded questor, Brother Camillo, who cheerfully greeted him with, "Bravo!" Camillo congratulated the new arrival on being faithful to the call of St. Francis. The initial period for new-comers at the Friary was called the novitiate, a time of spir-itual and character formation. At that time, the require-ments were very strict, with prayer vigils, fasting, penances, mortifications, hard work and imposed silences. The novices endured extremes of temperature with the seasons, since a heated monastic cell in the winter was considered an insult to the vow of poverty. For one of their meals, they were allowed but three slices of bread.[3] But this restricted diet was not a problem for Francesco, who willingly ate but little, and passed the untouched portions to his brother novices.

Francesco, who was used to a hard, peasant lifestyle, adjusted well to the new regimen and became a model fol-lower of St. Francis. However, many of his confreres were either asked to leave or did so of their own accord. His Novice Master commented, "This boy seems to know and observe the Rule better than we do."[4] He preferred to spend his time and energy in prayer, as much as his obedience to his superiors and the Franciscan Rule allowed.

Two weeks after admittance, the novices were officially clothed with their religious garments, to signify they would now "put on the new man." They were given a white cord to bind around their brown habit, as a reminder that the Lord had once warned St. Peter that he would be led where he would not want to go.[5] Part of this ritual was the bestowal of a new name upon the candidates, with the second part of their name being their town of origin. Francesco was given the name of Fra (Brother) Pio of Pietrelcina, which was to be his name in religion. It is not known whether he chose the name himself; however, he was apparently named after Pope

St. Pius V. During the Turkish invasion, this Pope had asked all the Christians of the world to pray the Rosary, and their prayers were credited with helping the Papal forces defeat the invaders at the battle of Lepanto in 1571. The traditional feast day of St. Pius V is May 5, and Padre Pio always observed this as his *"onomastico,"* or name day, which in Italy is a day of celebration comparable to one's birthday.

In the autumn of that novitiate year of 1903, Fra Pio's father made a return visit to Pietrelcina from America. A few days later, Grazio and Mamma Peppa visited the Friary at Morcone, and they were taken aback by the appearance and deportment of their son. His body was thin and emaciated, his face pale, and his attitude to his parents was very formal and detached. He kept his head bowed and his eyes glued to the floor, barely speaking a word. Grazio demanded to see Padre Tomasso, the Father Guardian, to find out what they had done to his boy, who was scarcely recognizable. He was ready to pull his son out of the seminary, but was reassured by Padre Tomasso that there was nothing wrong. Fra Pio just had to learn to moderate himself in his mortifications, and he would be back to normal. The Guardian then gave Fra Pio permission to talk as he wished, and immediately "he started to chatter very freely."[6] In later years Padre Pio, in reference to a visit by his mother that had occurred just before this one, said, "As soon as I saw my mother, my impulse was to throw myself into her arms. But the discipline of the novitiate did not permit this."[7] On another visit by his mother, the Superior of the Friary remarked to her: "Donna Giuseppina, your son is too good; we can find no fault in him."[8]

During his stay at Morcone, Fra Pio was well liked and respected by his peers and his superiors. He was cheerful and affable, with a good sense of humor, and was also obedient and very devout. One incident that reflected his sublime spiritual state occurred when the Novice Master prohibited him from receiving Holy Communion one day. Reportedly Francesco nearly died as a result, and thereafter he was always permitted to receive this spiritual nourishment.[9] Although he was considered by all to be deeply religious, there were few overt demonstrations of the supernatural charisms that later made him famous throughout the world. This apparent absence of spiritual gifts would eventually change as he progressed in his formation for the priesthood after the novitiate.

One notable exception to the scarcity of supernatural manifestations at that time was his "gift of tears." He would be seen shedding tears in abundance, either when worshipping on his knees or while praying as he made his way along the corridors. His meditations usually centered on the suffering that Christ endured at His crucifixion and death on the Cross. Padre Placido of San Marco in Lamis, who knew him as a novice, remarked: "His meditation was always on the pain of the Crucified. In choir during prayer he would weep many tears, so much so that very often the floor would be stained."[10] Padre Leone of San Giovanni Rotondo wrote that when he visited Fra Pio's cell he

> . . . almost always found him praying on his knees with his eyes red from crying . . . he was a student that prayed continually, and these prayers were made up of tears, and it was enough to look at his eyes to understand that tears were habitual visitors.[11]

From Padre Damaso of Sant'Elia a Pianisi:

> Spurred on by devotion mixed with curiosity, I stealthily placed my finger on a large white handkerchief he had at his side, and I thought of the gift of

tears (it was said that he had an eye problem as a result of the many tears he shed). I withdrew my finger, which was now completely soaked, as the handkerchief was drenched with tears. From that moment something particular was conceived in my soul for Brother Pio's goodness.[12]

Padre Antonio of San Giovanni Rotondo, his spiritual director at the Sant'Elia a Pianisi Friary, recalls that he cried

> . . . enough tears to form a dent in the floor, during prayer time and especially after Holy Communion. When asked the reason for those tears, the little brother would always withdraw into himself and become silent. As his spiritual director, I finally obliged him to speak: "I cry," he said, "for my sins and those of mankind."[13]

The novitiate lasted one year, and in January of 1904 Brother Pio and his classmates made provisional, temporary vows that were to last three years. These were the traditional vows of poverty, chastity, and obedience. Fra Pio pledged and promised to God, the Virgin Mary, St. Francis and all the Saints, that he would ". . . observe for three years the Rule of the Friars Minor, confirmed by Pope Honorius, living in obedience, without property, and in chastity."[14]

At the turn of the twentieth century, the Capuchins were still regrouping in the aftermath of a recent suppression by the government of all religious orders in Italy. Thus, there was no designated monastery in the Capuchin Province of Foggia, to which the Morcone Friary belonged, that could provide a complete seminary education. Candidates for the priesthood would be shuffled to a number of different friaries, depending on which of them offered the particular training needed for the candidate's next step in formation. There is almost something poetic in the names of the various communities that Fra Pio was sent to after his year at Morcone was over: Sant'Elia a Pianisi, San Marco la Catola, Serracapriola, Montefusco, Gesualdo. The period of provisional vows ended in 1907, and in January, at the age of 19, at Sant'Elia he made his solemn profession before the Superior of the Friary—his permanent, lifelong vows of poverty, chastity and obedience. His path to the priesthood was not complete, however, and he continued to take courses at the various monasteries.

Unfortunately, during this stage of his priestly formation, his health began to fail him. High fevers and bronchial problems frequently occurred, and he was unable to obtain any treatment that offered lasting relief while at the friaries. As a consequence he was frequently sent home for brief periods to Pietrelcina, where breathing his native air allowed him to recuperate. Then in 1908, while at the Montefusco Friary, he experienced a severe fever and hacking cough. A doctor diagnosed him with active pulmonary tuberculosis, and gave him only a few months to live. He was sent home once again to Pietrelcina, where his father Grazio was back on a visit from America. His parents sent him to a local doctor, Andrea Cardone, who gave a different diagnosis of chronic bronchitis, aggravated by Fra Pio's fasting and his ascetic life style.

Though this new diagnosis was confirmed by a specialist in Naples, soon an aura of mystery developed around his illness. He would be treated by Dr. Cardone at Pietrelcina, then returned to the monastery. Shortly afterwards, he would become ill again, and the cycle would repeat itself. The doctors were unsure of the cause and nature of the illness. Unexplainably, his fevers registered abnormally high temperatures. Stories exist of thermometers that broke because the column of mercury had nowhere else to go. (A few of these with accompanying documentation are now on display in the friary at San Giovanni Rotondo.) Large bath thermometers were used, which sometimes measured his temperature at over 120 degrees Fahrenheit. One of his confreres speculated that the high temperatures were a sign of his interior spiritual suffering. Fra Pio himself wrote later of a fire which burned his whole being, "a mysterious fire which I felt from my heart, which I couldn't understand. I felt the need to put ice on it to extinguish this fire, which is consuming me."[15]

He was assigned to different Capuchin monasteries in the hope his health would fare better at one of them, but there was always a relapse. It appeared that the only place where he would remain in reasonably good health was at Pietrelcina, since as soon as he was sent back to a friary, he would be seized by severe symptoms, which included violent stomach cramps, fevers and vomiting. Doctors examined him many times, and although they could verify the illness, they could give no explanation for it.

In May of 1909, he was once more sent home from Montefusco, for what was meant to be a short stay. But instead, this was the beginning of a long period lasting almost seven years, during which he was almost constantly confined to his native Pietrelcina. The Provincial Superior at the time, Padre Benedetto of San Marco in Lamis, had reluctantly decided to let him remain with his family indefinitely because of his habitual ill-health.

Fra Pio was given special permission to complete his studies for the priesthood while at home. But soon, even the native air of his home town was not fully able to alleviate his symptoms. He began to despair that he would ever be healthy again, and in addition to the fevers, he complained of pains in his chest and back. It seemed to him at times that his heart would burst through his chest.[16] As his condition worsened, he became convinced that his death was near, and he even welcomed it.

> The idea of being cured after all these storms sent by the Most High seems like a dream to me, indeed a meaningless phrase. On the contrary, the idea of death seems to attract me greatly, and I feel I shall reach it before long.[17]

Fra Pio asked if he could be consecrated as a priest before the required age of 24, because he was almost certain he would die before then. The Superior, Padre Benedetto, was also quite concerned, and he requested permission for an early Ordination. This was granted, and the Foggia Capuchin Province was allowed to proceed with Fra Pio's Ordination nine months sooner than usual.

Thus, on August 10, 1910, Fra Pio became Padre Pio. His Ordination to the Catholic priesthood took place in the Romanesque Cathedral of Benevento, in a rite performed by 83-year-old Archbishop Paolo Schinosi. (Sadly, more than 30 years later, Allied bombers during World War II almost totally destroyed the same Benevento Cathedral.) Mamma Peppa was present for the ceremony, along with some of the family, while his father Grazio was back in the United States working on Long Island, along with Padre Pio's brother Michele. That did not prevent Grazio from having a joyous party with his friends in America to celebrate the occasion— after all, it was his willingness to work overseas that had made possible his son's Ordination.

But the rejoicing in America did not compare to the welcome Padre Pio received on his return to Pietrelcina. The city band was there to greet him when he reached the edge of town, and the *Pucinari* cheered and tossed coins and little confections. At home, his mother had prepared a grand feast to be shared by as many as could fit into their small house. Through it all, Padre Pio remained his humble and reserved self. For him, the priesthood was a vocation of the utmost seriousness. To commemorate his new state in life, he had a little prayer card printed as a gift to family and friends. On it were these sobering words in remembrance of his first Mass: "Jesus, my life and my breath, today I timorously raise Thee in a mystery of love. With Thee may I be for the world the way, the truth, and the life, and through Thee, a holy priest, a perfect victim." And truly Padre Pio did become both a holy priest and a victim soul for others.

Although he was now a priest, his poor health compelled his Capuchin superiors to continue to allow him to spend most of his time in Pietrelcina. With some exceptions, he remained there until 1916. Often he would visit the little family farm at Piana Romana, and other times he would retire to a small room across from his birthplace on Vico Storto Valle. This room stands by itself, perched atop a rock, and is reached by a steep external stairway. Still visited today by pilgrims, it is known as *La Torretta*, or the Little Tower. However, his primary residence as a priest in Pietrelcina was a home which his father Grazio had been able to buy for the family with some of his earnings from America.[18] Just a short distance from their old house, it had an upstairs room, where Padre Pio spent quiet hours in prayer and study, and corresponded with his two spiritual guides. These were Padre Benedetto of San Marco in Lamis, who had become his official spiritual director, and Padre Agostino of San Marco in Lamis. The town of San Marco in Lamis has since honored these two mentors of the future Saint by erecting imposing statues of both Capuchins in the town square.

Though not able to live in a friary under the personal guidance of his superiors in religion, Padre Pio's spiritual development was guided and nourished by means of letters to and from these two directors. The extent and depth of this correspondence is indicated by the English language edition of the letters, which comprises over 1,300 pages, covering from 1910 to 1922.[19] The collection has already become a classic of spiritual literature, revealing the mystical heights, sufferings, joys and torments of a man on his way to sainthood. They also show how the initial disciple-director relationship began to reverse itself over the years, and eventually it was the disciple Padre Pio who often directed his two teachers. This exchange of letters with his spiritual guides comprises Volume One of the four-volume *Epistolario* of the Saint.

Chapter 4

The "Invisible" Stigmata

THE story of Padre Pio's life is also a journey into the mystery of suffering. He valued and even sought suffering, but not for its own sake. Rather, suffering was for him a sharing in the redeeming mission of Jesus Christ, which he could offer up in union with Christ for the salvation of souls. The words of St. Paul in his Epistle to the Colossians provide the Scriptural basis for this offering: "I now rejoice in my sufferings for you, and fill up those things that are wanting in the sufferings of Christ, in my flesh, for his body, which is the church." (*Colossians* 1:23-24). Padre Pio wished to offer his whole life for souls, and was willing to accept punishments that were meant for others, if it would benefit their salvation. A person who makes such a complete oblation of self in order to undergo sufferings for others is known as a "victim soul."

In November of 1910, Padre Pio wrote to his spiritual director Padre Benedetto asking explicit permission to offer himself as such a victim soul:

> Now, my dear Father, I want to ask your permission for something. For some time past I have felt the need to offer myself to the Lord as a victim for poor sinners and for the souls in Purgatory.
> ... I have in fact made this offering to the Lord several times, beseeching Him to pour out upon me the punishments prepared for sinners and for the souls in a state of purgation . . . but I should now like to

21

make this offering to the Lord in obedience to you. It seems to me that Jesus really wants this.[1]

In December Padre Benedetto's reply reached Padre Pio in Pietrelcina:

But Jesus, tempted in the desert and hanging on the Cross, is a clear and consoling proof of what I will tell you, that is, that for a soul that yearns for God, the storms of the present life are a sign of His special love and His exceptional mercy. Courage, then, and go ahead.

Make the offering of which you speak, and it will be most acceptable to the Lord. Extend your own arms also on your cross and by offering to the Father the sacrifice of yourself in union with our most loving Saviour, suffer, groan and pray for the wicked ones of the earth and for the Poor Souls in the next life who are so deserving of our compassion in their patient and unspeakable sufferings.[2]

However, the Lord had apparently already accepted his desire to become a "perfect victim," even before Padre Benedetto ratified this wish. Less than a month after his Ordination in August of that year, Padre Pio began to feel pains in his hands and feet while praying at his favorite spot at Piana Romana under an elm tree. On the 7th of September he went to his parish priest, Don Salvatore Pannullo, and showed him red puncture marks on the palm and back of both hands. Though they did not bleed, the sores appeared to go right through his hands. Padre Pio explained to Don Pannullo that he had been praying under the elm tree when Jesus and Mary appeared to him, giving him these wounds. Don Pannullo prudently had Padre Pio see a doctor, who diagnosed the lesions as tuberculosis of the skin. A second opinion was sought from Dr. Andrea Cardone, who had prior experience with Padre Pio's medical anomalies; he rejected the tuberculosis theory, but could offer no explanation of his own. He determined that the wounds were half an inch in diameter on both sides of each hand. As part of his examination, he pressed his fingers into the palms of Padre Pio's hands. In spite of the resulting pain, Padre Pio managed to quip, "Are you trying to be like St. Thomas?"[3]

Padre Pio did his best to conceal this phenomenon from others, and even his mother did not know about it. However, she came close to finding out as he entered the house one day, shaking his hands back and forth as if they hurt. She jokingly asked her son, "What's wrong, you look like you are trying to play the guitar!" He replied that it was nothing, just little stabs in his hands of no importance; but for the next couple of days, Mamma Giuseppa noticed that her son seemed to be trying to keep his hands hidden.

The sores disappeared after about a week, apparently because Padre Pio and Padre Pannullo prayed that the visible manifestation would go away: "Let's pray together to ask Jesus to take away this annoyance. I want to suffer, even to die of suffering, but all in secret."[4] However, during the next year, the visible wounds re-appeared for short periods of time. But even on days when they could not be seen at all, he often felt a sharp pain in his hands and feet, and occasionally in his side. He did not reveal these incidents to Padre Benedetto until a year after their first occurrence; he did it in a letter dated September 8, 1911, and even then he did so reluctantly.

> Yesterday evening something happened to me which I can neither explain nor understand. In the center of the palms of my hands a red patch

appeared, about the size of a cent and accompanied
by acute pain. The pain was much more acute in the
left hand and it still persists. I also feel some pain in
the soles of my feet.

This phenomenon has been repeated several times
for almost a year now, but for some time past it had
not occurred. Do not be disturbed by the fact that this
is the first time I have mentioned it, for I was invariably overcome by abominable shame. If you only
knew what it costs me to tell you about it now!

. . . I have no idea, dear Father, what these signs
mean.[5]

In a letter to Padre Agostino on March 21, 1912, he again
refers to these manifestations. Although this time he does
not mention that they appear visibly, he admits that he can
still feel their pain on some days:

From Thursday evening until Saturday, and on
Tuesday also, a painful tragedy takes place. My
heart, hands and feet seem to be pierced through by
a sword, so great is the pain I feel.[6]

Since in general they were not visible, except for intermit-
tent periods, the occurrences which began in September of
1910 are often called the "invisible stigmata." This is to distinguish them from the visible, bleeding stigmata that Padre
Pio received in 1918, which lasted fifty years, until his death
in 1968. Some call this first manifestation the "proto-stig-
mata," since they were a forerunner of the permanent
wounds that appeared later.

In a rather amazing letter of October 10, 1915, to Padre
Agostino, Padre Pio clearly delineates the heavenly favors he
had received, even using the word "stigmata" himself. As one

of his spiritual guides, Padre Agostino had insisted in two earlier letters to Padre Pio that he was to answer three questions about his inner spiritual life. "Answer me in a confidential letter; Jesus will make me keep this secret." After much hesitation and reluctance, Padre Pio finally wrote back, out of modesty referring to himself in the third person:

By the first question you want to know how long since Jesus began to favor this poor creature with His heavenly visions.

If I am not mistaken, these must have begun not long after the novitiate.

In your second question you ask if He granted this soul the ineffable gift of His holy stigmata.

To this, the reply must be in the affirmative, and the first time Jesus deigned to grant this favor, the signs were visible, especially in one hand. The soul was greatly terrified by this phenomenon and therefore asked the Lord to withdraw the visible signs. Since then, the signs are no longer to be seen; however, though the wounds disappeared, the intense pain has not ceased on this account, and it continues especially in certain circumstances and on certain days.

By your third and last question, you want to know if the Lord made this soul experience His Crowning with Thorns and His Scourging, and how many times.

The reply to this question must also be affirmative; as regards the number of times, I am unable to specify this. All I can say is that this soul has suffered these things for several years, almost every week.

It seems to me that I have obeyed you, haven't I?[7]

Thus, there is ample testimony that the invisible stigmata

were a very real phenomenon, and Padre Pio's response to them was quite rational and showed a healthy humility. We have seen that Padre Pio told Padre Pannullo that Jesus and Mary had appeared to him and gave him these wounds, and also that he and Padre Pannullo had prayed to have them taken away. Further, he stated in the letter just quoted that he was terrified by them and asked the Lord to remove their visible aspect. The visible signs were in fact removed, but still they continued to be painful.

Therefore, it would be difficult to accept the statement made only a few years after Padre Pio's death by Giorgio Cruchon at the First Congress of Studies on Padre Pio's Spirituality. He refers to the stigmata of 1918 as the "real and true stigmata," as opposed to the "other stigmata due to 'the meditations that he made' . . . at Pietrelcina." Cruchon concludes that the earlier manifestation of this phenomenon was " . . . like that of many dubious, neurotic stigmata, and caused by strong emotion, helped by religious sentiment and the wish to identify oneself with the crucified Christ."[8] In essence, Cruchon is alleging that the invisible stigmata were caused by auto-suggestion on Padre Pio's part. To accept this unlikely conclusion, one would have to question not only Padre Pio's integrity and the validity of his visions, but would also have to postulate that he had such great power of auto-suggestion that he could make the visible wounds disappear, but still allow himself to feel their pain!

Chapter 5

Foggia

DURING the years that Padre Pio remained at Pietrelcina for health reasons, his director, Padre Benedetto, made repeated attempts to return him to friary life. But, as had happened during his studies for the priesthood, whenever he was sent to one of the friaries, he became so ill that the only alternative was to send him back to Pietrelcina. Padre Pio himself felt that he was in exile from his own Franciscan community, but it was beyond his power to affect the situation. The doctors still did not know what to make of his sickly condition, especially his vomiting and inability to retain food while at the friaries. For example, at the Venafro Friary in 1911, he could retain no solid food for a period of 21 days, his sole source of nourishment being daily Holy Communion.

It was at Venafro that many of the supernatural manifestations in Padre Pio's life became known to his confreres for the first time. Padre Agostino, who was also a resident there, described in his diary many of the ecstasies that he witnessed, including Padre Pio's conversations with Jesus, the Virgin Mary, his Guardian Angel, and other celestial personages. However, not all of Padre Pio's experiences were of heavenly beings, and Padre Agostino noted ten diabolical apparitions.[1]

The demons would appear to Padre Pio disguised as beings of light, often posing as Saints, but he always experienced a feeling of disgust at these counterfeit visions. To test the spirits, he would ask them to praise Jesus, and if they

refused, he knew they were devilish. Once found out, they
would leave him alone for a time. As usually happened when
he stayed at a friary, his physical condition began to collapse,
and after about 40 days at Venafro he was back home once
again. In 1914, another attempt was made to return Padre
Pio to communal life. This time, he was ordered to Morcone,
but he became so ill that he lasted there only five days.

That same year the First World War broke out, and by May
of the next year, Italy had entered the fray. In the fall of 1915
Padre Pio was drafted by the military, which had no qualms
about emptying out the seminaries and monasteries in the
search for conscripts. Initially rejected by a medical officer
because of a diagnosis of tuberculosis, he was sent to another
locale for observation. Here a different doctor approved him
as fit for duty after a cursory examination, and he was
assigned to the Tenth Medical Corps based in Naples. But
his health was as bad as ever, and he wrote to Padre
Agostino,

> You can imagine, my dear Father, how I am feeling
> physically. I think I am getting worse each day. My
> condition is becoming unbearable, and I remain alive
> only by a miracle.[2]

Fortunately, good sense prevailed, and just before the
Christmas of 1915, a group of doctors in Naples found that
he had an "infection of the lungs" and granted him a one-
year leave of absence from the military as a convalescent.

The year of his leave from the Army, 1916, marked a critical turning point in the life of the future Saint. The fact that
he had been able to survive a few weeks in the military, away
from the beneficial environment of Pietrelcina, convinced his
spiritual director, Padre Benedetto, that he was ready to be
definitively assigned to a friary. However, Padre Pio was

determined to stay in Pietrelcina, concerned that his poor health would not allow him to survive another attempt at monastery life. As indicated by the excerpt below from one of his letters, his position was supported by others who knew his case well.

> I want you to know, moreover, that the fact of being obliged to live outside the cloister saddens my whole life. I have never relied on my own judgment in this matter. I have explained my case to learned persons who are enlightened as to God's ways and they have replied that in view of my exceptional position and taking everything into consideration, I cannot venture to live in the cloister . . .[3]

However, thanks to the efforts of Padre Agostino, he was prevailed upon to leave Pietrelcina, and take up residence at the Friary of St. Anne. This friary was located on the outskirts of the Southern Italian city of Foggia. For almost two years Padre Pio had been providing spiritual direction for a noblewoman of Foggia, Raffaelina Cerase, exclusively by an exchange of letters. In early 1916 Raffaelina had become very ill, since an operation to remove a cancerous tumor had not succeeded in arresting the disease. Padre Agostino, with Raffaelina's consent, urged Padre Pio to come to Foggia in person, to provide spiritual comfort to her in her last days and hear the dying woman's Confession.

Padre Pio finally agreed, and Agostino met him at the train station in Benevento, where they left for Foggia on February 17, 1916. This date marks the end of Padre Pio's nearly seven year exile from community life, although he did not intend it to be so, since he had with him a round-trip ticket, along with some personal belongings. But upon his arrival at St. Anne's, Padre Benedetto, who had made a special trip from his own monastery, was there waiting for him. Padre Benedetto promptly ordered Padre Pio to send his belongings back home, because "dead or alive, you're staying here at Foggia!"[4] Padre Pio would in fact remain at the Foggia friary for a little over six months.

Raffaelina Cerase clung to life until the feast of the Annunciation on March 25. Padre Pio visited her every day, providing spiritual counsel and comfort, and he often said Mass in the Cerase family's private chapel. In the two years prior to their meeting in person, when they communicated solely by mail, they wrote about one hundred letters altogether. The collection of these letters comprises the six hundred page Volume Two of the *Epistolario* of the Saint. Their correspondence reveals Padre Pio's masterful ability to provide spiritual direction to a soul that desires to attain perfection. In the preface to the English language edition, Padre Gerardo di Flumeri writes:

> These letters teach with certainty the ways of God, on the basis of reliable mystical doctrine and solid biblical information. They are therefore a proof of the Padre's cultural grounding and that he is not an improvised spiritual director, but an enlightened guide of souls, sustained by an enviable theological, ascetic-mystical and biblical training.[5]

The collection is considered a masterpiece on the science of the spiritual life, and provides a gold mine of resources both for spiritual directors and those who are receiving direction.

Raffaelina Cerase was the most notable of the early "spiritual daughters" of Padre Pio. In the short time he was assigned to St. Anne's Friary, his reputation as a spiritual guide blossomed, and an informal prayer group comprised of some of the Italian women under his direction was formed.

This was a harbinger of what would some day become a worldwide movement of organized prayer groups under Padre Pio's banner.

The demands on his time by those seeking his spiritual counsel continued to increase. Shortly before he was to leave Foggia for a new assignment, he ended a letter to Padre Agostino on August 23 by apologizing for not writing more often:

> If I don't send you my news more frequently, please don't blame me, Father, knowing that this is not due to lack of goodwill. . . . I must let you know that I am not left a free moment: crowds of people thirsting for Jesus are pressing upon me, so that I am at my wit's end.
>
> In the face of such an abundant harvest, on the one hand, I feel glad in the Lord because I see the ranks of chosen souls swelling and love for Jesus growing; on the other hand, I am dismayed by such a burden and almost demoralized, for many reasons which are easy to understand.[6]

Foggia, in the center of the *Tavoliere,* or great plain of Southeastern Italy, is normally unbearably hot and humid in the summer. The oppressive heat was an additional burden on Padre Pio's already delicate health. Seeing his suffering, Padre Paolino, a visiting priest from a tiny hill-top friary located at San Giovanni Rotondo on the Gargano mountain, invited him to spend a few days there. So on July 28, Padre Pio accompanied Padre Paolino to Our Lady of Grace Friary, a trek of about 25 miles, using horse and coach. The poor horses had to climb a steep winding road bestriding the cliffs of the mountain, in order to reach the 1,800 foot high town of San Giovanni Rotondo, and the journey took about twelve hours. Once at the medieval town itself, the little party endured another mile or so of rough, rocky mule trail before finally reaching the isolated monastery.

Padre Pio stayed at Our Lady of Grace for a week, returning on August 5. The cooler mountain air and fresh breezes proved extremely beneficial to his health, and the quiet and solitude were most agreeable to his spirit. Padre Pio, upon his return to Foggia, wrote to Padre Benedetto describing the improvement to his well-being, and he asked to be allowed to spend more time at this mountain Friary:

> I am going to ask a favor of you and I ask it because Jesus compels me to. He tells me that I must strengthen my body a bit in order to be ready for other trials to which He intends to subject me.
>
> The favor I want to ask of you, dear Father, is to let me spend some time in San Giovanni Rotondo, where Jesus assures me I will feel better. I ask you not to refuse me this charity.[7]

Padre Benedetto granted the permission, and on September 4, 1916, Padre Pio arrived once again at Our Lady of Grace Friary. In view of his past history of short stays at so many monasteries because of his medical problems, no one surmised that "some time" in San Giovanni Rotondo would amount to 52 consecutive years spent in the same friary!

Chapter 6

Mary McAlpin Pyle

NOTWITHSTANDING the spiritual wisdom contained in the collected letters to the Italian noblewoman Raffaelina Cerase, the most prominent and notable of all of Padre Pio's spiritual children was an American, a daughter of the "nobility" of America's wealthy social classes. She was Adelia McAlpin Pyle—better known as Mary Pyle after her conversion to Catholicism, or as Maria Pyle, *l'Americana*, to the Italians. Born only a year after Padre Pio, her origins were in total contrast to the Saint's humble and poor beginnings.

Until very recently, the city of her birth was not certain—it was thought to be either Morristown, New Jersey at her grandparents' estate, or Manhattan, where her parents resided. However, fresh research by Susan De Bartoli, who is collecting documentation on Mary Pyle's Cause for Beatification (see the Afterword), indicates that she was in fact born in New York City. The eight servants at the Manhattan town home indicate with certainty the financial and social standing of the Pyle family. Born April 17, 1888, Adelia McAlpin Pyle was baptized as a Presbyterian, and it was only much later, after becoming Catholic as an adult, that she took the name of Mary.

Adelia, one of six siblings, was the eldest daughter of James Pyle, who had made his fortune in the soap business, and of his wife Adelaide. Adelaide was one of the McAlpins, a family which was tied by marriage to the Rockefellers. They prospered in tobacco and real estate, and owned the

Hotel McAlpin in New York. This exclusive hotel, which was
built in 1904, had a rooftop health club, and a "silent floor"
for guests who worked at night and slept during the day. It
endures today as a residential building on the corner of
Broadway and 34th street.

Adelaide was ambitious for her children, and wished her
daughter Adelia to be properly brought up to become a "high-
society" matron. Therefore, her early education was under-
taken by private teachers. For foreign language instruction,
a tutor would come to live with the family, and Adelia was
not allowed to speak anything but the language to be
learned. In this way she became proficient at reading and
speaking French, Spanish, German and Italian.[1]

Rather than having her attend a university, her mother
sent her to finishing schools to learn music, dance, voice and
the art of teaching. Adelia recalled that as a child, the family was invited to the home of Calvin Coolidge for social gatherings. As a young adult, she attended the best society balls
in New York and became an avid horseback rider—that is,
until a riding injury ended her interest in that sport.

To Adelia, who was an intelligent, cheerful and sensitive
young lady, the life she was being groomed to lead had a con-
straining shallowness. She was an idealistic soul, to whom a
life of material pursuits and worldly social engagements had
no meaningful appeal. She felt an inner emptiness, even in
the practice of her Protestant religion, and began to seek
greater spiritual fulfillment. The spark for this religious
quest may have been kindled when she was a child of about
ten years old. One of the family maids, who was an Irish
Catholic, befriended Adelia, and on occasion the two of them
would attend Mass at the maid's Catholic parish. Her
mother put an immediate end to this when she found out,
since to her, Roman Catholicism was not a socially acceptable religion.[2]

Later, as a teenager, Adelia began to express a serious desire to become a Catholic. Her parents sought to dissuade her by inviting learned Protestant ministers to their home to speak to her. Finally, they prevailed upon the head pastor of the Brick Presbyterian Church, which they attended, to try to persuade her not to convert. Arriving at their house, he tried to impress on her the folly of converting to Catholicism. During the discussion, Adelia asked him if he truly believed and was convinced that his religion was the right one. He hesitated, then admitted that he was not really sure of the truth of his own religion. Adelia then responded with simple logic, asking why he would want to impose his religion on her if he himself did not fully believe in it.[3] After this and similar failures, Adelia's parents put an end to these visits, but not to their opposition to the Catholic Church. However, the young Adelia was not yet ready to make a formal break with the family religion in order to become a Catholic.

In 1912, when Adelia was in her twenties, her father passed away. Her mother Adelaide at that time was becoming quite immersed in the work of Maria Montessori, the famed Italian educator. Dr. Montessori, the first female licensed physician in Italy, had developed a new method of pedagogy for young children. She met with spectacular success working with the slum children of Rome and gained international acclaim for her teaching methods. Adelaide, who had shown such great interest in the education of her own children, established the Montessori Education Foundation in New York, in order to found schools in America that would be based on the Montessori Method.[4] Although biographers differ as to the exact sequence of events, Adelia's exposure to the work of Dr. Maria Montessori probably began at this time.

Shortly thereafter, her mother, in order to discourage Adelia's affections for a certain suitor that she did not think

proper for her daughter, encouraged her to take a trip to
Europe. Soon Adelia was on her way to Italy and arrived in
Rome, where she visited Maria Montessori. Impressed by
Adelia Pyle's linguistic abilities and intelligence, Dr. Montessori began instructing her on her teaching methods. Over
a year later, they both embarked for the United States, and
for a while each went her separate way.

Soon, the involvement of Adelia's mother in the Montessori system led Dr. Montessori to visit the Pyle residence.
Meeting Adelia again, and in need of an interpreter, she
offered the position to her. Adelia spent some time thinking
over the offer, and in the meantime her mother left for California. Finally Adelia made up her mind, and wrote to
inform her mother that she was leaving for Europe to be Dr.
Montessori's interpreter. But mother Adelaide, although herself committed to spreading the Montessori Method, wrote
back to her daughter, forbidding her to go.

In her letter, she said that Adelia was too young to be traveling for such long periods of time away from home. However, Adelia was already a young woman in her twenties.
Since it was no secret that Dr. Montessori was a devout,
practicing Roman Catholic, might there have been another
unspoken reason for Adelia's mother's opposition to her
daughter's association with Dr. Montessori? At any rate, the
letter forbidding her to go arrived too late, for Adelia was
already on her way overseas.

Adelia worked with Dr. Montessori for ten years, traveling
to the great capitals of Europe. In addition to interpreting
for her in many languages, she became a trusted collaborator, associate, close friend, and confidante. Taking advantage
of their journeys to countries such as France, Spain and
Germany, Adelia spent much of her free time visiting
Europe's magnificent Catholic cathedrals and Marian
shrines. One year during Holy Week, Dr. Montessori took her

to Rome, where together they attended many of the sacred functions held at the ancient basilicas.

Adelia was drawn to these places, not just because of their artistic beauty, but also because of her spiritual longing and her growing desire to learn more about the Catholic religion. In Spain, one of her favorite shrines was the sanctuary of Our Lady of Montserrat, not far from Barcelona, where she made daily visits to spend time in prayer and meditation. It was while praying at this church that Adelia Pyle finally decided to become a Catholic, and she began taking instructions from the Jesuit Fathers.

Arrangements were made to have her baptized conditionally[5] at the shrine in Montserrat by one of the Jesuit priests who had been instructing her in the Faith. But for some inexplicable reason, in spite of her indebtedness to the Jesuits, Adelia decided to have the ceremony performed by a Capuchin. She had no explanation for this request, and did not know herself why she made it. Perhaps it was because of the Capuchin friar who was a frequent visitor in Dr. Montessori's home, although it is not known whether this was the same Capuchin who baptized her. Also uncertain is the date the rite was performed. Dates of 1913,[6] 1918,[7,8] and even 1921[9] have all been proposed. (The difficulty in finding documentation for either her Catholic or Presbyterian baptism is unfortunate, since it might be an obstacle—hopefully a minor one—to her Cause for Beatification.) Adelia chose "Mary" as her baptismal name, and thereafter preferred to be known simply as Mary Pyle.

Her mother's reaction was severe but not unexpected. She was deeply hurt and disturbed that her daughter had renounced the family's Protestant faith to become a Roman Catholic. Consequently, Mary was disinherited from the Pyle-McAlpin fortune, and a generous allowance she had been receiving was cut off. Her mother also broke all ties with Maria Montessori, and the Montessori Education Foundation she had set up in New York she renamed The Child Education Foundation.[10]

Mary continued her association with Dr. Montessori, and became fervent in her new Catholic Faith. Together they tried to attend daily Mass and received Holy Communion whenever possible. Spiritual reading was part of Mary's regimen, and it was during a stay in London in 1921 that she came across a two-volume set of books by Fr. Jean-Pierre Caussade, entitled *Self-Abandonment to Divine Providence*. She liked the first volume very much, since it taught how to live each day according to the Will of God.

But it was the second book that made a special impression on her. This book was a collection of letters from Fr. Caussade, in which he gave spiritual guidance and advice to various cloistered nuns. Reading this made Mary realize the importance of having a director to guide her soul, so that she could progress safely in her spiritual growth and not deviate from the true path.[11] Mary felt this was especially necessary, because at that time she was trying to fight a tendency to a kind of spiritual lethargy, a malaise that was setting in after her first fervor.

She immediately began a novena to Our Lady of Pompeii to obtain such a guide. From London the two women traveled to Rome, where Mary continued her supplications. She went almost every day to the Church of the Holy Name of Jesus (*Chiesa del Gesu*, the Mother church of the Jesuits), where she prayed perseveringly to the *Madonna della Strada*, Our Lady of the Way, imploring her for a wise spiritual director. It was during this same period that she began to hear about a certain Capuchin monk in the south, whose fame for sanctity was spreading throughout Italy. It was said that he lived a very holy life, that he had received the wounds of Christ on his own body, and that he lived in an

obscure monastery near a remote mountain town called San
Giovanni Rotondo.

Chapter 7

From Spiritual Director to Soldier

T HE town of San Giovanni Rotondo is perched on a broad plateau, high on the Gargano mountain in southeastern Italy. On the map, the Gargano massif comprises the spur of the boot-shaped Italian peninsula, and is a large elevated promontory jutting out into the Adriatic Sea. The rocks and karst which form the mountain are similar in their pale orange color to the stones one finds in the mountain towns at the opposite side of the Adriatic.

When Padre Pio was assigned to the tiny Capuchin monastery at San Giovanni Rotondo in 1916, it was an unknown, forgotten farm village whose few thousand inhabitants lived almost a medieval existence in their stone houses. There was no running water and no electricity. The primary occupations of farming and grazing were made difficult by the rocky, barren slopes. Roads were few, and visiting the nearest main city, Foggia, entailed navigating a serpentine road of hairpin turns that ran alongside the steep southern side of the Gargano. Transportation was by mule or horse-cart when it was not on foot. Robbers and fugitives frequented the area, hiding out in caves and primitive huts in the many deserted tracts in the hills and valleys.

About a mile-and-a-half to the west of the town and a little higher up the mountain, stood a remote friary and church dating from the mid-1500's. Standing by itself on the lonesome hillside, with nothing but an old mule trail to connect it to the town below, Our Lady of Grace Friary was home to a handful of Franciscan Capuchins. In 1916 the Gargano mountain itself was almost an uncharted area of Italy, and the little Friary was the most forgotten and isolated of all of the Capuchin monasteries in the southern part of that country. Frequently, friars were sent to Our Lady of Grace as a punishment for some indiscretion or other, and no one ever volunteered to be assigned there.[1]

Although summers were quite pleasant in the breezy hills, winter winds often brought bitterly cold weather and blowing snow, sometimes completely cutting off the Friary. But the townspeople looked out for the monks, and if the snow got to be too high, they would dispatch a party of volunteers to reach the monastery with food and other needed supplies. However, even under the best of conditions, visitors to the church were few, because of the difficult climb up the rough mule path.

All this would change dramatically for the town and Friary over the course of Padre Pio's residence and continue even to the present day. Word of the arrival of the "holy monk" on September 4, 1916, spread rapidly through the handful of mountain communities. Soon the informal prayer group at St. Anne's in Foggia, some of whose members had been from San Giovanni, was re-established at Our Lady of Grace. Comprised of a dozen or more women, they met and prayed together with Padre Pio in the guest room of the Friary twice a week.

Among these was a woman who had also been part of the Foggia group, Lucia Fiorentino, somewhat of a mystic in her own right. A few years after Padre Pio's arrival, she wrote in her diary that in 1906 she had heard the voice of Jesus in her heart telling her that a priest would come from far away, symbolized by a great tree to be planted in the Friary. This tree would be so large, well-rooted and leafy that with its shade it would cover the whole world. Whoever faithfully took refuge under this tree would come to salvation, and those who despised and ridiculed it would be punished. Lucia was convinced that this prophecy was fulfilled with the coming of Padre Pio to Our Lady of Grace Friary in San Giovanni Rotondo.[2]

With his arrival at San Giovanni Rotondo, Padre Pio's ministry as a guide and director of souls blossomed, and his reputation for holiness made him a widely sought counselor. He was encouraged by his superiors to provide spiritual direction for those in the surrounding area who sought his advice. For many of the women, this was done as before, primarily by an exchange of letters (comprising the third volume of the *Epistolario*),[3] since women did not have the same access to the Friary and to his cell that was afforded to the men.

He was also put in charge of the "Seraphic College" at the monastery. This consisted of a group of young boys aspiring to the priesthood, who had completed elementary school and were continuing their education under the Capuchins. Padre Pio became their classroom teacher, in addition to being the spiritual guide of these dozen or so souls.

He varied his approach towards those he was directing and guiding, according to their dispositions and progress; to one person he was strict, at other times or with another person he was easy-going, and on occasion he could even seem indifferent. But he was consistent in the substance of what he taught.

He recommended meditative prayer twice daily, especially on the life, suffering and death of Christ. First, in the morning as a preparation for the events of the day, and then in the evening as a purification from any worldly attachment to those events. These half-hour periods of meditation should also include an examination of conscience, especially in the evening session, with reflection on how well the day was spent. Some form of prayer should continue throughout the day. He had written to Raffaelina Cerase:

> Never let your mind become so absorbed in your work or in other matters as to make you lose the presence of God. For this purpose I ask you to renew very often the right intention you had at the outset. Now and then you should say some short prayers which are like so many darts which wound the heart of God and constrain Him, if I may use such an expression, which is no exaggeration in your case, to grant you His graces and His help in everything you do.[4]

The importance of reading Scripture and spiritual books was emphasized—his favorite author was the Apostle St. Paul. He counseled weekly Confession, daily Holy Communion, and penance and fasting for those whose health could bear them. Frequent Confession was recommended, even if there were no major transgressions, because "a clean room will need to be dusted again after eight days, even if it is not in use."[5]

His direction and guidance extended beyond the strictly spiritual, and his advice was often sought on every-day matters, personal decisions to be made, or even what name a child should be given. In all of this, he endeavored to instill the principles of Christian living in every aspect of one's daily walk.

Unfortunately, after a few happy months at San Giovanni Rotondo, military obligations once again beckoned Padre Pio. His one year leave of absence from the Army for poor health ended in December of 1916, and on the 18th of the month he reported to the Army headquarters at Naples. He was sent to Holy Trinity Hospital for examinations to determine his fitness to resume military service, and he was once again declared unfit.

In a letter to Padre Benedetto on January 2, 1917, the ailing Padre Pio wrote:

> Thanks be to God! I had the medical examination this morning and they wrote down: infection at the apex of both lungs and widespread chronic bronchial catarrh. They confined themselves therefore to granting me six months convalescence. Never mind! This is better than nothing. I hope they'll give me my departure papers this evening. Tomorrow morning, God willing, I'll pay a visit to Our Lady of Pompeii and then, after putting in a brief appearance in Pietrelcina, I'll return to the community. As regards my health, I feel very bad. My stomach will no longer retain any food. I am also very dejected spiritually and the combat is increasingly relentless. I have to end here because my strength and my sight are failing me.[6]

When his six-month convalescence was over in July 1917, the Army sent a telegram to San Giovanni Rotondo addressed to Francesco Forgione, recalling him back to duty. No one knew who this Francesco Forgione was, so the telegram was returned to the Naples barracks. The Army then assumed he had gone to his home town of Pietrelcina to avoid military service, and he was considered a deserter. The Military Police were sent to look for him there, and had no luck until his sister finally explained that he was currently known by his name in religion, Padre Pio, and that he was at the monastery in San Giovanni. Finally, the local police of San Giovanni Rotondo came calling at Our Lady of Grace with the news that he was ordered to report to the Tenth Medical Corps in Naples. Padre Pio left the next day, and by now it was already August. The "deserter" gracefully explained that he had been told to await orders when the six months were up, the orders had just arrived, and here he was!

Again he was hospitalized to determine whether he was medically fit for the army. He was examined twice, and the verdict was that he was still too ill to serve. However, he was subjected to one final observation, by a Colonel, whose cursory examination consisted of just a glance at his face; he declared Padre Pio fit for indoor service. Private Forgione's new address: Fourth Platoon, Tenth Medical Corps, Sales Barracks, Naples.

But in a matter of weeks, he was back in the hospital, with high fevers, vomiting, and coughing of blood. On November 6 he was given yet another leave, this time for four months. Reporting to the Army after this latest period of convalescence was over, he was hospitalized once more, which by this time should have surprised no one in the military.

Padre Pio's hospital stays were quite unpleasant experiences. The wards were stark and gloomy, and medical treatments were given with a minimum of personal attention. The disagreeable memory of those cold, impersonal examinations, treatments and rooms, stimulated him to consider the type of environment a hospital should ideally provide. His ideas were ultimately realized in the design and operation of the magnificent hospital he himself would build many years later.

Finally, on March 18, 1918, he was permanently discharged from the Army for medical reasons and was given a good conduct report for serving his country honorably. He was also awarded a small pension for his service, but this he did not want to accept, since he felt he had done nothing to deserve it. However, when it was explained to him that the payments could be earmarked for the monastery and for the poor children of San Giovanni, he consented to the pension.[7]

Thus ended the military career of Private Francesco Forgione, which consisted of a total of one hundred eighty-two days of active service over a period of about two-and-a-half years.

Chapter 8

"My God, My God, Why Hast Thou Forsaken Me?"

ONCE again ensconced at our Lady of Grace Friary on the Gargano mountain, Padre Pio continued to suffer from general ill-health. However, since he was enjoying fresh mountain breezes, in lieu of breathing the foul city air of Naples, his physical condition did show some improvement. From now on it would be his spiritual experiences that would cause his worst trials and pains. In the succeeding months, he would undergo severe interior torments, a true "dark night of the soul," that would result in the mystical "transverberation" of his heart. These interior sufferings and heavenly touches were part of a crescendo of events that culminated in the reception of the visible, bleeding stigmata in September, 1918. The details of this spiritual ascent to his own Calvary are preserved in the remarkable letters to his directors, Padre Benedetto and Padre Agostino.

In March of 1918, he wrote to Benedetto that he himself did not understand his own interior state. It seemed to him that the Lord was withdrawing His grace from him more and more, condemning him to live in ever greater spiritual darkness. A month later, he lamented to Padre Agostino that he was on the verge of collapsing under the weight of this trial. But he was reluctant to reveal many details about his suffering because of his inability to describe in words what was transpiring within his soul. "I hesitate to put in writing the account of my interior sufferings and combats, because I find

47

I am far from describing what goes on within me, by no deliberate fault on my part."[1]

In May he sounded a brief, joyful note in a letter to Padre Agostino, describing how he spent a few happy days with Padre Benedetto in the latter's friary at San Marco la Catola. But by June, his interior sufferings had returned and were dramatically more severe. In a letter on the 4th to Padre Benedetto he described an agonizing martyrdom, and complained that the Lord's hand weighed heavily on him, causing his soul to be more perturbed than ever before. He implied that something had occurred at the end of May that caused him such extreme anguish that he felt forsaken by God. His soul was now enveloped in darkness, with only occasional and rare flashes of light to tell him God exists.

> My supreme Good, where are You? I no longer know You or find You, but I must necessarily seek You, You who are the life of my dying soul. *My God, my God!*— I can no longer say anything else to You—*why have You forsaken me?* I am aware of nothing but this abandonment, I am ignorant of all else, even of life, which I am unaware of living.[2]

But Padre Pio continued to be reluctant to reveal, even to his trusted directors, a complete description of his spiritual experiences. In his very next letter to Padre Benedetto, on June 19, he repeated his complaint that God had forsaken him. Convinced it was because of his own sins, he labeled himself a reprobate, undeserving of further help or guidance. Even when "a glimmer of knowledge flits by," it only made him thirst more for God. Although he bemoaned that he could not find his God, he made a heroic effort to unite himself to God's Will and to fulfill it perfectly. Once again, he alluded to something that had befallen him at the end of

May. "My day began on May 29 and has never waned. I feel crushed in soul and body . . ." He referred to this as a "new state" and confessed that he had to do violence to himself in order to reveal any details to Padre Benedetto.

Yet, he knew that he must sooner or later confide in his spiritual director, in order that his soul "may not feed on pure illusions." Padre Benedetto wrote to Padre Pio to assure him that God would not abandon him, that God was within him. He was aware that Padre Pio had in the past been granted great spiritual consolations, but now his soul was to be buffeted: ". . . after tasting honey it must continue to sip the chalice of Gethsemane."

By the end of July, Padre Pio's descent into the dark night of the soul reached new depths. In a letter to Padre Benedetto of July 27, 1918, he described himself as completely astray and forsaken, having lost every trace and vestige of the Supreme Good. Even the flashes and fleeting glimmers of light had disappeared.

> Completely cut off from the light of day, without a glimmer which might dispel my everlasting night, I crawl along in the dust of my nothingness, but I am powerless to move forward in the mire of my miseries of all kinds.[3]

In that letter he finally overcame the reluctance to reveal what had occurred within him at the end of May, on the feast of Corpus Christi. He wrote that at Holy Mass that morning he felt the Spirit of God, the Divine Presence, touch him mystically and interiorly, in the deepest recesses of his soul. "I was touched by a living breath," he said, but it lasted only for a fleeting moment. The experience left him shaken and in terror, and he almost passed out. This was succeeded by a sensation of great calm, such as he had never felt before.

This mystical experience is described in theological terms by the editors of the *Epistolario*[4] as an "interior stroke of love," an event purely spiritual and internal to his soul, with no external manifestation. Padre Benedetto's reply dwelt on the meaning of this "living breath":

> And what was the meaning of the interior touch on the morning of Corpus Christi? It meant that God adhered to your soul and shook it, infusing into it a stream of life, like an elixir to sustain you when you were placed on the gallows.[5]

Padre Pio experienced some relief from his unending spiritual struggles in the practice of his daily ministry, which consisted of celebrating Holy Mass, hearing Confessions, and imparting spiritual direction. On July 29, he apologized to Padre Agostino for not writing more frequently, explaining that he just did not have the time to write, for he spent the whole morning hearing Confessions. Notwithstanding the recent "interior touch," he once again cried out that he had been abandoned by God: "My God! My Father! I have lost all trace of the Supreme Good . . . Where has He concealed Himself?" Padre Agostino's wise words of reply came in a letter of August 3:

> But reflect that the suffering humanity of the Lord was never really forsaken by the Divinity. He suffered all the effects of being forsaken but He was never forsaken. Thus it is with souls who love Jesus' sufferings . . . You ask me if you can hope for Jesus' return within you! But He is within you![6]

On the 5th of August, 1918, Padre Pio received the most sublime of all the Divine visitations that he had experienced up to that time. This was the mystical gift of transverberation, a spiritual wound of love that transfixed his heart. True to form, Padre Pio, in his modesty and reluctance to speak about the heavenly favors bestowed on him, did not inform his directors Padre Benedetto and Padre Agostino of this event until weeks after it had occurred. He sent similar letters to them on the 21st, describing what he feared might be a new punishment inflicted on him by divine justice. The reason he gave for finally revealing what had happened was that his "case is so truly desperate."

Padre Pio wrote that on the evening of August 5, while he was hearing the boys' Confessions (the students of the Seraphic College), in his "mind's eye" he saw a mysterious celestial being (*misterioso personaggio*).

> He had in his hand a sort of weapon like a very long sharp-pointed steel blade, which seemed to emit fire. At the very instant that I saw all this, I saw that person hurl the weapon into my soul with all his might. I cried out with difficulty and felt I was dying. I asked the boy to leave because I felt ill and no longer had the strength to continue.[7]

The anguish and agony lasted through the next day, and continued until the morning of August 7. Padre Pio felt as if his very entrails were torn asunder and that he had been mortally wounded. He was in continual torment, as if he were suffering an open wound in the depths of his soul. In his humility, modesty and confusion he feared that this pain was the action of God's justice in response to his own shortcomings and ingratitude. "Is this not a new punishment inflicted upon me by divine justice?"

Padre Agostino was the first to write a response, assuring Padre Pio that the reason for this trial was not that he had offended Our Lord, but rather, it was a proof of God's love for him. Souls that truly want to follow Jesus must resemble Him in His sufferings. "The spiritual wound inflicted by that celestial person is the token of God's love for you." Padre Agostino pointed out that the painful, all-day suffering on the 6th coincided with the feast of the Transfiguration of Our Lord. It was a confirmation that Jesus wanted to "transfigure" the soul of Padre Pio with this wound of love.

A few days later, Padre Benedetto wrote to express similar assurances to Padre Pio. "It is a trial, it is a vocation to coredemption and hence a source of glory." In words that were similar to Padre Agostino's, he added that this phenomenon was not a purgation of the soul due to any shortcomings, but it was rather a painful union with the Lord, a pledge of love. Then, without considering that a further, more profound experience could possibly occur, he wrote, ". . . the wound completes your passion just as it completed the Passion of the Beloved on the Cross."

The phenomenon of transverberation is usually associated with Carmelite spirituality and is described in the classical literature on mysticism. St. Teresa of Avila, the Spanish Carmelite who lived in the 16th century, provided one of the earliest accounts of the event, which was very similar to Padre Pio's experience. In a vision, she saw an Angel holding a long golden spear, with a tip that seemed to be on fire. The iron tip of the spear pierced her heart several times, leaving her inflamed with the love of God. Her contemporary, St. John of the Cross, compared the experience to a cauterization of the soul by the arrow or dart of a Seraphim. The soul is painfully wounded by the dart, but at the same time feels ineffable delight. St. Therese of Lisieux, the Little Flower, also described an episode in which she was wounded by a fiery dart. She experienced simultaneously an ardent fire and such heavenly sweetness that she thought she would die.[8]

The question remains as to whether the transverberation produced a physical wound in his heart, since Padre Pio seemed to be speaking more in terms of something internal: "I feel in the depths of my soul a wound that is always open . . ." However, on September 5 he wrote to Padre Benedetto that "The wound which has reopened bleeds incessantly." A few lines later he again mentions the "open wound."

Almost a year later, after he had received the full-fledged visible stigmata, a clinical examination of his chest wound revealed that it was approximately in the form of an "X." The Father Guardian of the Friary, Padre Paolino of Casacalenda was one of the witnesses to this examination. In his memoirs he wrote that the "X" shape indicated ". . . that there are two wounds, and this fits in with the fact I have heard mentioned but cannot prove for lack of reliable documents, that long before the stigmata, Padre Pio received a sword-thrust through the heart from an Angel."[9]

Definitive confirmation that the transverberation resulted in an open wound is found in a deposition Padre Pio made in 1967, shortly before his death. In that statement he declared that ". . . a visible, physical wound in his side resulted from the experience."[10]

Interestingly enough, Padre Pio apparently experienced a recurrence of the transverberation. On December 20, 1918, he wrote to both Padre Benedetto and Padre Agostino about another visit from the "mysterious personage." For the past few days he had felt a sharp pain, as if a steel blade were extended from the lower part of his heart to his right shoulder. "It causes me extreme pain and never allows me to rest." This renewed experience occurred more than four months after the original transverberation, and two months after the appearance of the actual stigmata. In these latest letters, Padre Pio now referred to his celestial visitor as the "usual" mysterious person.

Chapter 9

The Imprint of God

T HE *misterioso personaggio*, or celestial being of the transverberation, paid him a special visit in September of 1918, which would mark Padre Pio in spectacular fashion for the rest of his life—as a beacon of hope for many and a sign of contradiction for a few. On the morning of September 20, the Friary of Our Lady of Grace was practically deserted. Most of the priests were serving in the military, the Superior, Padre Paolino, was out of town, and the questor, Brother Nicola, was off seeking alms. The students of the Seraphic College were in the monastery gardens, while their spiritual director, Padre Pio, was praying alone in the choir loft, making his thanksgiving after Mass. The following description of what occurred next is taken from Padre Pio's own letter of October 22, 1918 to Padre Benedetto,[1] and from an account he gave to his priest friend and *paesano* from Pietrelcina, Don Giuseppe Orlando.[2,3]

While engrossed in prayer that morning before the crucifix that adorned the choir loft, Padre Pio began to feel extremely calm and peaceful. Everything within and around him became indescribably still and quiet; he compared it to a sweet sleep. Without warning, that same mysterious person appeared before him as he had during the August 5th transverberation. But there was one difference; this time the hands, feet and side of the celestial being were dripping with blood, and shining forth rays of light and flame. Padre Pio was terrified. His pounding heart seemed ready to burst out of his chest, and he felt he surely would have died had not the Lord strengthened him at that moment. When the vision disappeared, he found himself on the floor and saw that his own hands, feet and side were dripping blood. He managed to crawl and drag himself back to his cell, unable to walk because of the pain in his pierced feet. He cleansed the wounds, and then remained alone in his room in prayerful weeping and thanksgiving. In his description of the prodigy to Don Orlando, he specifically mentioned that the apparition was of the "wounded Christ."

On the following days he did what he could to hide from everyone what he considered his great embarrassment. The boys in the Seraphic College could not understand why their instructor seemed to be hiding his hands under his garments during the classes that he was teaching. The Father Guardian, Padre Paolino, noticed that Padre Pio appeared to be covering up red spots on his hands with the sleeves of his habit. However, he was not too concerned since he and Padre Pio had recently received burns on their hands from carbolic acid. The boys had needed injections to fight the Spanish Flu, which was raging at that time. Due to a shortage of doctors, Padre Paolino and Padre Pio administered the shots, using carbolic acid as a sterilizing agent. So when Nina Campanile, one of the spiritual daughters of Padre Pio, told Padre Paolino that she had seen the marks of the stigmata on the Friar, Padre Paolino just shrugged it off as being the carbolic acid burns. But shortly thereafter, a second woman reported to Padre Paolino that Padre Pio, like St. Francis, had received the sacred wounds. Aware that his own acid burns had already healed, Padre Paolino began to think that he should examine Padre Pio's marks more closely.

Since he was the Father Guardian, he took advantage of his position, and entered Padre Pio's room one day without knocking. The Padre was writing a letter, and Padre Paolino was able to see his hands clearly. The wounds were definitely not from the carbolic acid. He was able to see marks on both sides of Padre Pio's right hand and on the back of the left hand. The palm of the left hand was resting on a piece of paper, so Padre Paolino could not see that wound. Without saying anything about the marks, the Guardian left Padre Pio's cell. He was now convinced that Padre Pio really had the stigmata. His next move was to write Padre Benedetto, who then wrote to Padre Pio.[4]

True to form, it was not until a month after the event that Padre Pio found the courage to reveal to his director what had occurred. (His director was also the Capuchin Provincial Minister.) In a letter dated October 19, 1918, he briefly mentioned that he was bleeding, and Padre Benedetto immediately wrote back and asked Padre Pio: "Tell me *everything* quite frankly, not just by allusions." Padre Pio replied in his now famous letter of the 22nd, in which he described in detail what had transpired in the presence of the mysterious personage. In the same letter he lamented not only his physical pains and agony, but the embarrassment and humiliation of bearing about him these visible signs.

> I am afraid I will bleed to death if the Lord does not hear my heartfelt supplication to relieve me of this condition. Will Jesus, who is so good, grant me this grace? Will He at least free me from the embarrassment caused by these outward signs? I will raise my voice and will not stop imploring Him until in His mercy He takes away, not the wound or the pain, but these outward signs which cause me such embarrassment and unbearable humiliation.[5]

The outer wounds did not go away or heal as the days passed, and to Padre Pio it seemed as if that celestial person continued to open them up afresh. "He continues his work incessantly, causing me extreme spiritual agony."

About a week after Padre Pio had received the stigmata, Padre Agostino made a visit to the Friary. He did not know about the recent event, but did notice a red spot on the back of one of Padre Pio's hands. Aware that he had on occasion experienced the wounds of Christ in prior years, and knowing Padre Pio's reserve and modesty, he discreetly kept quiet and did not ask about the mark. It is not known for certain when Padre Agostino did find out, but on March 5, 1919, Padre Benedetto wrote to Padre Agostino explicitly mentioning the phenomenon. After stating that some pilgrims from San Giovanni and neighboring San Marco in Lamis had started to arrive at Our Lady of Grace Friary in order to see Padre Pio, he wrote:

> In his case there are no spots or imprints, but real wounds which perforate his hands and feet. I have observed the wound in his side, a veritable gash from which blood or a blood-red secretion flows continually. On Fridays it is blood. I found him barely able to stand, but when I took my leave of him, he was able to celebrate and when he says Mass, this gift is exposed to the public view, since he must raise his bare hands.[6]

The news of the great prodigy at first spread very slowly. The Provincial Minister Padre Benedetto had wished to keep Padre Pio's condition as secret as possible, and asked the Superior, Padre Paolino, to observe strict silence. The spiritual daughters who had noticed the wounds were also to keep quiet, but in their case they were not under the yoke of religious obedience. Apparently it was Nina Campanile who first broke the news in San Giovanni Rotondo, informing her

mother and sister about the joyous event. Even Padre
Paolino could not contain himself, and quietly informed his
sister in Foggia. However, it was not until May, over seven
months after the stigmata appeared, that the trickle of visitors showing up at the monastery grew to a steady stream.
In the beginning of the month it was a small group of women
from Foggia, who had heard about the news from Padre
Paolino's sister. The next day a larger contingent from the
nearby towns arrived, and in subsequent days, more pilgrims continued to appear.[7]

Soon the floodgates would be opened for good. The press
had gotten wind of the event, and on May 9, 1919, an
unsigned item that appeared in a newspaper in Rome broke
the story. In 1986 an Italian, Gerardo Saldutto, published his
doctoral dissertation concerning this period of Padre Pio's
life. He relates:

> The first news article on Padre Pio goes back to
> Friday, May 9, 1919, and is from the daily Roman
> newspaper, *Il Giornale d'Italia*. A brief sketch, with-
> out a writer's name, entitled "The Miracles of a
> Capuchin of San Giovanni Rotondo," describes "the
> humble Capuchin," a "saint," esteemed by the people
> for his prophetic spirit, his clairvoyance, his ubiquity,
> his ecstasies. If these phenomena could be doubted,
> one however is quite visible: the stigmata. The com-
> mon people, who in crowds and on pilgrimage flow
> into the monastery, believe in the holiness of the
> monk, while "cultivated people and the clergy main-
> tain a strict reserve, waiting for the authoritative
> judgement of the Church."[8]

This article not only guaranteed that the tide of pilgrims
would increase, but it also attracted the attention of other

reporters, who wasted no time in jumping on the bandwagon with articles about the "Miracle Monk." On May 25 (the Padre's 32nd birthday) a Southern Italian paper was the next one to announce the news. The article reported that some expected Padre Pio to die at age 33, in imitation of Christ. As described in the Saldutto dissertation:

> The 25th of May, which was coincidentally the birthday of Padre Pio, it was the turn of *Il Foglietto*, the weekly newspaper of the area, edited at Lucera, which was the paper best known and most appreciated in the Province. It presented an organized and faithful portrait of San Giovanni Rotondo, a town which was now becoming famous, not for its brigands, but rather for the merit of a humble little friar, Padre Pio of "Pietra Arcina," who arrived about two years ago. He is esteemed as a saint by almost all the population, and many come from all parts of Italy. The 20th of September of last year, he received the stigmata, from which issue blood, especially from his chest, and in a particular way on Friday, on which day it is possible to perceive a rustic perfume which emanates from his person. The Father Guardian references that Padre Pio vomits all the food that he consumes, and Dr. Merla affirms that, when Padre Pio is ill, his temperature reaches about 120 degrees. He has come to be called "the Saint," is thirty-two and a half years old, and the people believe he will die, like Christ, at age 33. He has no special education but possesses an appealing manner.[9]

In short order, the crowds increased to the point that almost all of the activities of Our Lady of Grace Friary were centered around ministering to the pilgrims. Four priests recently discharged from the military were assigned to the monastery, and immediately they were plunged into the duty of hearing the Confessions of the women, while Padre Pio heard those of the men. Soon it would entail a two week wait among the men to confess to him. Letters addressed to the Padre began to pour in, and a special room had to be set aside to sort and handle them. The people who arrived from distant points were truly on a pilgrimage in the classic sense. In the little town of San Giovanni Rotondo, there were no hotels or inns, and many of the pilgrims simply slept out in the open in the nearby fields.

In the meantime, Padre Pio took to covering the hand wounds with dark brown fingerless gloves or mittens, which served the dual purpose of hiding the wounds and also making it difficult to see the blood stains on them. In the evening, back in his cell, he would switch to white gloves. The wounds themselves were not pleasant to look at, and as the blood dried, large unsightly crusts would form around them. In later years Padre Alessio Parente, one of the friars who attended to Padre Pio, was hoping he would get to see the stigmata clearly. But when he finally was able to observe them, they looked so horrible that he prayed that he would never have to look at them again. This same friar reported that one time when Padre Pio was trying to clean some of the sharp, pointy crusts off of his hand, he fainted away from the pain.[10]

Padre Pio's usual reply when he was asked if the wounds hurt him was, "Do you think the Good Lord gave them to me as a decoration?" Sometimes visitors would speculate that the wounds were caused by long hours spent in thinking and meditating on the Passion of Christ. On one occasion, when a friend told him that a famous doctor had said as much, Padre Pio responded, ". . . Tell him to think intensely about being an ox. Let's see if he grows horns."[11]

In the summer of 1919, Padre Pietro of Ischitella became the new Provincial Minister, replacing Padre Benedetto. Later that year Padre Pietro remarked that almost all of the printed news about Padre Pio was coming from the secular press. Catholic publications for the most part were still silent, which was in keeping with the new Provincial's desire to keep publicity at a minimum, continuing Padre Benedetto's course of action. Padre Pietro observed that most of the visitors at the Friary were motivated by a true spirit of devotion, rather than by curiosity, and that Padre Pio spent sixteen hours a day in the confessional. Visitors often numbered in the thousands each day, somehow accommodating themselves to a church which could only contain a couple of hundred at a time. He noted that many people had returned to the practice of their religion, and that there were also many converts to the Catholic Faith. "All this, in my opinion, constitutes the true prodigy, and witnesses to the fact that the Lord desired to reveal this to His elect for the good of souls and for the glory of His Name."[12]

The visitors to Our Lady of Grace represented every level of society, from farm workers and peasants to the educated classes, including doctors, lawyers and the clergy. Royalty was no exception, and eventually Queen Maria Jose of Italy, Empress Zita of Austria, and the Queens of Spain, Bulgaria and Portugal all made their appearance.[13] King Alphonso XIII of Spain wrote to him asking for prayers and healing for his children.

In November of 1919, the Friary received a letter from the Vatican Secretary of State, Pietro Cardinal Gasparri, recommending his personal friends, the Rosi family, who were arriving at the Friary in order to receive the Sacraments of Confession and Holy Communion from Padre Pio. Cardinal Gasparri also wished to have Padre Pio pray every day during his Mass for the intentions of Pope Benedict XV and for himself, so that the Lord ". . . may enlighten and sustain us in our many difficulties."[14]

Pope Benedict XV was very favorably inclined towards Padre Pio and defended him against those who accused him of being a fraud and charlatan. He referred to Padre Pio as one of those few extraordinary men that God occasionally sends on earth for the conversion of sinners. He also said that although it is important to be prudent, it is not good to be too incredulous. On one occasion he ordered a Monsignor who had spoken ill of Padre Pio to go to San Giovanni Rotondo himself to learn how wrong he had been.

Chapter 10

The Doctors Are Summoned

T HE prudent approach of the Holy See and of the Capuchin authorities in discerning the true nature of Padre Pio's wounds was nowhere more evident than in their arrangements for medical doctors to examine him. The first was Dr. Luigi Romanelli, who was commissioned by Padre Benedetto to examine the wounds in May of 1919. Dr. Romanelli was the Chief of Staff at the City Hospital of Barletta, and he made five studies of the lesions from May to July of that year. After his first examination of the wounds, he issued a report that admitted of no scientific explanation for them:

> ... from the month of September up to the present day, Padre Pio's wounds have maintained the same form and state, and what is more marvelous, they do not present any difficulties or disturbances to the limbs as do common wounds. It is to be excluded that Padre Pio's lesions are of natural origin, but one must look for the productive agent without fear of moving to the supernatural. In itself, the fact constitutes an inexplicable phenomenon for human science alone.[1]

In an extremely painful experience for Padre Pio during this first study, Dr. Romanelli placed one of his fingers over the wound on the back of one of Pio's hands. He then positioned his thumb on the lesion in the palm of the same hand, and slowly pressed his fingers together. He perceived noth-

ing but empty space between the two fingers, finding no
resistance from either bone or tissue. From this he concluded
that there was literally a hole in between the lesions on the
front and back of the hands. In his final report, issued
November 1920 after completing the five examinations of
the stigmata, he concluded, ". . . I have never been able to
classify them in any known clinical disorder."

About two months after Dr. Romanelli began his studies,
the Vatican sent Dr. Amico Bignami, an atheist and a profes-
sor at Rome University, to report on the nature of the
wounds. He studied the stigmata for two days in July, 1919
and based his conclusions in part on the fact that Padre Pio
had occasionally used iodine to disinfect them and to try to
stop the bleeding. Bignami explained that repeated applica-
tions of iodine would act as an irritant, which would cause
the wound to persist instead of heal. His concluding hypothesis was that the wounds originated from neurotic auto-suggestion and persisted through the use of the iodine. Any
supernatural explanation was ruled out: "In any case, one can
confirm that there is nothing in the alterations of the skin
which cannot be the product of a morbose state or the use of
well known chemical agents."[2] Ironically, he issued his report
before waiting for the results of an experimental cure that he
had ordered to be performed on Padre Pio. When the results
of his experiment were compiled, they conflicted with his own
hypothesis that the wounds should show signs of healing.

Dr. Bignami had ordered that for eight days it was entirely
prohibited to treat the wounds with iodine, and they were to
be examined, then bandaged and sealed daily, in the presence of two friars. This was a great emotional trial for Padre
Pio, who was always deeply embarrassed when the stigmata
were viewed by anyone, even by priests from his own friary.
At the end of the eight days, the priests issued their report.
They observed that the condition of the wounds had

remained the same. Each day when the bandages were changed, it was evident that all the lesions had shed blood, and more so on the last day when the wounds were a bright red color. No healing was observed, and no iodine or other medicine had been applied. One of the observers was Padre Paolino, and he wrote in his memoirs that Padre Pio ". . . suffered intensely in his heart at revealing the wounds, which he always tried to hide from the eyes of all."[3]

Faced now with two conflicting medical diagnoses, the Minister General of the Capuchin Order dispatched Dr. Giorgio Festa to the monastery. Dr. Festa was a surgeon from Rome and had a reputation as one of the city's best doctors. He began his work on October 9, 1919. In November, he issued a long and detailed report in which he discounted any known natural cause for the wounds. "We are faced with an extraordinary phenomenon that we are unable to explain with the knowledge we possess." In his report he described the "goodness, affability and gentleness" of Padre Pio's character, of his life dedicated to personal sacrifice for the good of others, and his long hours spent in prayer and meditation. He concluded: "Hence, that which for science would seem to be an enigma, can be explained by faith."[4]

One of Dr. Festa's medical observations was that the aroma of the wounds was often not that of blood at all, but rather like a perfume or fragrance. During his investigation he took back to his office in Rome for closer examination a piece of cloth that had covered the heart wound. While *en route* in an automobile from San Giovanni, other passengers in the car commented that they could smell the distinctive perfume that emanated from the person of Padre Pio. They were not aware that Dr. Festa had the cloth along with him in a closed case. He stored the piece of cloth in a cabinet of his Rome office, and patients would often ask him why the air of the room was filled with perfume.

Another characteristic of the wounds that Dr. Festa observed was that sometimes light could be seen through them. In one of his reports he wrote that he was certain that he ". . . would be able to read something or to see an object if it were placed behind the hand."[5] During his Mass, Padre Pio did not wear the fingerless gloves, and some would notice a shaft of light passing through his hands when he raised them during the ceremony. Other witnesses claimed that at times the blood seemed to emit an unusual shine. Many years later, one of Padre Pio's confreres, Fr. Joseph Pius, would comment, "It is true that if you were very close and there was a light behind his hand, you could see a light shining through the holes in his hands."[6]

The early work by these doctors has assumed greater significance with the passing of time, since the Vatican later placed many restrictions on Padre Pio, including the prohibition of further medical examinations and studies of his stigmata.

Chapter 11

"l'Americana" Arrives

WHEN Mary McAlpin Pyle first heard about Padre Pio and his stigmata in 1921, she was in London working with Dr. Maria Montessori, translating educational tracts on the Montessori Method into English. She wrote later that she did not at that time want to go to see him merely to satisfy her curiosity. "I believed in him, and that seemed to me, in my state of lethargy, to be sufficient."[1] Two years later, Mary and Dr. Montessori traveled to Capri, where they spent the summer and early fall. While at Capri, a close friend of Mary's, Rina Caterinici D'Ergin, came to visit her. Rina, a member of the Eastern Orthodox Church, was trying to decide if she should convert to the Catholic Faith and told Mary that she wanted to hear personally from Padre Pio whether she should convert. Mary answered that since the Padre was a Catholic, of course he would tell her to convert. Rina was not satisfied with that reply and insisted on going to see Padre Pio, but only if Mary would accompany her. Reluctantly, Mary set out with Rina from Capri in October of 1923, and the two traveled via Naples and Foggia to San Giovanni Rotondo. Although Mary had been praying for a spiritual guide for quite some time, it had not occurred to her to seek out Padre Pio on her own initiative. ". . . I was so deaf that the Lord almost had to pull me by the ear to awaken me and force me to come and find that for which I had been searching for so long."[2]

Their meeting on October 4 with Padre Pio was a dramatic, emotional event for both women. Rina burst out cry-

ing, and asked him how to prepare to become a Catholic.
Padre Pio gave her a little catechism with various prayers
and teachings, and then gave Rina her most important
instruction: "It is necessary to love, love, love, and nothing
more."[3] As for Mary, she now realized this trip was more
than just a journey to accompany a friend to San Giovanni
Rotondo. When she saw the stigmatized Friar for the first
time, she was overcome with emotion and fell to her knees
saying, "Padre!" Mary Pyle and Padre Pio looked at each
other, and his eyes seemed to penetrate her soul. He placed
his gloved hand on her head in blessing, and said: "My child,
stop travelling around. Stay here."[4] The seed was planted.
The sophisticated, 35-year-old socialite could not sleep that
night, thinking that here she had met a Saint, but her duties
still called her elsewhere.

Mary returned to Capri with her friend, after explaining
to Padre Pio that she could not stay because she was
employed by Maria Montessori. He reportedly replied, "Who
is this woman that she should keep you tied up in this manner? You must stay here!"[5] From Capri, Mary and Dr.
Montessori continued to work together, traveling to London
and Amsterdam. But the image of Padre Pio blessing her
with his wounded hand began to hound her, and she felt restless and dissatisfied. Finally, she said to Maria Montessori,
"There is a living saint in this world, and it saddens me not
to be near him."[6] She asked her employer to come with her
to meet Padre Pio for herself. Thus, only a few weeks after
her first visit, Mary once again made the journey to San Giovanni Rotondo, this time in the company of her friend and
employer.

The afternoon of their arrival, they met with Padre Pio in
the sacristy of the little church. During the conversation,
Padre Pio surprised Mary by saying to her, "I will put a chain
around you and I will bridle you!"[7] This instantly reminded

her of a vivid dream that had occurred some time before, and she recounted it to him. In the dream she and Dr. Montessori were speeding away in an out-of-control stagecoach led by galloping horses. Suddenly, a mysterious figure appeared, who boldly grabbed the reins and stopped the horses. When the coach halted, a new road became visible on one side. The mysterious figure said, "Blessed are those who take the right road, for they will be saved."[8] After hearing the dream, Padre Pio smiled and said to Mary, "Remain here!" Mary replied that she had indeed been thinking about ending her employment with Dr. Montessori and settling in San Giovanni Rotondo. As if to confirm her decision, Padre Pio then said, "Obey your mother!" Mary was astonished, since the Padre had no way of knowing that her mother had tried to stop her from working for Dr. Montessori, and had written a letter forbidding her to do so. Mary saw this as a sign of what she must do. She looked toward Maria Montessori, who understood the situation perfectly; she graciously said to Mary, "If that is what you wish, what else is there to do?"[9]

When it came time to leave, Mary intended to go with Dr. Montessori in order to gather her belongings. But when the bus arrived, she found herself strangely rooted to the spot, unable to board the bus with the Doctor. Maria Montessori urged her to hurry and get on, but Mary cried back: "I can't, I feel paralyzed, as though someone had nailed my feet to the ground."[10] So it was that Mary Pyle remained behind while Dr. Montessori left on the bus alone. It was to be the last time the two would ever see each other. Later, it was reported that Dr. Montessori was resentful toward Padre Pio for taking away her valued collaborator and interpreter, who had been a reliable employee for the past ten years. As for Mary, she had joined that growing group of people who chose to move permanently to San Giovanni Rotondo in order to spend the rest of their lives near the holy man of the

Gargano. She described what happened to her and the others: "They came, they returned, and finally they stayed. When you find a precious pearl, with what joy you discard all earthly goods in order to acquire it!"[11]

Mary's immediate need was to find a place to stay, a difficult task, considering that San Giovanni Rotondo was still a backward town with few modern conveniences and no hotels. She managed to find a room in the house of a local family, about two miles down the hill from the monastery. It was a humbling experience for a woman born into high society and who had traveled Europe with the world-famous Maria Montessori; she had to settle for quarters in what was at best a small rooming house. She soon adapted to the routine of the other women devotees of Padre Pio, who made their way up the primitive road each day to hear Padre Pio's Mass, which at that time was at seven in the morning.

Like the rest, she would spend the entire day at Our Lady of Grace, bringing along her lunch in a paper bag. At noon they would sit on a small stone wall that surrounded an elm tree in front of the Friary and have their meal. The day would be spent in prayer, in waiting to confess to Padre Pio and in attending the various religious functions at the church. In short, they desired to bask in the spiritual atmosphere of that peaceful sanctuary, joyful in the presence of the stigmatized friar whom they all considered a saint. Mary jotted in her notebook: "Here in this calm beside Padre Pio, one understands things better . . . for me his presence teaches more than a library full of books."[12]

Pietro Cugino, the child of a poor local family, was a favorite of both Mary and Padre Pio. He visited the monastery regularly and performed small chores and favors for the friars. When Mary would see him, as she sat under the elm tree, she would offer him part of her lunch. He would protest that the friars had fed him, but she insisted, happy to spend time with this fortunate boy, who spoke to Padre Pio almost every day. In fact, it was through Pietro that Mary was often able to communicate with the Padre, asking his advice, since she seldom had an opportunity to speak with him in person outside of Confession.

Pietro was probably not the only child to share Mary's lunch bag, for she soon began to lose enough weight that Padre Pio noticed it. Eventually, he had to advise her to go home every day for a full lunch and then return in the afternoon. While waiting for the church to reopen, Mary would teach Pietro many of the basics of the Catholic religion as they sat under the shade of the elm tree. In the evening Pietro and another boy, Cusenza, would visit Mary at her lodgings for more lessons, and ". . . when supper time arrived, she would not dismiss us without first giving us a hearty snack."[13] When it came time for Cusenza's First Holy Communion, it was Mary who provided him with his brand new suit.

As for Pietro, he soon became blind, and was destined to spend all of his life as an adopted son of the monastery. He is familiar to pilgrims who may have seen him kneeling near the altar during Mass, and is known by all as Pietruccio. (As of this writing, he is still living.) One day Padre Pio said to him, "Blessed are you Pietruccio, that you are blind and do not see the brutality of this world." He then asked him if he would like to regain his sight, for Padre Pio was prepared to intercede before God, to ask for the grace of sight for his blind friend. Pietruccio replied ". . . if it is harmful to my spiritual salvation, then I prefer to remain blind. For me it is enough to know that you are near me." Padre Pio, respecting his friend's wish, and knowing full well of the dangers to salvation that come through the eyes, did not pray for this grace. From then on he would speak with pride of Pietruccio, who had chosen not to endanger his spiritual vision by having his physical vision restored.[14]

Meanwhile, back in America, Mary's family was both disturbed and curious about her decision to end her employment with Maria Montessori, in order to live on a lonely hillside in a remote part of Italy. At that time virtually no one in the United States had any inkling that a stigmatized priest across the ocean was being called another St. Francis and a miracle worker. These were the "roaring twenties," a time of materialistic pursuits and exuberant diversions. Mary Pyle's actions seemed so strange to her socialite family that soon David, one of her brothers and a successful attorney, made the trip to San Giovanni to find out exactly what had happened to her. Upon his arrival he was taken aback by Mary's living conditions and way of life, which he considered completely inappropriate for her, in view of the family's social standing. Returning to America, he besought their mother Adelaide at least to restore Mary's allowance, which had been terminated, along with her inheritance, when Mary converted to Catholicism.

The strong-willed Adelaide, determined to see for herself who this Padre Pio was, went to San Giovanni Rotondo herself. But the initial encounter between the Friar and the matron was a disaster. With her beribboned dog at her feet, she and Mary waited in the sacristy of Our Lady of Grace Church for Padre Pio to walk by and greet the people. As he came near, the frisky dog ran out and got in his path, and the Padre instinctively shooed it away with a little kick. The horrified Adelaide picked up her four-footed friend and charged out of the monastery.[15] In a sequence of events now lost to history, Mary somehow managed to smooth things out, and her mother's subsequent encounters with Padre Pio had more favorable outcomes. In fact, she became quite taken with him, and decided to have her daughter's allowance resumed.

Resigned to Mary's new way of life, her mother began to

make annual visits to San Giovanni, not only to see her daughter but also to confer with Padre Pio, who had become a good friend. Because of the language barrier, Mary had to be present when the two met and talked. On one occasion, Adelaide bared her soul to Padre Pio to such an extent that he remarked later that he could have given her absolution. One day Mary received a letter from her mother, who was in northern Italy at the time, asking her to thank Padre Pio for visiting her there. It was an instance of Padre Pio's incredible gift of "bilocation," since he never physically left San Giovanni Rotondo after receiving the stigmata in 1918.

To Mary's disappointment, her mother never embraced the Catholic religion. Originally a Presbyterian, she had become a firm Baptist, and her daughter was concerned about her spiritual state. Padre Pio told her not to worry, assuring Mary that her mother would be saved ". . . because she is in good faith."[16] On what was to be Adelaide's last visit to the Saint shortly before she died, his parting words to her were prophetic: "Let's hope we meet again, but if we don't see each other here, we will see each other up there."[17]

Mary's newly restored allowance came to about $6,000 a year, an immense amount in the 1920's, and even more so for poverty-stricken Southern Italy. She began thinking about building her own home close to the monastery, so that she would no longer have to climb the rugged unpaved trail back and forth from the town to the church. Padre Pio agreed with the idea, and told her to build a good house that would serve herself and others, because ". . . here will remain the imprint of your work."[18] After finding a local architect, she picked a site that was quite close to the Friary, but near the bottom of a very steep hill. She did not follow Padre Pio's suggestion that she build it elsewhere, and regretted her decision many years later when the frailty of old age made the climb extremely difficult.

When facing the monastery, the house, which is still standing, is on the left side a few hundred feet in front of it. The
hill is so steep that from the road leading to the Friary, the
top of the three-story building is at eye level. (Some books
call it a two-story home, because to Italians the "first" floor
is the one above the ground floor, which is called the
"*pianterreno*.") The sturdily built house looks like a little castle with its roof-top turrets, and Mary had it painted pink,
giving it an inviting appearance. It was completed around
1927, and Padre Pio, who could not walk well on his
wounded feet, rode a donkey down the hill in order to bless
it. Until recent years, it was still easily identified by its distinctive pink hue, but unfortunately it has now been
repainted a dull beige.

This home would serve as a gathering place for many.
Pietro Cugino and the other youths continued their catechism in the new home and often stayed for dinner. Mary
generously invited children, orphans and the needy to be fed
and also to learn about the Faith. Often, people who were ill
would be invited to remain for extended periods of time.
Sometimes there were so many women living there that it
was like a small community of nuns.

Visitors from many different countries found their way to
her little "castle" during their pilgrimage to the monastery.
One of them wrote: "She performs the role of Public Relations Officer at San Giovanni Rotondo."[19] Both of Padre Pio's
parents spent their last days living in the pink house, and
there they passed away. During the War, many American GIs
were recipients of her hospitality, and the large kitchen table
was often packed with soldiers at meal times.

Mary's kindness was unbounded, and it was said that no
one who knocked on her door for some kind of assistance was
ever turned away. Her generosity was known even to the
thieves and brigands who lived in caves on the sides of the

mountain and in the woods. They used to come directly to her home and she would give them food.

Often by the end of the month, she had no money left, and she had to wait patiently for the next monthly allowance check from her family to arrive. She would then bring the check, along with any American currency she had, to San Giovanni's community treasurer, Andrea Russo. She would gently say to him, "Mr. Russo, will you please change the dollars for me, because if you don't I won't know how to help all the people who are pressing me."[20] There was no way of knowing the exact exchange rate, so Russo would approximate it. Whenever he traveled to Foggia, the capital of the province, he determined the exact rate and he could then balance the account with Mary.

A day in Mary's house would begin quite early in the morning, in preparation for attending Padre Pio's Mass, which had been moved to 5:00 a.m. Afterwards, she would remain in church in prayer and thanksgiving. An excellent musician, she had begun to learn the organ, and sometimes she played it for church functions later in the morning. When she finally returned home, it was time for breakfast. During the day, there were a multitude of tasks to be performed. Those living in the household would wash and iron the vestments and altar cloths for the Capuchin friars. Since she was proficient in five languages, Mary would assist the monastery with their foreign correspondence, translating the letters into Italian and typing them out. Often, visitors would come from around the world seeking information about Padre Pio, and she would usually be able to respond in their own tongue.

On some days there was choir practice in the house, and on others the household prepared the hosts for Holy Communion. Lunch was at noon, accompanied by a Scripture reading, and concluding with a special set of prayers. In the

evenings it would be back to the church for either Mass or
other religious functions, and prayer afterwards. Carmela
Marocchino, one of the women who lived with Mary, noted
that in the evenings, at the monastery ". . . often we could
hear Padre Pio sobbing as he prayed alone in the balcony."[21]
Before bedtime Mary would pray the Divine Office; sometimes she remained awake, writing late into the night. If she
were scheduled for Confession with Padre Pio the next day,
she would prepare envelopes with all the donations that visitors had left with her for Padre Pio's various works, to give
to him at the church.

Little by little *l'Americana* began to discard some of the
personal items that pertained to her wealthy background,
such as jewels and expensive clothing. Padre Pio used to
playfully tease her at times by saying things like, "Oh, how
elegant we are today!" Maria Montessori had been caring
for Mary's jewels. Mary asked Maria to mail them to her so
that they could be sold and the money used for the poor. Dr.
Montessori, however, was fearful of entrusting these precious items to the postal service, and instead went to the
Capuchins in Rome. Thinking that they were directly connected with the monastery in San Giovanni Rotondo, she
asked them to take the package to Mary. But they were
reluctant to get involved, stating that they did not approve
of all of this devotion to Padre Pio. They finally accepted the
jewels, on the condition that they would be used to decorate
a statue of the Madonna in Rome, which is what finally
occurred.[22] Mary still held on to one item, however. It was a
gold watch encrusted with precious diamonds, which she
kept only to tell the time. One day her mentor commented,
and this time not playfully: "So, you still have the gold
watch with the diamonds, eh?"[23] Mary at once left the
church, took the watch in her hand, and smashed it to bits
against a wall. She picked up the pieces and diamonds, went

back inside the church, and handed them over to Padre Pio.

To formalize her new life of Franciscan simplicity, Mary became a member of the Third Order of St. Francis (also known today as the Secular Franciscan Order). This order was founded by St. Francis for the laity, single or married, who wish to follow more closely a religious way of life, while living in the world. At first, Mary thought that Padre Pio would want her to join a convent, but it was he who advised her to join the Third Order, telling Mary, "The convent is not for you." She became a novice in the Third Order in the summer of 1924, and a year later was accepted as a professed member by Padre Pio himself, who was the spiritual director of the chapter. She took the name of "Pia" as her Franciscan name.

Normally Third Order members, sometimes called Tertiaries, wear items signifying their commitment, such as a cord around their waist and a small habit or scapular around their shoulders. But Mary received special permission to wear the actual Capuchin habit itself, complete with brown garment (but without the hood), Rosary on the side, and sandals. To this she added a pectoral cross. She even slept in her habit.[24] She resembled a friar to such an extent that some thought of her as "Brother Mary." She eventually became a teacher and guide for others who wished to enter the Third Order fraternity that was directed by Padre Pio. Often she would invite the women members over to her home for breakfast. She wrote in her notebook: ". . . Padre Pio is preparing a net of souls in order to encircle the entire world, fishing for souls for Jesus . . . How lucky for me to have met with the greatest Saint since Saint Francis."[25]

It was Padre Pio who had asked Mary to learn to play the old reed organ in the church. She was also an accomplished singer, an art which she had studied while a young girl in America, and she soon took charge of the choir, or *schola can-*

torum. Padre Pio and the congregation were extremely pleased with the added decorum to church functions provided by the organ music and choir. In fact, recordings were made of Mary at the organ, with the *schola* performing under her direction. The records were sold at the local shops that offered religious goods. Mary continued to play the organ until Elena Bandini, an accomplished organist, arrived in San Giovanni. She replaced Mary at the keyboard for church functions, and Mary humbly and gracefully accepted the transition and became Elena's pupil. Later on Elena became ill, and Mary again resumed her former post for most daily Masses and ceremonies, except for major feast days, when a concert pianist from central Italy led the music.[26]

When asked about her former aristocratic life in America, Mary would say that she did not miss it at all. She was quite content to live a much simpler existence in San Giovanni Rotondo, without servants and elaborately prepared meals. She enjoyed the simple Italian fare, and astonished her American relatives who came on occasional visits, with her relish for pasta, ricotta cheese, and similar staples of Southern Italian cooking. She considered her former way of life, when she had had eight servants at her disposal, as much too comfortable. Her former social status would not even allow her to light a match, the servants were to do everything. To one of her friends, she confided: "Now, on the other hand, I am happier because I am free of that life which I consider a form of slavery. I prefer the simple things in life . . ."[27]

Chapter 12

Opposition and the First Suppression

WHEN Mary Pyle arrived at San Giovanni Rotondo in the fall of 1923, it was in the wake of attempts by Church authorities earlier that year to have Padre Pio transferred to another friary farther north. The reasons had to do with wild tales and rumors about him which had reached the local and regional clergy, and spread all the way up to the Vatican. There were innuendoes about his personal life, reports of fanaticism among the devotees, accusations of financial irregularities, alleged improprieties among the friars at Our Lady of Grace, and a host of other specious stories.

Until Padre Pio received the stigmata in 1918, his trials had been primarily confined to physical sufferings and spiritual battles. People were generally friendly and kind to him; he was not particularly persecuted by others nor did he have any serious enemies. But once he became publicly portrayed as a "Holy Man," his sufferings took on a new dimension, characterized by unrelenting personal attacks against him. Even within the hierarchy of the Church, animosity towards him developed, aroused by jealousy, suspicion, or misunderstandings. To his devotees, he was a saint and miracle worker, suffering in union with Christ and bearing a copy of His wounds. But the very existence of such an exemplar of holiness was a silent rebuke to others, particularly those in religious garb, who were not so committed as he was to applying Christian principles to their own lives. While some were sincere in their doubts as to whether he was the genuine article, others openly became detractors. To the latter, he was a fraud and a charlatan, siphoning money into the coffers of the Friary, a sham whose wounds were the result of neurosis, hysteria, or chicanery.

Two names among these critics of Padre Pio loom out because of their prominence. One was Padre Agostino Gemelli, a priest, a PhD, and the founder of Sacred Heart University of Milan. He was held in great esteem at the time as an authority on psychology, medicine and theology. The other was the head of the diocese that encompassed the friary at San Giovanni—the Archbishop of Manfredonia, Msgr. Pasquale Gagliardi. Padre Pio had other enemies, including some of the priests assigned to the local parishes, who made their opinions known to Rome; but Padre Gemelli and Archbishop Gagliardi were by far the most influential, and their accusations seem to have done the most damage.

In the spring of 1920, Padre Gemelli visited the Friary in the capacity of a private person and not as a medical doctor. It had been made clear to him that since he did not have written permission from Rome, he would not be able to study Padre Pio's stigmata. However, once in the presence of Padre Pio, he asked if he could examine his wounds. Padre Pio had no choice but to decline, since Padre Gemelli did not have the required authorization. Padre Benedetto and some others were also present at this encounter. According to Padre Benedetto, Padre Gemelli then made an impolite comment, telling Padre Pio to "cure yourself" of the wounds. At that point, Padre Pio walked out of the meeting, and Padre Gemelli shouted ominously after him, "All right, Padre Pio, we will meet again!"[1]

Dr. Giorgio Festa saw Padre Gemelli a year later, and remarked that from his own conversation with him, he could easily understand why Padre Pio would have felt uncomfortable in the man's presence. Padre Pio, observed Festa, must have sensed that his visitor had no intention of being objective. (Of course, Padre Pio's main reason was his obligation of obedience.) According to Festa, Padre Gemelli regarded Padre Pio as a mentally disturbed person, but one that he himself would be able to cure, using his own knowledge of psychology.[2]

Upon his return to Rome, Padre Gemelli wrote a report for the Vatican's Holy Office in which he gave a negative verdict on Padre Pio. Soon, word began to spread that the well known and respected Padre Gemelli had actually examined the wounds, and had written a damaging report on them. A few years later, he published a widely-circulated article stating that the only genuine stigmatist in the history of the Church was St. Francis—and possibly St. Catherine of Siena. All other cases, he wrote, could be reasonably diagnosed as induced by hysteria.[3]

Padre Pio's other accuser, Archbishop Gagliardi of Manfredonia, was a very complex, enigmatic figure. Initially he appears to have been neutral or even favorable toward Padre Pio, but at some point he turned completely against him. The exact cause of this turn-around is not known, but it was probably fueled by the contrast between the lifestyles of the two men. Rumors were rife that the Archbishop's personal behavior was immoral and that he neglected the duties of his office. Apparently he failed to administer the Sacrament of Confirmation at many of the parishes under his jurisdiction. He also had a reputation for requisitioning many valuable works of sacred art from his parishes, and then selling them off. The proceeds were supposedly to benefit the poor, but he kept much of the money for himself.[4]

He was extremely unpopular among the Catholic laity under his charge. He sought to blame his problems on Padre Pio, perhaps realizing that his own ministry was being cast in a rather poor light compared to the beacon shining from

San Giovanni Rotondo. He wrote countless letters of complaint about Padre Pio to the Vatican, at times making
absurd allegations. For example, he insisted that while on a
visit to Padre Pio's monastery, he had seen him perfume
himself and put makeup on his face when in his cell. But
Padre Agostino was also present the entire time of this visit,
and Padre Agostino makes it clear in his diary that the Archbishop never entered Padre Pio's room.[5]

As long as Benedict XV remained Pope, the opposition had
little effect on the ministry of Padre Pio or on life at Our
Lady of Grace Friary. This Pope had dispatched at least
three major apostolic visitors and his own personal doctor to
San Giovanni Rotondo, and had received favorable reports
all around. He considered Padre Pio a true man of God and
once remarked that since Padre Pio's mission was to bring
souls to God, his own mission would be to remain at his side.[6]
Unfortunately, Benedict XV met an untimely death from
pneumonia in January 1922. He was succeeded by Pius XI, a
serious business-like man, who had risen from five years of
obscurity in the Vatican Library to become the Archbishop of
Milan before being elected Pope.

Equipped with a practical outlook, Pius XI was immediately thrown into the midst of the turmoil of post-war
Europe and the rise of Nazism and Fascism. With global
issues at hand, he had little time or inclination to delve into
the case of the mystic of San Giovanni Rotondo. Padre Pio's
detractors seized the opportunity to influence the opinion of
the new Pope, who had limited prior knowledge of the
Capuchin, other than a pre-conceived notion that he was a
fanatic.[7] Various letters denouncing Padre Pio began pouring
into Rome, and the new Pope, instead of rejecting them as
Benedict XV had done, had all such correspondence forwarded to Rafael Cardinal Merry del Val, head of the Holy
Office.

This Cardinal had the unpleasant duty of trying to sort out the truth about Padre Pio. On the one hand, he had to consider the very serious accusations raised by Archbishop Gagliardi, who appeared at the Vatican in person to make his charges. Gagliardi accused the Friar of a host of indiscretions, mixing vicious gossip with imaginary scenarios. Padre Pio was said to spend evenings indiscreetly in the Friary guest room in the company of various young women. The Archbishop even went so far as to contend that Padre Pio was possessed by a devil.[8] He accused the other friars in the monastery of coming to blows over large sums of money, which he alleged the Friary fleeced from the naive pilgrims. He informed the Cardinal that the monks would plant lies and false stories with the newspapers about miracles and conversions that had never occurred, in order to draw large, gullible crowds to San Giovanni Rotondo. Cardinal Merry del Val also heard negative reports from Padre Agostino Gemelli, from some of the local priests of the San Giovanni Rotondo area, and even from a bishop connected with the Vatican. On the other hand, Padre Pio had his defenders, too. Among them were Pietro Cardinal Gasparri, who was the Vatican's Secretary of State, the Vatican official Agosto Cardinal Silj, as well as some bishops.[9]

The furor surrounding Padre Pio was such that Cardinal Merry del Val had no choice but to take action in order to calm the situation. It had reached the point where he deemed it necessary to initiate a formal inquiry, and he convened a hearing in order to hear from witnesses for both sides. As a result of this investigation, a series of stern directives was issued by the Holy Office. Unfortunately, it was Padre Pio himself who had to bear the brunt of them, since it seemed that the only way to control the events in San Giovanni Rotondo was to restrict his ministry severely.

Thus, on June 2, 1922, the Holy Office (which today is

known as the Congregation for the Doctrine of the Faith)
issued its decrees. Padre Pio was to be kept under strict
observation, and his activities were to be in conformity with
the other friars. He was not to show the stigmata to anyone;
he could not speak about the wounds or allow them to be
kissed; and he was no longer permitted to bless the pilgrims
from the monastery window overlooking the piazza. In order
to avoid the mad crush of humanity forcing its way into the
tiny church to attend his Mass, he was to vary the time of
Mass every day, preferably celebrating it very early in the
morning, alone in a private chapel. In addition, it was forbidden for Padre Pio or his assistants to reply to any letters
from devotees asking for his counsel, thus putting an end to
the correspondence with his spiritual children that he had
carried on for years.

To all this was added the devastating order that Padre
Benedetto was no longer to be his spiritual director; all communication between the two, even by letter, was to cease
immediately. This was an extremely hard blow for both men,
yet they submitted to this injunction without complaint. For
the remaining twenty years of his life, Padre Benedetto
never saw, spoke to, or corresponded with his beloved
friend—at least not in conventional ways. When on his
deathbed in 1942 his superiors asked Padre Benedetto if
they should send for Padre Pio, "No, it is not necessary," he
replied, because "He is here beside me."[10]

Far more serious than any of these severe regulations and
curbs, in the eyes of the citizenry of San Giovanni Rotondo,
was the final directive. It stated that in order to be certain
that all of the restrictions on Padre Pio would definitely be
carried out, it would be necessary to transfer Padre Pio out
of San Giovanni Rotondo, preferably to a different religious
province in the north of Italy. But the Holy Office had not
taken into account the determination of the *Sangiovannese*

to keep their saint with them at all costs. Petitions were circulated, and a People's Association was formed. Civilian watchmen were posted near the monastery to make sure their saint was not secretly taken away, and armed violence was threatened in order to prevent his removal.

The Mayor himself, Francesco Morcaldi, stated his intention to renounce his office and join the demonstrators if necessary. He presented to the religious authorities a 50-page list of signatures protesting against attempts to send Padre Pio to another friary, and warned that "his removal would give way to serious and grave inconveniences, as the people have decided to obstruct, with every means, the transferal."[11]

The situation festered for the next year, with neither side willing to back down. A friary in Ancona, on the Adriatic coast of central Italy, was targeted by the regional Capuchin authorities as the most likely spot to send him. The Vatican took a further step in May of 1923, when the Holy Office issued an official warning or *monitum* to the public on Padre Pio and his ministry. It stated that there was nothing supernatural in the occurrences involving said Padre Pio, and that the faithful should act in accordance with this decree. The Vatican hoped that this statement would discourage visitors from considering Padre Pio a saint and would keep them from besieging Our Lady of Grace Friary, thereby putting an end to what they saw as fanaticism.

But the *monitum* had little, if any, effect on the populace. The same was not true, though, of Padre Pio himself. The Friary Guardian tried to keep the news of this official warning from him, until Padre Pio happened to see it in a Capuchin publication. After reading it, he set his face like flint, then walked into his room and wept. Variations of the same *monitum* were issued by the Vatican four more times over the next decade. Ironically, these warnings, designed to keep people from esteeming him as a saint, were never officially revoked by the Vatican, and technically were still in effect when he was canonized as St. Pio of Pietrelcina on June 16, 2002.[12]

Matters came to a head in the summer of 1923, when the Friary attempted to implement for the first time the directive that Padre Pio's Mass should "preferably" be held in a separate chapel, with no congregation present. On June 25, Padre Pio was forced to say Mass privately in the internal chapel of the monastery. That morning, the people in the main church were waiting for Padre Pio to appear there for his daily Mass. Only after one of his assistants, with tearful eyes, entered the church alone, did they comprehend that the orders to completely segregate Padre Pio from everyone were now being carried out. Their ultimate fear was that the transfer of their beloved priest would be the next and final step.

The citizens wasted no time in making their displeasure known. Almost immediately word spread through San Giovanni Rotondo and to neighboring areas, and soon a crowd estimated at between three and five thousand people marched on the Friary. Mayor Morcaldi, the town fathers, civil and military authorities, and even a marching band, accompanied the throng. The multitude was on the verge of becoming a mob, with some raising threats to burn down the homes of suspected enemies of Padre Pio. The friars were both intimidated and amazed at seeing such a long line of marchers, extending halfway down the hill towards the town.

The mayor and other civil authorities met with the monastery superiors, and convinced them to suspend the order, and allow Padre Pio to resume saying Mass in the main church. Padre Ignazio, the Guardian of the monastery, was forced to make the decision on his own authority. He later explained to his Capuchin superiors that he acted:

". . . to avoid grave consequences and to pacify the excitement of the people."[13] The next day, June 26, to the great joy of the populace, Padre Pio appeared once again in the main church to celebrate Mass in public.

Church authorities nonetheless persisted in their determination to effect the transfer of Padre Pio, but the very real threat of civil violence was preventing them from actually carrying it out. For his part, Padre Pio was ready to obey any relocation order and was resigned to the apparent inevitability of his transfer. However, he did not want any violence to occur over his removal. He wrote to the Mayor pleading with him not to interfere with the decision of the Church authorities. In a now-famous letter, he expressed the great love he had for the people of the town and made known his desire to have San Giovanni Rotondo be his final resting place.

> I will always remember these generous people in my prayers, imploring peace and prosperity for them. As a sign of my predilection, being unable to do anything else, I express the desire to be buried in a quiet little corner of this land, provided that my Superiors are not opposed to it."[14]

The most chilling episode of this first suppression of Padre Pio occurred in August, 1923, when an assassination attempt was made against the Friar. It took place on the tenth of the month, the anniversary of Padre Pio's Ordination to the priesthood. An around-the-clock guard had been posted at the doors of the Friary, in order to prevent any attempt to whisk the Saint away to another location. It was early evening, and Padre Pio was just finishing the ceremony of Benediction of the Blessed Sacrament before the packed church. Suddenly, out from the crowd strode a bricklayer, Donato Centra. He rushed toward Padre Pio pointing a pis-

tol at him, shouting: "Dead or alive, you're going to stay with
us here in this village!"[15] Confusion and fear reigned everywhere, but some in the crowd were able to grab Centra
before he had time to pull the trigger. What finally happened
to Centra is not known, but later that night Padre Pio composed a missive to the Lord, pouring forth his emotions and
thoughts about recent events, and asking that his assailant
be forgiven:

> I have no clear idea of what will happen tomorrow:
> I am not certain what my superiors will do, to which
> religious community they are going to send me. I,
> your son, who is devoted to Holy Obedience, for my
> part, will obey without opening my mouth.
>
> Assuming such, I have good reason to suppose
> what my final end will be, knowing the intentions of
> my dearly loved people of San Giovanni Rotondo to
> keep me with them, if not alive, then at least dead. . . .
> I desire that the civil and judicial authorities do not
> apply the penalty of the law against them.
>
> I have always loved everyone, I have always given
> pardon, and I don't wish to go to my grave without
> having pardoned whoever has wanted to put an end
> to my days.[16]

He consigned this letter to one of his spiritual daughters,
telling her to keep it in a safe place, because by the next day
it might be needed. This faithful daughter held on to it for
45 years, turning it over to the Friary Guardian shortly after
Padre Pio's passing in 1968.[17]

A few days after this dreadful event, there was another
threat of violence, this time by a group of armed men. The
Guardian, Padre Ignazio, wrote in his diary: "The evening
came to an end with the threat of eight fascists armed with

clubs, to make known that the Padre must remain in San Giovanni Rotondo; otherwise, 'we will crucify Padre Pio,' they say, 'and the Father Guardian!'"[18] Concern for everyone's safety was now paramount. The head of the Italian police, General Emilio DeBono, sent one of his deputies to investigate the situation and to submit a report on the risks involved in attempting to transfer Padre Pio.[19] The deputy reported back that "forceful action would be necessary, with the certainty of spilling blood."[20] General DeBono then began to work through channels to have Church authorities revoke the transfer orders.

Finally, Rome accepted the reality of the situation, and on August 17, 1923, the Capuchins received a communication from Cardinal Merry del Val of the Holy Office, announcing that for the present at least, the transfer order was suspended. It took another month for the populace to quiet down, but behind the scenes some Church officials continued to plan for the eventual relocation of Padre Pio. The Pope was still unfavorably disposed toward him, and the usual accusations against him continued to be spread. But for now, violence had been averted and some semblance of calm was returning to Our Lady of Grace Friary and to San Giovanni Rotondo.

Chapter 13

"l'Americana" as Collaborator

B Y THE fall of 1923, shortly after the order to transfer Padre Pio had been rescinded, Mary McAlpin Pyle had made her first visit to San Giovanni Rotondo. It was a time of great loss for Padre Pio—he was now deprived of his spiritual director, and could no longer communicate by letter with his spiritual children. But the providence of God ordained that just at this moment, the person who would become his most prominent spiritual child and collaborator, took up residence in the same town. Here was a woman who gave up her wealth and former worldly way of life, in order to learn spiritual truths at the feet of a great master—and there was no need for an exchange of letters in order to direct her soul.

By Christmas of 1923, Mary was already living in San Giovanni Rotondo.[1] Her calling as Padre Pio's collaborator began a year or two later, when a group of residents from Pietrelcina approached her and asked if she would build a Capuchin friary and church in Padre Pio's home town. Although the actual date is not certain, this probably occurred after her mother had restored Mary's allowance, since those asking her must have known she had the means to contribute to this project. She replied that she would first have to confer with Padre Pio and obtain his approval for the undertaking. When she informed him of the project, he readily gave his consent: "Yes. Do it quickly. Let it be dedicated to the Holy Family."[2] The Holy Family (*Sacra Famiglia*) Friary was also to house a "seraphic sem-

90

inary" for young boys aspiring to become Capuchin priests.

Padre Pio's good friend, Emmanuele Brunatto, was recruited to supervise the overall effort. Much of the money came from the townspeople of Pietrelcina, including those who had emigrated to America. The rest came largely from the Pyle fortune, with Mary's mother Adelaide also contributing. Brunatto obtained the permits and approvals to begin construction and also arranged for the acquisition of the land. The spot chosen for the new monastery was an open field and pasture. This particular field was the subject of a prophecy made by Padre Pio about fifteen years before, in 1909, when he was still known as Fra Pio. The prophecy was the first of three prodigies—some might consider them supernatural signs—associated with the building of the Holy Family Friary and Church in Pietrelcina.

While he was still a Capuchin brother residing in his home town for health reasons, Fra Pio would go for an evening walk in the nearby countryside with a small group of friends. This group usually included the parish priest, Don Salvatore Pannullo, and some seminarians. On one occasion Don Pannullo made everyone stop and listen for what Fra Pio was saying he could hear. Stories vary as to exactly what Fra Pio did hear—some say it was a "choir of angels singing and bells ringing."[3] Others report he heard the chanting of friars and smelled the aroma of incense.[4] He predicted to the group that someday a monastery and church would be constructed on this spot, with prayers and hymns rising up to Heaven. His companions laughed since they had heard no unusual sounds or singing. But Don Pannullo remarked: "If it is the desire of Heaven, it would be the greatest fortune for Pietrelcina."[5] Many years later, after the Friary and church had been built at that very spot, one of these former seminarians asked Padre Pio if he remembered that day when they all made fun of his prophecy, since ". . . now for sure there is

singing and the bells ring continuously!" To which Padre Pio
pensively replied "How can I forget!"[6]

The actual work on the Pietrelcina monastery began in
1926, at the location pointed out by the aged Don Pannullo,
who indicated where he had been walking with Fra Pio when
the prophecy was made.[7] The first stones for the new edifice
were brought to the site by enthusiastic townspeople from an
ancient, crumbling chapel known as the Purgatory Church.
In only one day, all of the available stones from the old Purgatory Church were transported uphill to the new site, carried on the heads and shoulders of the *Pucinari*. Even the
women were seen balancing stone blocks of up to 100 pounds
or more on their heads, laboring until sunset until the job was
finally completed.[8] A mound of stones several yards high
loomed in the twilight. As evening fell, the second portent
occurred. A great light in the form of an immense cross was
seen over the pile of stones. It gradually rose up from the top
of the pile, and appeared over Pietrelcina. The cross was visible to the townspeople for about half an hour, as it slowly
climbed into the sky and eventually disappeared.[9]

On June 13, 1926, the cornerstone of the Friary was
blessed by the Archbishop of Benevento, Luigi Cardinal Lavitrano. The locals continued to participate in scouring the
surrounding area for the additional stones needed for the
building, meeting weekly for this purpose. Even old Don
Pannullo, who died only a few months later, was seen stag-
gering up the hill under the weight of the rocks he carried on
his shoulders. Mary Pyle resided for a time in Pietrelcina
during the Friary's construction. When there were problems
that needed Padre Pio's advice or consent, she sent word to
him through his father Grazio.[10] In a little over two years,
the monastery was completed, but due to many difficulties it
would be another twenty years before it would actually be
occupied by the Capuchins.

During the Second World War, it served as a barracks for whichever troops happened to be in the area, whether German, Italian, or Allied soldiers. As a result, by the end of the war the building was heavily damaged and covered with graffiti in several languages. But even with repairs underway, ecclesiastical approval for the Capuchins to move in was lacking. Agostino Mancinelli, who had become Archbishop of Benevento, refused to give his permission on the grounds that the offerings of the people for a friary associated with the name of Padre Pio, would significantly reduce the contributions taken in by the local clergy in their own parishes. In addition, a neighboring Franciscan friary in the town of Paduli objected for basically the same reason. In other words, it was "Monks against monks!"[11]

Padre Pio was understandably concerned about this delay. Once he even remarked that the Cathedral of Benevento was bombed and heavily damaged during the Second World War as a punishment for the Archbishop's stubbornness. He also felt that the Capuchin presence was urgently required in Pietrelcina, in order to combat an incursion of Jehovah's Witnesses into the area. The Witnesses wanted to purchase the unused friary and turn it into a "Kingdom Hall."[12] The stalemate was ended with the intervention of Cardinal Lavitrano, who was now based in Rome. The Archbishop of Benevento dropped his objections after receiving a communication from the Cardinal—the contents of the message to this day are not known. Approval from the Vatican was received next, and in April of 1947 the first Capuchins arrived. Afterwards, a pilgrims' hall in honor of Mary Pyle was erected next to the friary, called *Casa del Pellegrino Mary Pyle*.[13] Emmanuele Brunatto and most of the *Pucinari* were hoping that the establishment of a Capuchin friary in Padre Pio's home town would result in his transfer to Pietrelcina. However, this was not to be; otherwise, it would have been *Pucinari* against *Sangiovannese!*

Construction on the adjoining Holy Family Church began in 1928, two years after work on the Friary had commenced. One reason for the late start was lack of water, not only on the site, but in Pietrelcina itself, which created a serious handicap for the builders. The workers had made many attempts to find water nearby, but were always unsuccessful. When word reached Padre Pio in San Giovanni Rotondo, he pointed to a specific location on the blueprints that were shown him and promised that, if they dug in that particular spot, they would have all the water they needed. The well was dug at the spot indicated by him, and the abundant spring of water that was discovered served not only the new monastery and church, but eventually even part of the town.[14] Thus came about the third prodigy connected with the Holy Family Friary and Church.

A later episode concerns the formal dedication of the church, which was finally scheduled for May of 1951, decades after construction had commenced. Padre Pio himself was planning to join Mary Pyle and a contingent from San Giovanni Rotondo, who were preparing to travel to Pietrelcina to attend the ceremony. But when word leaked out, the *Sangiovanese* reacted as they had years before, posting guards at Our Lady of Grace Friary, and threatening to riot if Padre Pio set foot outside of San Giovanni Rotondo. They feared that once he was in his home town of Pietrelcina, which now had its own Capuchin friary, he would never return. Padre Pio, realizing that violence was a possibility, canceled his plans to attend the dedication in Pietrelcina, to his great disappointment.

On one of her return trips to San Giovanni Rotondo from Pietrelcina, Mary Pyle had been accompanied by Padre Pio's mother Giuseppa. It was early December, 1928, and Mamma

Peppa wanted to spend Christmas with her son. She stayed in a small room on the second floor of *l'Americana's* pink castle and had a wonderful view of the almond trees and cultivated fields of the Gargano. She could see in the distance the outline of the Adriatic Sea, the coastal town of Manfredonia, and the great plains of Apulia, the *Tavoliere*. Mary wrote about this visit in her notebook, describing how fortunate she was to have such a guest and praising Padre Pio for giving the gift of his mother to San Giovanni Rotondo. "Now I understand why this house was built . . .," she wrote.[15] Taking advantage of Mamma Peppa's presence as a guest, Mary often asked her to regale those present in the pink house with stories about Padre Pio's childhood.

But the winter of 1928-29 was biting cold. Giuseppa, who was about 70 at the time, had arrived on the mountain with only light clothing. She was frail and in poor health, and plagued with a constant cough. It seemed to many that she had actually come to San Giovanni Rotondo to die close to her son.[16] Mary and her friends offered her a heavy fur coat and woolen dress to wear during her trek up the steep hillside, often in the snow and frigid wind, to attend her son's daily Mass. But she politely declined, saying she did not want to appear to be a "great lady." She preferred to wear her simple peasant garb, especially when talking to her son.

When mother and son first met that December, it was outside on the square (*sagrato*) in front of Our Lady of Grace Church. She took her son's hand and kissed it for each of their many family members, about ten times altogether. Finally, she tried to kiss his hand for herself, but Padre Pio raised his arm saying: "Never! The son should kiss the hand of the mamma, not the mamma the hand of the son!" After that she would no longer try to kiss his hand; but whenever his Mass had finished, she would quietly kneel down and kiss the floor where her son's stigmatized feet had been standing.[17]

Christmas Eve of 1928 was greeted by a snowstorm and freezing temperatures, but Mamma Peppa did not want to miss her dear son's midnight Mass, and trudged up the hill that cold night, wearing her usual light clothing. During the ceremonies Padre Pio passed by carrying the statuette of the Baby Jesus, which she tenderly kissed. Back at Mary Pyle's home on Christmas morning, she started sneezing and came down with a high fever. She was put to bed, and the next day a doctor was summoned, who diagnosed double pneumonia. For the next few days family and friends gathered around her bedside, including her husband Grazio and son Michele. Padre Pio came many times to comfort her, and sometimes personally administered medicines to his mother. When he did so, those who were present could see the blood from his wounds trickling down his fingers.[18] As she worsened, many wondered if Padre Pio would be able to intercede for her, asking God for a miracle. He certainly must have prayed for this, but when directly asked about it by the doctor, he looked up to Heaven, was quiet for a time, and then said, "God's Will be done."[19]

The end came peacefully on January 3, 1929, as she kissed the crucifix. Padre Pio, who had administered the Last Rites, was inconsolable and fainted. Placed on a bed in a nearby room, he ". . . soaked a pile of handkerchiefs with his tears and made those present cry also with his painful lament. . . ."[20] When someone tried to comfort him by mentioning that sorrow is an expression of love, he replied, "But these are precisely tears of love. Nothing but love."[21] His mother was laid out that afternoon in Mary Pyle's home, clothed in the habit of the Third Order of St. Francis. Great crowds came to pay their respects, even from out of town, although she was personally known only by a few people in that area.[22]

After an impressive funeral on the next day, she was

interred in the Capuchin Chapel in the village cemetery of San Giovanni Rotondo, located at the opposite end of the city from the monastery. For days, her bereaved son was so upset and shaken that he was in no condition to return to the Friary, and was not even able to attend her funeral. He watched the cortege, led by the Mayors of Pietrelcina and San Giovanni Rotondo, from Mary's window, as he sobbed and cried out, "My mother, my beautiful mother!" Not long after Mamma Peppa's death, some of those who knew her began to ask her intercession for their special intentions. When Padre Pio came to know about these prayers to his mother, he remarked: "You have found the path to the grace."[23]

Mary Pyle's home had been bustling with so much activity during that Christmas season, and she was so preoccupied with Giuseppa's final illness, that there had been no time for her to write to her mother Adelaide in America. Finally she found a few moments and was able to send her a telegram informing her of "Aunt Giuseppa's" death. Adelaide replied that Padre Pio had come again to visit her recently (in bilocation), but she did not understand then that the reason was his mother's passing. Mary asked Padre Pio, who was still staying at her house, if it were true that he went to see her Mother. He replied, "I always go there!"[24]

On one of his final days in Mary Pyle's home, he noticed that Mary was crying, apparently troubled about something. When pressed by him, she said that she was worried about what would become of her house in the future. To calm her, Padre Pio affirmed that, "Even if this house were to crumble, it would be rebuilt stone by stone for something beautiful."[25] Mary was overjoyed at these words and always remembered them. She later gave full legal title of the house to the Capuchins so that memories of all that occurred there would be preserved. Padre Pio remained in Mary's house until he was finally summoned back to the

Friary by his superiors. He obeyed, though he was still so weak and disconsolate that he fainted three times before reaching his monastery cell.

Chapter 14

The "Imprisonment"

THE spring of 1931 saw the second major suppression of Padre Pio's ministry. The chastisement of ten years ago put an end to the correspondence with his spiritual children, and forced the removal of Padre Benedetto as his spiritual director. However, the Vatican had not succeeded in their efforts to prevent him from saying Mass in public, nor in having him transferred. Mary Pyle had moved to San Giovanni just as the furor surrounding the first attempt to transfer Padre Pio was abating, and thus was not a part of those events of the early 1920's. Unfortunately, she would be an innocent victim of the sad story of the constraints and curbs imposed on Padre Pio in the 1930's.

Rumors were afloat in the spring of 1931 that a new Father Guardian of the Friary was to be appointed to replace the current Guardian, Padre Raffaele of Sant'Elia a Pianisi. His replacement was to be a "foreigner" from northern Italy, and according to the scuttlebutt, this was to be the first step in a new initiative to have Padre Pio moved from San Giovanni Rotondo. Unlike so many of the other rumors concerning him, this one had some factual basis. Padre Raffaele had been secretly informed on March 31, in a private meeting with his superior, that he was to be replaced by a priest from Milan. However, Emmanuele Brunatto had received the same news from his contacts in Rome, and soon Mayor Francesco Morcaldi and the rest of the town were privy to the "secret." In a repeat of what had happened ten years pre-

vious, the riled up *Sangiovannese* quickly barricaded the
streets around the Friary, and a twenty-four hour watch was
posted to sound the alarm if any attempts were made to
remove Padre Pio from Our Lady of Grace Friary.

Into this hornets' nest stepped an unsuspecting Franciscan priest from another town, Padre Eugenio Tignola, who
had taken a bus into San Giovanni to talk to Padre Pio about
spiritual matters. Unfortunately for Padre Tignola, Mayor
Morcaldi was a passenger on that same bus. The Mayor concluded that this stranger must be the new Father Guardian
that was to replace Padre Raffaele, and he quickly spread
the word to his constituents. An unruly mob of a hundred
men "armed to the teeth" gathered that evening in front of
the Friary, shouting that this "foreigner" must be turned
over to them so they could send him back where he came
from.[1] Padre Raffaele of course refused them and tried to
explain that the visiting priest was simply a guest for the
night.

The demonstrators did not believe him, and around midnight they took action. Tearing down a light pole from the
piazza, the riotous crowd used it as a battering ram and
broke through the doors of the Friary, entering the private
cloister area of the monastery. In a bold move, equal to the
brazenness of the armed mob, Padre Raffaele stood up to
them: ". . . with an imperious voice I commanded them to
leave the Friary. I took a risk as they were all armed, but it
worked . . ."[2]

After they moved back into the piazza, Padre Pio spoke to
the throng from a window, assuring them that the visiting
priest was not the new Father Guardian, but just a harmless
guest. The crowd then shouted that Padre Pio was only saying this out of obedience to his superiors and refused to disperse. Finally, Mayor Morcaldi arrived on the scene, and
entered the Friary with some other leading figures of the

town to determine the true identity of the visitor. Convinced that he was not the new Guardian, Mayor Morcaldi and the local head of the *Carabinieri* (the Italian state police) persuaded the crowd to disperse. Leaving some townspeople behind as guards, the crowd started on their way home at 2:30 a.m.[3] At 5:00 in the morning, poor, frightened Padre Tignola somehow got past the guards, and safely boarded the bus for Foggia.

Padre Raffaele immediately filed complaints with the civil authorities about the break-in, and also reported the incident to his Capuchin superiors. It was not long before high Vatican officials learned of this latest incident of the "fanaticism" surrounding the person of Padre Pio, and they decided upon stern and quick action. In short order, the Holy Office issued the sweeping and stunning directive that Padre Pio was to be stripped of every one of his priestly functions except that of saying Mass! Even his Mass itself was restricted; it had to be celebrated in the private Friary chapel, with no one else present except one assistant. This time, unlike the 1920's, Mayor Morcaldi was aligned with the local police and the *Carabinieri*, instead of threatening to join with the rioters. Perhaps that is why the threat of mob violence did not deter the Capuchins from carrying out their instructions from the Vatican, as it had a decade ago.

Padre Raffaele received the directive regarding Padre Pio on June 9. On the following day he made an emergency trip to his superior in Foggia in an attempt to have the orders delayed or rescinded, but he was told that nothing could be done except to carry them out. That evening he had the unpleasant duty of informing Padre Pio that he could no longer say Mass in public, and was prohibited from hearing any Confessions, including those of the friars. This was a hard blow, since celebrating Mass and hearing Confessions were the cornerstones of his ministry of directing souls and

guiding them towards Jesus. He took the news silently, saying only, "May the Will of God be done!" Then he covered his
eyes with his hands, and bowing his head, retired to pray
before the crucifix in the choir, where he remained until after
midnight.[4]

Thus, on the next day, June 11, 1931, Padre Pio's segregation and "imprisonment" began. He said a three-hour Mass
in the private chapel of the Friary, attended by only one
server, with the chapel door closed to prevent anyone else
from entering. The news of these strict measures against
their beloved saint spread throughout the whole Gargano
region like a thunderbolt. There were protests, telegrams
and indignant letters, and the usual threats of violence. But
the *Carabinieri* were on the ready, and their numbers were
enough to dissuade any major demonstrations in front of the
Friary.

Padre Raffaele, who feared that the people would try to
take Padre Pio by force and compel him to say Mass for
them, traveled to Rome in July to give a first-hand account
of the situation. The Vatican wanted to determine the risk
involved in installing his replacement as Guardian, the "foreigner" from northern Italy. Fortunately, Padre Raffaele succeeded in persuading them to cancel any such plans. But
Rome went ahead with other repressive and humiliating
measures, removing Padre Pio as director of the Third Order
Franciscans and transferring the Seraphic College of aspiring seminarians out of Our Lady of Grace Friary. As far as
the Vatican was concerned, the restrictions on Padre Pio
would be permanent, and his removal to another friary in
the future was still being considered.

A first hand account of these terrible days is described by
one of his closest spiritual daughters from San Giovanni
Rotondo. Cleonice Morcaldi's diary, *La Mia Vita Vicino a
Padre Pio* (*My Life Near Padre Pio*) was published in Rome

in 1997.[5] According to Cleonice, at the beginning of the segregation, the devotees of the Saint gathered at 10:00 a.m. in
the church, where they prayed at length for his liberation.
At that same hour, Padre Pio was in the choir at prayer and
meditation, but no one was able to see him because he was
even forbidden to go near the balcony rail. The only person
allowed contact with him was his blind friend Pietruccio,
who was permitted to visit him once a day. On one occasion,
Cleonice entrusted Pietruccio with a little note for Padre
Pio, in which she wrote that everyone was peacefully
resigned to carrying the cross of being deprived of him.
Padre Pio in return sent a short reply, which said in part,
"You realize that the Lord chooses the priest for the altar
and for the confessional. I am not suffering because of
myself, but for these souls. But may God's Will always be
done."[6]

Her diary records that after some months, the faithful
came to believe that the restrictions were going to be permanent, and that Padre Pio would never again enter the
main church, so they went back to attending their own
parishes. Our Lady of Grace Church became desolate, left
alone except for the friars. She wrote that even the Padre's
close spiritual children stayed away, except for those living
close to the monastery (a veiled reference to Mary Pyle).
"The meek victim was left to himself, as was Jesus in the
desert, in the garden and on Calvary."[7] There was also talk
that he would be sent away in exile, and people were terrified at the thought that Padre Pio might be forced to leave
his adopted home of San Giovanni Rotondo. Cleonice made a
vow to walk to the Shrine of St. Michael at Monte Sant'Angelo should Padre Pio be freed, a distance of about fifteen
miles.

But such a feat had already been accomplished by Mary
Pyle. During the first year of the segregation, she went on

foot both ways to the shrine at Monte Sant'Angelo in one day. The next year she repeated the pilgrimage, but this time stayed there overnight before returning the next day.[8] Mary, however, was suffering her own personal banishment in a way, because the townspeople had come to hold her responsible in large part for what had befallen Padre Pio. This was the probable reason why Cleonice Morcaldi did not mention Mary Pyle by name in her diary.

The villagers laid some of the blame for the restrictions placed on Padre Pio's ministry on sensationalized stories about him in books and magazines. They thought that these stories were fed in part by Mary Pyle's enthusiastic tales of Padre Pio's wonders. Mary loved to talk about her spiritual father, but the Capuchins had been asking people not to publicize Padre Pio, hoping that a low profile would work in his favor. Mary did her best to follow their advice, but one day she exclaimed, "How can I be silent about Padre Pio? . . . I want to shout, to tell everyone who this man is!"[9]

There were two events involving Mary that caused people to point an accusing finger, even though there was no actual proof that she was at fault. The first involved interviews with journalists, who would come ostensibly to interview her, but were actually seeking information on Padre Pio.[10] Whether stories published by the writers Mary Pyle spoke to actually influenced the decision to restrict Padre Pio is not known, but the townspeople felt that l'Americana should not have been talking about the Friar at such a difficult time for him.

A second incident involved a book written in 1932 by two supporters of Padre Pio, with the provocative title of *Padre Pio of Pietrelcina: Messenger of the Lord*. The book did not have ecclesiastical approval, and was published after the Vatican had repeatedly declared that there was no evidence of the supernatural in his life and ministry. However, the book spoke openly of miracles attributed to him, and presented him in a way that could only encourage the kind of fanaticism that the authorities were trying to prevent. Again, the townspeople blamed Mary Pyle because they thought she had supplied the authors with some of the miracle stories, although there was no proof that she had done so. Unfortunately for Mary, Padre Pio's director, Padre Agostino, also made the same accusation.[11]

Mary Pyle thus became *persona non grata* in San Giovanni Rotondo. No one would speak to her, with the exception of the friars and a few people living with her in the pink house. Even in church, when she approached the Communion rail, the others would move away from her. Wherever she went, stares and stony silence greeted her. Reportedly, some women even used the prayers of exorcism against her.[12] The friars felt sympathetic and would chase away some of these ladies. Mary's sufferings were compounded by being deprived of all contact with Padre Pio and of the spiritual direction he would give her during Confession.[13]

How did she react to this personal trial? We may be able to learn the answer by reading a short portrayal of her character, given as a testimony by a woman who knew her for many years.

> Because she had great spirit and exceptional moral fortitude, she overcame trials that only a saintly person like her could overcome. There were all kinds of trials, yet she never breathed a word about them. There were injustices, persecutions, slander, calumny and deceit. The persons who had made her their target were treated by her with the same gentility and affability; she always pretended to be unaware of what they were doing.[14]

Padre Pio's banishment lasted for two full years. It ended only after Pope Pius XI sent his personal representatives to San Giovanni Rotondo to investigate the situation. In addition, Padre Pio's friend Emmanuele Brunatto had compiled a book of scandalous information and gossip about the Church hierarchy and Padre Pio's accusers, and was threatening to publish it unless the restrictions were lifted. In the summer of 1933, the Holy Father ordered an end to the isolation of Padre Pio, admitting that although he had not been badly disposed toward him, he had been badly informed about him.[15] The Pope also remarked, "Now you Capuchins will be glad. It is the first time in the Church's history that the Holy See [has retracted] its decrees."[16]

In mid-July of 1933, Padre Pio entered the main church for the first time in two years to offer Mass before the people. In her diary, Cleonice Morcaldi vividly described that morning:

On the morning of July 16, 1933, while alone and feeling desolate, I was at the back of the friary church praying to the Virgin Mary. I saw a friar preparing the altar at an unusually late hour, and he was in the process of placing the chalice on the altar. What could this be about? Only when Padre Pio celebrated Mass did they set up the chalice beforehand! My God!

I kept looking, wondering . . . my heart was pounding! Then a multitude of townspeople started arriving—men, women, children. Many of them went down on their knees in tears, kissing the pavement . . . instantly the little church was filled. They had learned that Padre Pio was to celebrate Mass! It was the Provincial who had carried the news to them.

I don't know how to describe what went through me, I had to go outside to give way to my sobbing, I just could not contain myself. I had suffered so much

. . . and this joy was so great. I was powerless to worthily thank the good God who had come to our aid against all hope.

. . . The Padre came forth, with his face full of emotion, and tears streaming down his eyes. He began the Mass amidst the sobs and tears of his children. He was crying, as all of us were crying. When it came time to bring us Jesus in Holy Communion, every so often he would say: "Enough. No more crying!"

After that Holy Mass, I went on foot all the way up to the grotto at Monte Sant'Angelo to render thanks to the Archangel Saint Michael.[17]

On the way to attend Padre Pio's first Mass in two years, Mary Pyle stopped to pick a daisy from her garden. After the Mass, she offered him the flower; kissing it, he held it close to his heart, and then gave it back to Mary. Back home, she wrapped the flower in a sheet of paper upon which she wrote, "The day that Padre Pio came down to celebrate Mass in church on July 16, 1933, he kissed this flower and held it close to his heart."[18] Although Mary always enjoyed the love and affection of Padre Pio, it would be a long time before the townspeople befriended her as before, and forgot her alleged indiscretions with the press.

The next May, Padre Pio was given permission to hear Confessions of the women, and they lined up in the church. When it was Mary's turn in the confessional, Padre Pio shouted at her, "Wretched one!" (*"Sciagurata!"*) a few times, loud enough for all to hear. The shocked disciple could not understand why he was saying this to her. Upon leaving the confessional, she saw that many of the women wore smirks and smiles. Later Padre Pio explained to Mary that he shouted at her, not for anything she had done wrong, but because, ". . . some of these women would have killed you, (because of) the terrible resentment of you that they had in their hearts."[19] Apparently, they considered such a stunning rebuke from their Padre punishment enough for *l'Americana*.

Chapter 15

More than a Mystic

PADRE Pio's life was not exclusively devoted to prayer, meditation, and to his spiritual ministry; he also had a down-to-earth practical side, and was deeply affected by the physical sufferings of others. Like many followers of the Master, he sought ways to alleviate the afflictions of those undergoing pain, infirmities, and sickness. He saw Jesus in everyone, especially those who were poor and those who were ill. The words of the Gospel . . .

> For I was hungry, and you gave me to eat; I was thirsty and you gave me to drink; I was a stranger and you took me in: naked, and you covered me: sick and you visited me: I was in prison, and you came to me. (Matthew 25: 35-36).

. . . were echoed by Padre Pio:

> In every sick person there is Christ who is suffering. In every poor person there is Christ who is languishing. In every sick person who is poor, Christ is doubly there.[1]

Perched on the Gargano Mountain, San Giovanni Rotondo in the early 1920's was still a primitive town, bypassed by the march of progress. Amenities were few, and basic services such as health care were barely adequate. The nearest hospital was at Foggia, a hair-raising trip down the mountain, about 25 miles away. Only the most urgent cases would be taken there, since the journey was over rough roads, and the available motorized vehicles were few. Padre Pio realized there was a pressing need for a medical facility at San Giovanni, and he envisioned a small hospital in the town's center. As far back as March, 1922, in the midst of the first attempts to suppress his ministry, he was involved in an effort to make this dream a reality.[2] From his followers, he enlisted collaborators who collected funds and procured part of an abandoned Poor Clare Convent, conveniently located near the middle of town. Thus, in January 1925, the "Civil Hospital of Saint Francis" was born.

The little hospital had an operating room, equipped with surgical instruments paid for by a local benefactor. There were two wards, one for men and the other for women, each with seven beds, and also two private rooms. Those who could not afford to pay were treated free of charge.[3] Dr. Angelo Maria Merla from the monastery was on call daily, and nursing was provided by the Sisters of the Sacred Heart and Sisters of the Precious Blood. Surgery was performed by a Dr. Bucci from Foggia, who made the trip twice weekly.

A plaque was erected on an outside wall listing the names of the co-operators. It began with: "Padre Pio of Pietrelcina wished that this town would have a hospital. From his faithful followers he gathered the necessary funds for the establishment of the same."[4] This hospital served the people for thirteen years, until a severe earthquake struck in 1938. The tremor caused much of the building to collapse and buried the operating room, forcing the clinic to close its doors.

However, Padre Pio's dream was not shaken. The town had grown substantially since St. Francis Hospital had opened its doors, and the increased demand for medical care was more critical than ever, now that it was closed. The poor and the sick continued to flock to the monastery, many hoping for a miracle cure from their saint. Even before the earthquake, he had thought of building a new and greater hospital, one that would have its own permanent staff of physicians and nurses. In 1935, he spoke about it to his friend Dr. Guglielmo Sanguinetti, who was visiting from his home in northern Italy. Prophetically he told Dr. Sanguinetti, "You are the man who will come here and build my hospital."[5] But the doctor had his practice in Tuscany and could not afford to relocate. Then Providence intervened, as so often occurred in events revolving around Padre Pio. Dr. Sanguinetti learned that he had won a large sum of money in a lottery; along with his friend Dr. Mario Sanvico, he was able to build a small cottage near the monastery, which they took turns using. It was one of the first homes to appear along the old mule trail that led from the Friary to the town.

Once the little clinic was gone, Padre Pio reflected in earnest about his dream for a newer, larger hospital. This institution would serve not just the town of San Giovanni, but the whole Gargano region, and beyond. He discussed with the Superior, Padre Raffaele, the possibility of building it close to the monastery, squarely into the side of the mountain.[6] Then in late 1939, a little over a year after the destructive earthquake, a few friends gathered in Padre Pio's cell, where the talk turned to the need for a new clinic. Among those present were Dr. Sanvico and Pietruccio. Padre Pio spoke at length of his ideas for the new hospital, in such a way that he inspired his listeners with the determination to put his plans into action.

A short time later, on January 9, a small group of Padre Pio's supporters gathered at the Sanvico-Sanguinetti home near the Friary. Present were Dr. Sanvico and his wife Maria, Dr. Carlo Kisvarday and his wife Mary, and Ida Seitz. The time had come to formalize the project and set up a working committee. It was agreed that all undertakings and decisions would be put to Padre Pio for his approval, and he was designated as "Founder of the Work." Dr. Sanvico was appointed Secretary, Dr. Sanguinetti (it seems he was not present at this meeting) was to be Technical Medical Director, the Treasurer was Dr. Kisvarday, and the Director of Internal Organization was Ida Seitz.

After the meeting, some of the group went to Padre Pio's cell to tell him the good news. Padre Pio approved wholeheartedly, and pronounced that "This evening my earthly Work has begun. I bless you and all those that will contribute to the Work which will become bigger and ever more beautiful."[7] He also talked of the ills afflicting humanity, and laid the groundwork for the moral dimension of this Work: "The man who, overcoming himself, bends over the wounds of his unfortunate brother, elevates to the Lord the most beautiful and noble prayer, made of sacrifice, of lived and realized love . . ."[8] He wanted this hospital to be more than an impersonal sick-bay for the treatment of physical ailments. It would be a place where a person would receive not only medicines, but also love and compassion from the staff. There would be a chapel and priests on the premises. Rooms would be places of light and harmony, offering a pleasant ambience to make the patient feel comfortable. The word "hospital" would not be used; instead, it would be called a home, the House for the Relief of Suffering (Casa Sollievo della Sofferenza)!

That very evening the committee began raising funds for the project. Padre Pio made the first donation, a gold coin that he had received that same day from an impoverished woman, who had insisted that he accept it. Among the others who donated that first night were his blind friend Pietruccio, and his spiritual daughter Cleonice Morcaldi. A six-page brochure was designed, so that Padre Pio's followers around the world would know about the project and could contribute to it. On his 53rd birthday, May 25, 1940, it was printed and distributed in several languages. On the brochure's first page was Giotto's portrayal of St. Francis giving his coat to a poor man. Inside, it detailed how the lack of a hospital in the whole Gargano region meant that often nothing could be done for the needy sick, and they "just die at home." In contrast, this new hospital would be a "grandiose" expression of God's charity, where those who could not afford to pay would not have to. It would in some small way give thanks to God for the graces given to this region of the Gargano; ". . . San Giovanni Rotondo is for us the feast of the hearts . . ."—the brochure's authors proclaimed.[9]

At this stage, the committee's main function was to initiate the fund-raising effort. In this they were quite successful, until the storm clouds of the Second World War engulfed all of Italy. Only a few weeks after the brochure appeared, Benito Mussolini's government entered the conflict on the side of Germany, declaring war on France and England. Padre Pio wisely understood that the war would result in drastic inflation, making the donations already received almost worthless. Therefore at his suggestion, the committee invested the funds they had collected in a landed estate in Lucera, an agricultural center located on the great plain of the *Tavoliere* south of the Gargano.

Then on December 11, 1941, Mussolini declared war on the United States. This was an unpopular move, because most Italians either had relatives there, or they hoped some day to emigrate to the United States themselves to partake of the "American Dream." For now, all plans for building a "grandiose" hospital had to be put on hold, and it was possible the project would never be resumed. But ironically, it was the War itself, and America's involvement in it, that would keep alive the hope that one day the great *"Casa"* would arise on the slopes of the Gargano.

Chapter 16

Mary Pyle "Interned" at Pietrelcina

NOW that Italy and the United States were at war with each other, the Italian authorities were obligated to detain and question Mary Pyle, since she had kept her American citizenship. It was likely she would be sent to an internment camp for political prisoners. Late in 1941, she was called to the Minister of Internal Affairs in Rome, where she was accompanied by a Capuchin who could vouch for her character, Padre Emilio da Matrice. The commissioner conducted a perfunctory interview, scarcely paying any attention to Mary's answers. He only showed some emotion, that of embarrassment, when it came time to ask her for permission to conduct a search of her home. At this request, Mary tearfully remained silent for while, and then slowly collapsed in her chair as if she were going to faint.[1]

The commissioner and the Padre rushed over to help her, and unbuttoned her winter coat so she could have some air. To the astonishment of both, underneath the coat Mary was dressed in her Capuchin habit, which she had special permission to wear. The overwhelmed commissioner eyed the pectoral cross, the knotted cord, Rosary, and brown habit. All he could say as he stood there staring at her was, "She looks like Our Lady of Sorrows." As Mary began to compose herself, the commissioner sat down and admitted to Padre Emilio that she was no ordinary person—she seemed to be a woman who should belong to a religious order. He even asked her to pray for him; she replied that she was not a saint, but that her beloved Padre Pio was.

114

The official did not pursue his request to have Mary's house searched. Padre Emilio, apparently sensing a reluctance to incarcerate her, proposed that she be put under "house arrest" at the home of Padre Pio's family in Pietrelcina. The commissioner was agreeable to this solution, and on December 27, 1941, Mary Pyle arrived in Pietrelcina to begin serving her "sentence" at the Forgione home. Although nothing could compare with living near Padre Pio in San Giovanni Rotondo, she was thankful and quite happy to be staying with his family in the home where he had been born.

Initially, the orders from the local police chief prohibited her from entering any other home in the town except for the Forgione residence. However, Mary was allowed outside for walks, and could attend church. In the afternoons she would go for long strolls with a friend, Caterina Florio, during which Mary used to thank her for "bailing her out of jail."[2] She also spent time in spiritual reading and in playing the harmonium, or reed organ. Every morning Caterina and Mary would attend Mass together. Afterward, Mary would remain in the church to say the Divine Office. In the evening it was back to the church again, this time for the full fifteen-decade Rosary, and any other evening functions scheduled for that night, such as Benediction of the Blessed Sacrament.

Mary was well-received by the good people of Pietrelcina, and eventually even the police chief relaxed the restrictions on her, and she was allowed to visit the villagers in their homes. Although she was a woman of great culture and spirituality, Mary never made the ordinary townspeople feel uncomfortable in her presence. In the words of one of the local women, "She was truly everything to everybody, in order to help everybody, and never let people feel the difference in their birth and education."[3] She was always smiling and friendly, and did not hesitate to perform works of charity.

There was a young mother in the village whose husband had been taken as a prisoner of war. She had a small baby to care for, which meant she was unable to attend Mass on Sundays, although she had a great desire to do so. When Mary found out about her situation, she offered to take care of the baby when she returned from the early Sunday Mass, so that the mother could attend the later Mass. Of course the mother gratefully accepted the offer. It was this kind of compassion and concern for others that endeared her to the *Pucinari*. Padre Pio's former doctor, Andrea Cardone, used to converse with her often, and praised her in glowing terms: "This woman, Mary Pyle, is truly exceptional. I have never known a woman so kind, so good, so detached from the grandeur of the world . . ."[4]

Pietrelcina itself was never bombed in the War,[5] but bombardments of neighboring areas, including Benevento, did occur. During these times of danger the Forgiones and Mary took refuge at the country farm cottage at Piana Romana. Mary would still attend daily Mass, and had to cross the fields to get to the church. One morning as she was returning from Mass, a German soldier suddenly jumped out from the nearby woods. Pointing his gun right at her, he ordered her to stop, and demanded to know where she was coming from and where she was going. To the soldier's complete surprise, Mary calmly answered him in perfect German. The delighted soldier put down his gun and began a conversation with her. He accompanied her to the Forgione's farm house, where the family served him a hearty meal. However, Mary became uneasy when she noticed he was showing a little too much interest in Pia Forgione. Pia was Padre Pio's niece, the attractive young daughter of his brother Michele. Sensing his intentions, Mary began to pray silently to Padre Pio for Pia's safety. The soldier ended up behaving himself, and when the meal was over he peacefully departed from the little farm house.[6]

In September of 1943, after Mussolini was deposed, Italy surrendered to the Allies, and a month later declared war on its former partner, Germany. Allied troops were moving north up the Italian peninsula, and on October 3 the American soldiers reached the outskirts of Pietrelcina. Mary was overjoyed because this meant her internment would be at an end. She ran to the bridge that led into town to meet the troops, many only in their teens, and hugged them as if they were her own sons. A few days later, she packed up her belongings and hoisted them into a farm wagon belonging to Davide Aucone, and together they started on the long trek back to San Giovanni. Mary did her best to keep their spirits up, even though roads and bridges were bombed out, rivers had to be crossed on foot, and a torrential downpour drenched the two travelers. In the mornings, after fasting from the night before, they would make their way to the nearest church to receive Communion. Davide Aucone would later observe that,

> After Holy Communion all traces of fatigue would disappear as if by magic. Her prayers along the way gave her comfort and courage. Maria was always smiling and happy, truly content, and more so whenever the trip became difficult.[7]

After three arduous days, they finally reached San Giovanni Rotondo. Her exile over, she was back in her own home, the "pink castle," and more importantly, she was reunited with her beloved spiritual father, Padre Pio.

Chapter 17

The Holy Man on the Mountain

A S THE Allies pushed the deeply ensconced German troops out of southern Italy in 1943, thousands of American GIs poured in from the 15th Army Air Force, the primary occupier of the Italian region of Apulia (or Puglia), whose capital is Bari. The military realized that the vast plains of Apulia, known as the *Tavoliere*, were ideal for constructing airfields. Many of these air strips were placed in and around Foggia, in such places as Cerignola and Amendola. There were a total of seven satellite air fields built in a circle around Foggia, located in the heart of the northern Apulia region. The region is bordered on the East by the Adriatic Sea, enabling planes to enter formation over the Adriatic for bombing runs in the north of Europe.

Apulia is primarily an agricultural area, dotted with almond groves, olive trees and grape vines. But the crop-growing flatlands of the *Tavoliere* do not extend to the northernmost part of the region. Instead, as one travels north from Foggia, there suddenly arises a line of sharp cliffs that form the slopes of the mountainous terrain known as the Gargano.

As the Americans settled into their bases and began to mix with the Italian locals, rumors emerged about a "holy man" somewhere up in the Gargano hills. Occasionally GIs heard about such a man during trips to nearby towns, where they bartered candy and cigarettes in exchange for fresh food such as eggs, poultry, and vegetables, in order to supplement their Army rations. On his return from one such bartering excursion to the town of San Giovanni Rotondo, Joe De Santis, a sergeant with the 15th Air Force in Cerignola, brought back to his camp the story of a priest up in the hills who had the wounds of Christ.[1]

Joe had been exploring the town, looking for fresh food, when he noticed groups of older women climbing up a rough hilly trail on their knees, praying the Stations of the Cross that were erected along one side of the unpaved road. Following them out of curiosity, he neared a church and monastery that was at the top of the hill and began talking to an old Italian lady, who amazed him by speaking perfect English. She told him all about a very holy priest who lived in the monastery, and who bore on his hands, feet and chest the wounds of Christ. The sergeant, based with the 484th Bomb Group of B-24 Flying Fortresses, returned to his base and began talking about this stigmatized priest to his fellow GIs. He found an interested listener in one of his men, Ray Ewen. Ray was a Catholic from the New York City area, and he was intrigued enough to accompany the sergeant back to San Giovanni Rotondo a few days later.[2]

They went to look for the English-speaking local woman to get more information about the priest, and had little trouble finding her. The name of that "old Italian lady" was Mary McAlpin Pyle, the American who befriended Padre Pio! Ray, who was familiar with the McAlpin hotel in New York City, felt very comfortable talking to Mary and they "hit it off" right away. Mary, for her part, was overjoyed to meet someone from New York. On that trip the two soldiers did not get to see Padre Pio, but it wasn't long before they journeyed back up the mountain again. They left very early in the morning, to be sure they could attend the Mass, which began at 5:00 a.m. The church had been jammed for an hour before the start time, but Mary took them in by a back way through the sacristy, and when they entered the church, they were right at the altar, where soldiers were allowed to remain. Ray was glad he did not have to contend with the local women for a seat in the pews!

Ray recalls that Mary was the organist. During the Mass, Padre Pio did not have his gloves on, but he wore his alb such that the sleeves covered the wounds. However, during the Offertory, when he raised his arms, Ray could clearly see the blood and "scars" on his hands. After the Mass, Mary took them to the sacristy, where Italian men were confessing face-to-face to Padre Pio. A little later, Padre Pio, Mary and the GIs who were present went out into the friary garden for conversation, with Mary as interpreter. Ray told Mary that he wished he knew enough Italian to have Padre Pio hear his Confession.

Ray Ewen made the trip to San Giovanni at least seven times. He would often sit on the little stone wall surrounding the elm tree in front of the Friary, listening to Grazio Forgione talk about his famous son. Grazio, now in his 80's, had come to live in San Giovanni in 1938. He spoke English fairly well, and was a "great guy." Grazio, often known as Orazio, slept in the same room in Mary Pyle's house where his dear wife Mamma Peppa had spent her last days.

On one of his visits to San Giovanni, Ray was inside the church while Confessions were taking place, and he heard Padre Pio order someone out of the confessional. After hearing Padre Pio say this, some of those waiting their turn in line lost their nerve, got out of the line, and left. They had witnessed one of the distinctive marks of Padre Pio's ministry of bringing souls to God. He would refuse to hear a Confession on those occasions when he was aware that the penitent was insincere, or required a jolt to make him realize that he needed to examine his conscience. It is said that invariably such people would undergo an inner conversion, and eventually return to make a sincere Confession either to Padre Pio or to another priest.

Usually, after Mass and the visit to the Friary were over, the soldiers would gather at Mary's "pink castle," sitting at her spacious kitchen table, chatting over coffee—preferably American coffee, supplied by the GIs! Ray remembers Mary as "adorable and jolly" and he felt right at home in the Pink House. They got along so well that Ray was invited to attend Thanksgiving dinner at the Pyle home in November of 1944. Grazio was present, along with his son Michele Forgione, and Count Telfener from England. The Count was quite a "character," sporting a patch over one eye and puffing on his pipe. His wife was a cousin of Irving Berlin,[3] and Count Telfener was soon to become very active in supporting the future hospital at San Giovanni Rotondo.

Ray was at Padre Pio's midnight Mass on Christmas Eve, 1944. Electric lights were not to be used because of a war blackout, and the entire ceremony was by candlelight. When Padre Pio processed into the church of Our Lady of Grace, carrying the statuette of Baby Jesus cradled in his arms, Ray described it as "so edifying, so unbelievable, I will never forget it!" During that Christmas season, some of the GIs in Ray's group asked Padre Pio when the War would end. He did not give a direct answer to that question, but did tell them that this would be their last Christmas in San Giovanni Rotondo. Padre Pio's prediction turned out to be true, for the war in Italy was over by the spring of 1945, shortly after Mussolini was captured by the Italian freedom-fighters (*partigiani*) and executed in April.

Ray's chaplain back at the Cerignola base camp was Fr. Walter Junk (spelled that way, Ray insists). Fr. Junk was a Capuchin, and following the directives in force at that time, he was not allowed to promote Padre Pio in any way. In fact he would say that Padre Pio was a "phony." When he found out that Ray had attended Padre Pio's Mass, and had even taken other GIs there, he made Ray go to Confession for going to a "phony Mass" and telling others about it! Even after the War, when Fr. Junk visited the Ewens' home, he actually asked Ray to take down the pictures of Padre Pio from his wall. Finally, after many years had gone by, Fr. Junk completely reversed his position. Then one day, on another visit to their home, he remarked about how fortunate the GIs had been to be so near to Padre Pio during the War. At this, Ray's wife Mildred almost took a poke at him!

Ray and Mary Pyle corresponded on a regular basis when he got back to the United States. He used to visit Mary's American secretary, a Mrs. Prendergast, at an office near Our Lady of Victory Church in the Wall Street area. There he assisted the secretary in sending packages back to Mary in Italy. Prendergast was basically in charge of handling Mary's estate, although the two met in person only once, when Mary visited America in 1948.

In May of 1956, Ray received a letter from Mary with some suggestions as to how he could explain Padre Pio to his children. In it she also mentioned the inauguration of Padre Pio's new hospital and described a miraculous cure.

Dear Ray and Company,

I gave your very generous offering for Masses with the intentions to Padre Pio on April 18. Late in giving it and still later in answering you. But never mind, Padre Pio reads your letter while you are writing it, or perhaps he reads it in your heart before it reaches the paper.

When your children want explanations about Padre Pio, just tell them that he loves Jesus so much, and Jesus loves him so much, that they have become very much alike. Jesus has given Padre Pio His wounds, so that they can both suffer together to make us all be good. When God sees that he is suffering so much, He gives him everything which he asks for—he makes people get well and makes bad people become good. We must all pray with him and try to be very good.

The inauguration of the hospital on May 5 was wonderful, and the patients are beginning to arrive. The best part of the inauguration was the accertation (I don't know if that word exists) of a great miracle which our beloved Father had performed.

A sixteen-year-old boy came here, having been sent by a doctor who said that nothing could be done for the boy, who had a tumor behind his eye—cancer. His eye was already deformed and his suffering was atrocious. The mother said that she would not move from here until her boy was healed. On the 5th of May the boy was examined again by the doctor who had sent him, and who is now here at the hospital, and the tumor had entirely disappeared. Deo Gratias!

Love to all,
Maria Pyle

In a letter from Mary dated February 14, 1946, She thanked Ray for playing a big part in "saving our dear friend's life" on Thanksgiving Day. This letter from Mary Pyle to Ray Ewen reads:

Dear Ray,

Many thanks for the lovely Christmas card and above all for your thought. I am very glad that you are home with your dear family but we miss you all very much.

Padre Pio remembers you all, one by one, and says that you are living in his heart and that distance cannot diminish the love which he felt for you when you were near. He once said to one who was leaving and who asked how she could communicate with him from afar: "Kneel in front of Jesus in the Tabernacle and you will always find me there." Isn't that a comforting thought?

We are still so grateful to you for what you did for us on Thanksgiving Day a year ago. You really took part (a big part) in saving our dear friend's life. We are also still grateful for all the etc., etc., etc.

This carries cordial greetings from all of my household and from all of those who knew you, and from all of the Pio family, of which you are also a member, and it carries love and many blessings from our beloved and mutual Father for you and yours.

God bless you,
Maria

Years later, in a letter to Ray and his family dated January 1, 1956, Mary passed on a request from Padre Pio for prayers on his behalf because he was not feeling well. Even though by now at least eleven years had gone by since the incident, Mary once again recalled how Ray helped save their friend's life.

Dear Ray, Mil, Eileen and Eddy,

Many many thanks in Padre Pio's name for the generous Christmas offering from you and yours, and Padre Pio's thanks always mean prayers and more prayers and blessings. He is not feeling well, and asks us all to help him with our prayers. All of the world is turning to him for help, and he wants his children to help him.

It is nice to see that you still remember us. We can never forget you, Ray, and think of you especially every Thanksgiving Day. Do you remember when you succeeded in bringing us the benzine or gasoline, at ten o'clock at night, which enabled us to save our friend's life? We can never stop thanking you for that act of charity.

My most cordial and affectionate greetings to all of the family with a big "God Bless you!"

Maria Pyle

Ray had all but forgotten about the time he helped save someone's life, and even today can barely recall what the incident was about. He remembers that there was a Third Order Franciscan woman who was seriously ill, and she had to get to a hospital immediately or she would die. But this was in the middle of the War and there was not enough gasoline available in the town for the doctor to take her to a hospital in Naples. Ray was told later by others that he kept saying, "Something's gotta be done; something's gotta be done!"

That night, back at the base, somehow Ray managed to sneak a few five-gallon containers of gasoline past the guards and transport them up the mountain to San Giovanni. By 10:00 p.m. the doctor and patient were on the way to Naples with a full tank of gas! Ray felt he could have been court-martialed for giving military supplies to civilians and relates that his buddies covered for him while he was absent from the base. Today Ray believes that it must have been Padre Pio, now St. Pio, acting through him.

Ray Ewen was a great friend of Mary as evidenced by their

post-war correspondence. But she also wrote to another of
Ray's war buddies from the same outfit, Joe Revelas.[4] Joe
went alone to San Giovanni on his first visit. He had heard
beforehand about Mary Pyle's generous hospitality and help-
fulness, so instead of going right to the Friary, he stopped at
the pink house and knocked on Mary's door. She answered it
herself and invited Joe inside. They talked for hours, mainly
about Padre Pio, and at one point she asked him if he had
met the Padre yet. Joe replied that he hadn't, but tomorrow
he was planning on attending his Mass and meeting him if
possible. However, Mary insisted on taking him to meet
Padre Pio right away, that very evening.

She walked Joe over to the Monastery, where they met an
English-speaking friar who took Joe upstairs to a room near
the choir area. Soon Padre Pio entered the room, and they
conversed, with the other friar interpreting. The talk was
casual, with Padre Pio asking Joe what outfit he was with
and where he was from. Joe's description of Padre Pio is full
of superlatives. "It was shocking and awesome to see some-
body like that. He was phenomenal, terrific, like a saint to
me." After about ten minutes, they left the room, and Padre
Pio knelt down in the choir, and remained there praying. Joe
Revelas went back to Mary's house, wondering where he was
going to spend the night. To his pleasant surprise, she
invited him to stay at her home that evening, and fixed up a
place for him to sleep in an upstairs room.

Early the next morning, Joe attended Padre Pio's Mass. He
was able to sit right by the altar, since the Italian ladies
present were telling the soldiers to go up front. Tears were
streaming from Padre Pio's eyes during the two-hour ceremony, although it didn't really seem that long to Joe. "You
could hear a pin drop in that church," he said, "except for the
parts where people beat their breasts—they hit their chests
so hard you could hear it through the whole church."

(According to one author's description: ". . . Padre Pio struck his breast with such conviction that the thump could be heard throughout the chapel.")[5]

On their visits to San Giovanni, Joe Revelas and Ray Ewen used to bring food from the mess hall for Padre Pio, Mary, and the friars. Sometimes Joe would bring over "goodies" that had been sent to him from back home. After Mass, they would go over to Mary's to relax and have a snack. On one occasion, Joe went shopping at a nearby religious goods store, and purchased a crucifix. He went to the Friary to have Padre Pio bless it. The Saint not only blessed it, but he kissed it "really hard." Joe understandably keeps this crucifix near him to this day.

Joe's claim to fame, however, is that when Mary Pyle came to the United States in 1948 to raise money for the church and monastery at Pietrelcina, she stopped at Joe's house in Philadelphia. "One day, just out of the blue, there was a knock at the door, and there she was!" She had a woman with her (probably Anita Lodi), and a soldier who seemed to be the one showing her around during her visit. Mary was wearing her Franciscan habit, and they stayed at Joe's for about an hour. He had been corresponding with Mary after the War, and she mentioned that she was coming to the States for a visit, but Joe had no idea that she would show up at his home.

Following are two undated notes that Mary Pyle wrote to Joe Revelas after her visit, and once again a miraculous cure is mentioned.

Dear Joe,

I have not thanked you for your greetings but I recommended you to Padre Pio and I still remember your visit to us and my visit to you. Don't forget to send your Guardian Angel whenever you want his blessing—he hears his children from afar and remembers them.

God bless you both; Padre Pio's blessing and my love,

Maria Pyle

Dear Joe,

With you, I always have to start every letter with a huge THANK YOU!!!

This is just a short little note to tell you that I have sent you one hundred little Sacred Heart cards with a novena, which I have had printed because it is the translation of one which Padre Pio says every day with the whole community, for all of those who ask for his prayers. I thought it would be nice for all of his far away spiritual children to join their prayers to his. Let us pray with him and according to his intentions.

Padre Pio is becoming more wonderful every day. Consequently, the crowds who come to him for help increase, and it is a real problem to be able to approach him. Two weeks ago, he healed a paralyzed woman, who had been carried into the church and went away walking without help. You can imagine the excitement, but still more wonderful are the conversions, and there are many of them. Do let us try to do our little bit in helping him with our poor little prayers.

How is your dear mother? Please give her my most cordial greetings and Anita's too.

Be good, God bless you,
Maria

One day back at the base near Cerignola, Joe's buddy Bob Mohs had a free day and decided to head for San Giovanni. Joe asked him if he would take some Miraculous Medals up with him. The medals had been given to Joe by some nuns he had met when he was in training in Colorado. They had asked him that if he ever got to Italy, to try to have them blessed by Padre Pio. Carrying the envelope of Joe's medals, Bob Mohs began to hitchhike the long trek from Cerignola, to Foggia, and then to San Giovanni Rotondo. Unfortunately, he was not offered a single ride, and ended up walking the entire way, a distance of over 25 miles.

Nearing the end of his journey, Bob climbed the old mule trail which had the Stations of the Cross erected alongside it, and this led him right up to the Monastery. Seeing no one around, he knocked on the door of the Friary. A monk with a black beard and glasses opened the door and asked him in broken English what he wanted. Bob simply handed him the envelope full of medals, which had a message from the nuns written on it. The monk asked Bob to wait, and in a few minutes returned and invited him into the Monastery, where they walked down a hall. He opened a door on the right and entered Padre Pio's cell. He came out again with two chairs which he placed in the hallway. Within a few minutes Padre Pio walked out of his cell, and Bob Mohs describes in his own words what happened next.

His hands were covered with fingerless gloves over his wounds. He sat down on one chair and the monk who let me in acted as interpreter, relaying Padre Pio's message to me. Padre Pio said, "You were a sucker for your buddy, as he was supposed to bring the envelope here." He opened the envelope and blessed the medals, then be blessed some of his own medals and gave them to me. He then said to me,

"You walked here, but you will not walk back." How did he know that? I had not mentioned anything to anyone about that walk! I thanked him and was led out of the monastery.

As I headed on the road away from the monastery, to my right there came a jeep which stopped and asked if I wanted a ride to Foggia. "Yes, thank you," I said. The jeep dropped me off at Foggia, and as I headed out of town, an Army weapons carrier stopped, and I was off to Cerignola. As I headed out of Cerignola, another weapons carrier stopped and took me right to my base. Wow! Thank you Padre Pio!

As word of my experience with Padre Pio at San Giovanni Rotondo got around our camp area, our commanding officer (a fallen-away Catholic) made available two weapons carriers for trips to Padre Pio's Mass. When we GIs went to Mass at the monastery church (which was always packed with people), wooden folding chairs were set up on the altar side of the communion rails. We were led from the sacristy to our chairs, and were not more than ten feet from where Padre Pio prayed the Mass without the finger-less gloves on.

After Mass we were privileged to go to the sacristy with Padre Pio, always packed with people. I recall kissing Padre Pio's open wounds, and the aroma of roses filled the air. I recall after kissing the wounds on his hands the taste of blood filled my mouth. To have been blessed with such a rare privilege as this experience gives me "chills" as many times as I recall this blessing.[6]

Ray Ewen, Joe Revelas, Bob Mohs, and Joe De Santis were all from the same squadron, based near Cerignola. For the record, it was the 484th Bomb Group, 826th Squadron, 49th Wing, of the 15th Army Air Force. The 15th had its headquarters in Bari, and the Wing headquarters were in Foggia. There were four squadrons in the bomb group, each squadron was composed of about four hundred men, with sixteen B-24 "Flying Fortress" planes. From the ranks of these soldiers came some of the first American witnesses to the greatness of the "Holy Man" on the mountain. Furthermore, in a letter to Ray Ewen sent after the War, their chaplain, Fr. Walter Junk, indicated that five soldiers from Ray's outfit had entered the priesthood, undoubtedly inspired to a large extent by their encounters with Padre Pio.

Chapter 18

"Struck" by Padre Pio

NOT all of the American soldiers had the chance to see Padre Pio more than once. Eugene McMahon[1] and Tony Afflitto[2] were part of a group of about half a dozen GIs who made the trip up the mountain to attend his Mass. It was February 1945 when these two men of the 463rd Bomb Group, which flew B-17s, went with their chaplain, Fr. Rice. The pair signed up to make the trip because Fr. Rice had told them that they were going there "to see a saint." The custom had grown among the troops to bring a present or a gift for the friars at Our Lady of Grace. Eugene and Tony chipped in and purchased a case of American beer and some cigarettes. Yes, Padre Pio was known to occasionally allow himself a small glass of beer, and thanks to the soldiers' gifts, his preference now was for the American brands.

Because of the harsh realities of the War, this was to be the only time the pair would ever see the Saint. They were allowed to remain on the steps of the altar during Mass, kneeling at the top step. After Mass, Padre Pio met with the group, permitted them to kiss his gloved hands, and gave them his blessing. Padre Pio gave Tony a medal, which he was still wearing over 50 years later, and also told Tony that he would be on the way home by Easter. To Tony, Padre Pio was "great, tremendous; I will never forget him." He wrote a letter to his wife that same evening, telling her, "Today I met a saint!"

Although he did not get to kiss Padre Pio's hand, Eugene was able to go to Confession and receive Holy Communion from him. "I never set eyes on a man like that." For Eugene, Padre Pio's mannerisms and his eyes, mainly, were something special. "His eyes looked right through you, I never saw anything like it in my life." Eugene reports that the church was mobbed; there were people in wheelchairs, on crutches, blind and injured. "You could see on their faces they were waiting to be cured." On and around the walls of the small church, he noticed the discarded crutches and wheelchairs of people who had been healed!

The graces Tony and Eugene received that day from meeting Padre Pio and attending his Mass gave them the strength to endure what befell them two days later. Flying over Austria in a B-17, their plane was shot down and all of the crew members were eventually captured and taken as prisoners of war (POWs). Some months later, Tony Afflitto managed to escape the POW camp. After walking three or four days, he ran into American troops under General George S. Patton . . . and was in Paris on the way home by Easter, as Padre Pio had foretold.

Eugene McMahon was able to avoid capture for almost two weeks, and wrote a vivid description of his experiences. His narrative of the reality of war is in sharp contrast to the oasis of peace he had experienced at San Giovanni Rotondo.

All the crew were captured in a few days by Austrians, except myself. I bailed out at about 25-27,000 feet. The Germans were shooting at us and I was hit in the arm and wrist. I landed in 2-3 feet of snow. Hearing voices and dogs barking, I began running and making my way to the Hungarian border. Hunger was gnawing at me, and with little or no food, I became a mere skeleton. My feet, hands and ears were frozen from the intense cold, sleet and snow, while fleeing over 200 miles before being captured.

In an attempt to secure information, my feet were beaten; but I refused, giving them only my name, rank and serial number. Even though my feet were lacerated, I was forced to march from Hungary to Vienna, then marched to Nuremberg and later to Frankfurt, Germany. I was later sent by boxcar to the Mooseberg POW camp in Germany where I was finally liberated about May 1, 1945, by General George Patton's Army. When liberated, I weighed only 96 pounds, and was sent to the military hospital in Atlantic City, New Jersey, where I spent three months recovering.

Horrible memories of being in a Quonset hut with mere skeletons of bodies staring at you, just starving to death, still haunt me, as does seeing the SS camp guards shooting prisoners for begging for food, and then laughing as they died, while I could do nothing as the guards taunted and shot at us.

The most treasured memory of the war, however, was my visit with Padre Pio, and to be witness to the many miracles of curing people. We attended Mass, and just to be in his presence was so inspirational, and receiving Communion from him gave me such peace at that time. I feel Our Lord has always been watching over me. I'm proud of having served my country in helping preserve our freedoms and would do it again.

On June 13, 1997, Eugene McMahon received New Jersey's Distinguished Service Medal, the highest honor that state can bestow on a citizen. Our Lord and Padre Pio have truly been looking after him.

Carl Amato[3] was another soldier from the 463rd Bomb Group who met Padre Pio. He arrived in a truck that carried about 15 soldiers and their chaplain, Fr. Rice. He remembers seeing the blood running down Padre Pio's hands during the hour-and-a-half Mass. When they met with Pio later, Mary Pyle was there to interpret. Carl's observation was that "Padre Pio was a living saint. You knew when you looked at him—his eyes made you want to come back." Later they went as a group to the "pink castle," and relaxed around the long kitchen table. Carl signed Mary Pyle's guest book.

After the war, when his son Carl Jr. received the Sacrament of Confirmation, the Confirmation name chosen for him was "Pio," in honor of Padre Pio. Soon afterward, Carl Jr. received a card from Padre Pio, via Mary Pyle, conveying his thoughts, congratulations, and gratitude for this honor, and offering his blessing. But there is a typical Padre Pio mystery here—as far as the Amato family knows, no one had ever informed Padre Pio about the Confirmation ceremony, and the name of "Pio" that was chosen!

Pete Mier,[4] another GI from the 463rd Bomb Group, believes he first heard about Padre Pio from an article in the overseas military newspaper *Stars and Stripes*. Pete's last name was actually Miragliotta, but the family changed it because they ran a business, and their clients could barely remember or pronounce it. He and two others visited the monastery in July of 1945, when the war in Italy was over. They were the only soldiers there that day, and the church was not completely full. Nevertheless, when they arrived inside, an usher took them up to the altar area and gave them folding chairs to sit on.

"You could tell Padre Pio was in such pain during the Mass, which he said slowly," observed Pete. When Mass was over, the three GIs met with Padre Pio in the sacristy, where Pete "reluctantly" kissed his hand, which was crusted with blood. While he kissed the stigmatized hand, he could detect the aroma of roses. He describes Padre Pio as "So gentle, so kind, so nice. He could be strict but he was not rough like people said." Pete to this day enjoys giving out medals and holy cards of Padre Pio. The Saint must be pleased with him, because Pete is occasionally rewarded on some evenings with Padre Pio's perfume of roses.

Pete Mier did not give in to his reluctance to kiss the Padre's stigmatized hand, but one solider who did hesitate was in for a big surprise. Nineteen-year-old Joe Haines[5] was an aerial photographer, whose assignment was to record the results of the B-17 bombing missions of the 416th Bomb Group. While stationed at an airfield near Foggia, Joe heard some of the men on his base talking about a "Holy Man" who lived on the mountain. To Joe, "Holy Man" sounded like someone from India. He knew absolutely nothing about Padre Pio, not even his name, and certainly was not aware of his stigmata. But Joe, who was Catholic, and two of his Protestant friends, made up their minds to find this so-called "Holy Man." Their airfield was close to the Gargano, and since they were young and energetic, they decided to climb the mountain on foot!

The cliffs were steep, and once on the upper plateau there was a long road to town, and from the town it was another mile or so uphill, to the friary of Our Lady of Grace. Of the three GIs, only Joe made it all the way there. Entering the church, he discovered that it was packed with worshippers. "The next thing I knew, I was sitting on a small stool on the altar side of the railing, in the center." When the Mass started, out came Padre Pio, walking so close that Joe could have reached out and touched him. During the hour-and-a-half Mass, Joe could see the tears falling as Padre Pio cried.

After Mass Joe followed him along with the crowd into the sacristy. He was able to get close to Padre Pio, and he blurted out "Padre!" Padre Pio turned around, took a good look at

Joe, and extended his hand, palm up. It was covered with scabs, rough looking, and it smelled like roses. "I saw his palm full of crust and purple, and thought to myself that he wants me to kiss his hand." But Joe hesitated, and Padre Pio sensed his reluctance. Then, the very next moment, Padre Pio made a fist, and actually punched Joe in the middle of the forehead—hard! Joe Haines knelt down like he was hit by a bolt of lightning, and thought to himself, "I'd better kiss that hand NOW!"

"Bingo! The next thing I knew I was back at camp!" Joe has no memory of anything that happened from the time of his dramatic encounter with Padre Pio until he was back at the base. (Later he learned that he would remember only what Padre Pio wanted him to remember.) He did not question what had happened, he just accepted it, unaware of its meaning. He was still not sure who this priest was, or even if he was the "Holy Man."

Back in the United States after the war, he heard that a speaker named Charles Mandina was giving a talk at a local church on Padre Pio and Foggia. The name "Padre Pio" meant nothing to him, but Joe went to the talk because it was about Foggia, where he had been stationed in Italy. He was able to meet and speak to Charles, who explained to him that Padre Pio was in fact the "Holy Man" of the mountain, and that the blow on the head he gave Joe was actually a very special blessing.

Joe knew that someone must have been praying for him while he was on his bombing runs. He had a streak of good luck and missed many close calls. He showed up for one mission not feeling too well, but was ready for the flight. However, the captain said that he looked sick and had him replaced. That plane blew up right after take-off.

As a mission photographer, he was the "odd man" on a bombing flight, and airmen are very superstitious about who is flying with them. Normally he would be considered bad luck because he was not part of their regular crew, since he was assigned to various planes. But Joe's reputation was just the opposite, and the airmen actually wanted him on their flights, as a good luck charm.

After he came home, Joe's "striking" experiences with Padre Pio were not yet over. Sometime after Padre Pio had died, Joe and his wife were visiting Naples, while on a trip to Europe. They were casually window shopping along a city street when a thought came to Joe. Since they were in southern Italy, he told his wife that he would like to go to visit Padre Pio's tomb, and she agreed. They continued walking down the street when suddenly Joe heard Padre Pio's voice in an annoyed tone. Joe reports that Padre Pio hit him on the back and knocked him down, right in the street. Then Padre Pio said to Joe: "You fool, you don't have to come to my burial place to get a blessing. Why don't you do something good?"

Joe was not hurt, but he was understandably "a little shook up." His first reaction was to tell his wife that they would still go to the burial place. But instead, they figured out how much money it would cost for train fare to Foggia and for hotel expenses in San Giovanni Rotondo. When they returned to America, they donated that amount to the poor. "I learned a valuable lesson I still hold to."

As a postscript, Joe added that one day while at home, his wife called him from the master bedroom. She was confused about the strong aroma of roses that filled the room, since there were no flowers at all in the house. Joe states: "I knew it was Padre Pio!"

An interesting story is told by Robert Simmons,[6] of the 99th Bomb Group out of Foggia. In the spring of 1945, Robert and his friend Rudy Tucci, both gunners on B-17s, had a day off from flying. They had heard the tales about Padre Pio in the camp, and decided to drive up to San Giovanni Rotondo. When they arrived, there were only a few people in the church waiting for the Mass to start later on. The two GIs were able to meet with Padre Pio, and he blessed them, placing his hand on their heads. They were also able to see his cell, which Robert described as very sparsely furnished. When Padre Pio found out they were both altar boys back in the States, he asked them to be the altar servers for his Mass. Robert said the Mass was attended by only a few old women, and there was nothing unusual about it, just a "normal Latin Mass." Padre Pio did speak a few words to the congregation, but it was not a homily.

While they were at the Friary that day, Robert and Rudy noticed that there were two men in civilian clothing who appeared to be waiting on Padre Pio, almost as if they were his servants. They were two German soldiers who had defected, and were apparently receiving some sort of sanctuary at the Friary. Robert and Rudy talked to one of the local Italian men who spoke some English, and he told them that the American army knew the two Germans were there, but let them alone. Since this was the only trip the two GIs made to San Giovanni, Simmons has no idea of the Germans' ultimate fate. As deserters, were they able to return to their own country, did they stay in Italy, or did the Allies eventually apprehend them? Hopefully, under the protective mantle of Padre Pio, they left the monastery safely. Apparently, they did not stay long at the Friary, since this appears to be the only report of their presence there. However, there are stories in the Padre Pio literature about two German soldiers, armed and in uniform, who came to the Friary during the War, making everyone nervous. After paying their respects to Padre Pio, they left peacefully. The power of an encounter with Padre Pio should not be underestimated, but one can only speculate whether the men

Simmons saw were these two armed soldiers who had later defected.

An interesting illustration of the power of even a simple encounter with Padre Pio is provided by Ed Karnes.[7] Ed, like Robert Simmons, was with the 99th Bomb Group out of Foggia. One afternoon in 1943, Ed and the men in his crew were invited to a party in San Giovanni Rotondo. Ed, who was not Catholic, had heard of Padre Pio, and wished to take advantage of the fact that he was so close to the Friary that day. He decided to leave the party a little early, and went up by himself to the Monastery to see if he could somehow meet Padre Pio. Arriving at the Friary, he saw one of the Capuchin friars and asked him in all simplicity if he could have an audience with Padre Pio. Ed was conducted to a tiny visitor's room and told to wait there. In a few minutes Padre Pio himself arrived, and sat down just two feet away from Ed Karnes. Ed could not speak Italian, and Padre Pio could not speak English, so the two just sat there looking at each other and not saying a word for about 30 minutes!

Ed does not recall kissing the wounds, but remembers that he did touch Padre Pio's hand. Ed knows that Padre Pio did something special for him, and to him, by allowing him to be in his presence for this half-hour of silent communication. The two men just sat together quietly, not even engaging in mutual prayer; he does not recall Padre Pio praying the Rosary during that time. Padre Pio sent him away from that encounter feeling wonderful and peaceful. "We were just trying to acknowledge each other. It was a marvelous experience; it couldn't have been more peaceful, I left there feeling so good; it was an experience in my life I'll never forget. Thank God he had the courtesy to come and sit with me; I walked out of there knowing something very, very special had happened." Ed went on to pilot fifty-one B-17 missions, both combat and supply, and not one member of his regular crew was injured. Perhaps it was because of that something special that the Saint of the Gargano did for Ed Karnes.

Padre Pio's gift of prophecy was occasionally used to confirm American soldiers in their religious vocation, or lack of one. Two friends stationed in Cerignola, Leo Fanning and Joe Asterita, visited Padre Pio often. They had found out about him from Padre Paolino, who was the Superior of Our Lady of Grace Friary when Padre Pio first arrived there in 1916, and was now assigned to the Capuchin church in Cerignola. When Padre Pio met Leo Fanning for the first time, he was introduced to him as "Leone" Fanning. Padre Pio told him, "Some day it will be Father Leone."[8] Fanning had been thinking about the priesthood since the fourth grade, but no one had told this to Padre Pio. He eventually did become Fr. Leo Fanning in 1954 and was assigned to parishes in New Jersey and Florida. After his Ordination, he was frequently asked to give talks about Padre Pio to parish groups.

At the time of this writing, Fr. Fanning is residing in a home for retired priests in Chester, New Jersey.[9] He is quite active, assisting with Mass and Confessions at nearby St. Michael's parish, and still occasionally giving talks about Padre Pio, attended by from fifty to two hundred listeners. About three years ago, he made his first visit to San Giovanni Rotondo since the War, attending a pilgrimage that spent a few nights at the shrine. He had waited so long before returning because he did not want to spoil his many happy memories of his time with Padre Pio. He was warmly welcomed by the new batch of friars and was able to sit at the same table in the old monastery where he had often dined with Padre Pio in the 1940's. The Friary's superior, understanding that Fr. Fanning had had a close relationship with Padre Pio, opened the iron gates protecting the Saint's tomb, allowing Fr. Fanning to enter the restricted area to spend time in veneration and prayer. Incredibly, he was also fortunate enough to meet a priest who had been a good friend during the War, Padre Paolo Covino. While stationed in Cerignola, Fr. Fanning used to play the harmonium for Padre Covino while the Padre was teaching the local children their singing lessons. The two men met again in Padre Covino's room in the upstairs infirmary of Our Lady of Grace monastery, and the old friar's face lit up when he recognized the American soldier he once knew.

During the war, Fr. Fanning and his friend Joe Asterita had a week's furlough, and they decided to spend it on the Island of Capri. On an exceptionally hot and sunny day, the two soldiers took a boat ride to the famous blue grotto, spending most of the day boating and sunning themselves. The next morning, Leo Fanning could barely get out of bed because his sunburn was so severe, especially on his legs. Joe Asterita called the medics, and they put Leo on a stretcher to take him back by boat to a hospital in Naples. As he was put on the boat he became very concerned about his condition, and prayed: "Padre Pio, help me!" Within five minutes Padre Pio made his presence known by wafts of his special perfume, which accompanied Leo Fanning all the way to port and was with him in the ambulance as it headed toward the hospital. He spent two weeks there, his legs wrapped in treated gauze, and during that time on three separate occasions he again was gifted with the Saint's mystical aroma. Later, when he finally saw Padre Pio again at the Friary, he thanked him for visiting him in the hospital. Padre Pio looked at Leo Fanning, nodded his head, and gave a knowing smile.

On one of his visits to the Saint, Leo Fanning asked him about the message of Fatima regarding the conversion of Russia. Padre Pio's reply was that Russia would be converted as the Virgin Mary had said, and that "Russia will teach the United States a lesson in conversion."[10] On a different occasion, another Air Force Chaplain, Fr. John Duggan, asked a similar question. Padre Pio answered that the Russian people would be converted, and it would happen quickly. However, "The conversion of the United States will be slow, but sure."[11]

Leo Fanning's friend, Joe Asterita, was an aide to chaplain Fr. John St. John of the 15th Air Force in Foggia.[12] When Joe, a frequent visitor to the monastery, told Padre Pio that he wished to become a Trappist monk, Padre Pio just laughed, since Joe Asterita was not known for the gift of silence. The Padre said that he should get married instead and raise citizens for Heaven. Joe Asterita objected, insisting that no one would have him for a husband. Padre Pio then promised that he would take care of it himself, and find a nice Italian girl for Joe.

When he returned to America after the War, Joe wrote to the Friary to let them know that everyone had arrived home safely. He soon found a job and met and started dating a young Italian-American girl named Adeline. A short time later, he received a letter from the Friary, written by Padre Agostino, which included a message for Joe from Padre Pio. The message essentially was this: "Joe, recently you have been acquainted with a girl named Adeline, that is the girl you are going to marry."[13] But when Joe had written to the Friary, he had not mentioned that he was dating, and there was no "human" way Padre Pio could have known about Adeline. Within a year, Joe Asterita and Adeline Bellini were married, and they later named their two children after Padre Pio and St. Francis.

On the last visit that Joe Asterita and Leo Fanning paid to Padre Pio before leaving for America, Leo asked Padre Pio if he had any advice for him. "Yes," the Saint said to the future priest. "Just as Joe feels so strongly that he is not going to get married, you should think just as strongly that you are going to the Altar of God, and nowhere else!"

Another GI that Padre Pio gave a prophetic message to was John McKenna.[14] While stationed in Italy, he read about Padre Pio in an Italian newspaper and convinced his chaplain to make the trip with him to San Giovanni Rotondo. After their arrival at the Monastery, he was asked to serve Padre Pio's Mass the next morning. That night, John McKenna was so nervous he could barely sleep. At 4:00 a.m. he started preparing for the service, which began an hour later. When Padre Pio entered the church, John could hear his heavy breathing and moaning, as the Saint commenced to relive the Passion of Christ. John McKenna was awed when blood started to ooze from the Friar's hands as the Host was raised at the Consecration.

Afterwards, he joined the other GIs in the sacristy to receive Padre Pio's blessing, and hopefully a few words of encouragement about his upcoming engagement and his professional baseball career. Instead, he received a shock, as Padre Pio simply said to him: "You will be a priest." John McKenna had difficulty comprehending this message, which was pointing to a life completely different than what he had planned. He wandered about the monastery for half an hour thinking about what Padre Pio had said, and finally decided to approach him again. He found a translator, and together they went to the room where Padre Pio withdrew to pray after each Mass. The translator asked the Saint to explain what he had said to John McKenna. Padre Pio's reply was brief and to the point: "Tell him he's going to be a priest, and he can take it or leave it!"

Fr. John Bernard McKenna was ordained a Catholic priest in 1954, faithfully responding to the vocation that Padre Pio had revealed to him. He was a popular priest with a reputation for delivering inspiring sermons, and often spoke about his miraculous call to the priesthood. He was quite active in promoting Padre Pio in the greater California area up until his death in 1987.

Chapter 19

Padre Pio "Remembrances"

B
OB Coble[1] was a Protestant when he first met Padre
Pio in 1944. He described his experiences almost
50 years later in an article he wrote for *The Voice of
Padre Pio* magazine.[2] Bob was in the 345th Signal Company
Wing based in Foggia. About a half-dozen men from that unit
regularly went to San Giovanni Rotondo on Sundays to
attend Padre Pio's Mass, where some of them acted as altar
servers. When asked to accompany them, Bob would politely
decline. His Protestant upbringing did not make him at all
curious, although he had been told that Padre Pio bore the
wounds of Christ. But, due primarily to the persistence of
Joe Peluso, one of the "regulars" who went up to see Padre
Pio, Bob finally agreed one Sunday to join them.

He attended Padre Pio's Mass, but since at that time he
did not understand what the Mass means to a Catholic, he
came away unconvinced that he should be as excited about
the Padre as his friends were. But he understood that he had
witnessed "something real, and something strange," and 50
years later still recalled the image of Padre Pio with the
wounds on his hands, partially covered by the lacy cuffs on
the sleeves of his priestly garment. After the Mass, the group
of GIs went over to Mary Pyle's house, and Bob talked to her
for a long time while sitting at the kitchen table. He remembers her as a "warm, loving, and caring woman," who regaled
her guests with delightful anecdotes about the human side
of the man everyone revered as a saint.

After the War, he came back to America and began to take

instructions in the Catholic Faith, largely due to his engagement to a Catholic girl, Alice. But like many who start on the road to conversion, he had problems accepting some Catholic beliefs. For Bob, the most troublesome point was the teaching that bread and wine are really and truly transformed into the Body and Blood of Christ at the Consecration in the Holy Mass—the doctrine of Transubstantiation. Bob made many attempts to resolve his problems with the Faith, but the books he read and instructions he took did not kindle any inner response.

He was going nowhere in satisfying his spiritual hunger, until a short note Margie MacMillan[3] wrote on a Christmas card provided the spark he needed. Margie, the wife of one of his army buddies Ronald MacMillan, wrote in the note that there was a new book out about Padre Pio that he should read. Bob obtained the book, and as he read it, "things started falling into place." The book renewed his interest in learning about Catholicism, and soon he was able to make an act of faith in the Real Presence of Christ in the Eucharist. He resumed his instructions in the Catholic religion, this time carrying them to completion, and entered the Church on Easter of 1988.

After his conversion, Bob experienced on more than one occasion Padre Pio's "sweets for his children"—the aroma of perfume and even that of tobacco. During the time of their son's serious illness, when Bob and Alice traveled across the country to see him, a "shadowy" Padre Pio appeared to Bob during the journey. Since the apparition was smiling, Bob knew that it was a sign that his son would be all right. He also received some unasked-for help with his own physical condition. A former Polio patient when he was younger, he still suffered from some infirmities, but he began to improve in 1993.

That was the 25th anniversary year of Padre Pio's passing,

and he attended Jeanette and Joan Salerno's Padre Pio pilgrimage that September. The trip back to southern Italy awakened in Bob many special memories, as he saw once again the places he had known while in the service 50 years before. He thought of the visits in trucks and jeeps by the troops in his outfit, clambering up the mountain to attend Padre Pio's Mass.

Even before this pilgrimage, Bob had conceived the idea of contacting some of his old buddies, and collecting their stories and recollections about Padre Pio. While on the trip, Jeanette Salerno, who has published many articles on the Saint, suggested to Bob that he ought to assemble the information and letters into a book that could be shared with others. When he returned to the United States, he forwarded some of the letters that he had collected to Jeanette, who wrote back, "Reading the accounts you sent, I began to get a sense of those War times, of Padre Pio's warmth and friendliness to GIs, of a spirituality that a few GIs became aware of on a mountain that was still most primitive."

Bob was in the process of finalizing his little book, which he called *Padre Pio Remembrances*,[4] when he passed away in 1994. Bob's wife, Alice, graciously consented to entrust his compilation to the present author, in order that some of the material could be included in this book about Padre Pio and America. Part of Bob's manuscript consists of biographical information on the life of the Saint. In addition, there are three long letters—two signed by Joe and Rita Peluso, and one by Raymond Bunten. Both Joe and Raymond were in the 345th Signal Company Wing with Bob Coble, and were stationed with him about eight miles south of Foggia, in Cerignola.

Bob Coble's intention was to allow the letter writers to speak for themselves, and we have followed his wishes. In an Afterword to his book, Bob wrote:

I resisted the urge to change their writing. It would be all too easy to try to write the book myself, editing everything that was given to me. That would have been a sham, and would not have properly conveyed the real feeling of the soldiers in question . . . In every case you are getting a first-person account, not hearsay filtered through another person's biases, and are getting the feeling of awe that the writer experienced.

Joe Peluso's undated letters as they appear in Bob Coble's manuscript were written around 1990. He had been one of Padre Pio's closest friends and had been allowed to take many movies of him during his trips to the Friary at San Giovanni Rotondo. Upon his return to America after the War, he became very active in making Padre Pio known in this country by presenting frequent talks, and showing the movies to various church groups and gatherings. Joe, who lived in Western Pennsylvania, passed away in 1996.

Joe's experiences and adventures with Padre Pio, Mary Pyle, and their friends and relatives are presented here with only minor editing for clarity. His charming, informal and heartfelt words will reveal a very warm and kind Padre Pio.

As an American soldier stationed in Italy in World War II, I had the honor and privilege to meet Padre Pio, his family and his close friends. This beautiful friendship of ours has endured over the years.

My first meeting with Padre Pio was on October 6, 1944. I had many visits with him over the following ten months, ending on July 15, 1945, when my army unit was transferred to France. At our first meeting, I felt that by some unexplainable force we were drawn together, as if Padre Pio had always been part of my earlier life.

In those ten months, a close relationship developed with Padre Pio, his father Orazio—known by his nickname of "No-No" to his family and close friends—Padre Pio's only brother, Michael [Michele Forgione], and Mike's daughter Pia and her fiancé Mario [Pennelli].

Our relationship became so closely knitted that Mike wanted to legally adopt me as his son, which was not feasible due to the War. When this failed, Mike's next wish and desire was to have his grand-children marry my children. [It didn't happen!]

After my return home to America following the War, my dream had always been to return to Italy to be reunited with my adopted family, Pia and Mario. This dream became a reality in March 1988, when the Padre Pio Foundation in Cromwell, Connecticut, invited me to accompany them on a trip to Italy. The purpose of the trip was to make a video recording of Padre Pio's birthplace and the monastery where he lived from 1916 until his death in 1968, and where he now lies in rest on the lower level of the newer church.

Four of us made the trip back to Italy: Joe Peterson, an ex-soldier who was a close friend of Padre Pio's, myself, Brother John (the cameraman), and Fr. Bob McQueeney. Fr. Bob, who was then in charge of the Padre Pio Foundation of America, supervised the project. With this taping we were complying with a desire of Padre Pio's, when he told me that *he wished to make all of America his spiritual children*. This video would bring Padre Pio back from Italy into the homes of the Americans who would otherwise never have been able to make this fabulous pilgrimage. [Unfortunately, the Padre Pio Foundation was unable to produce this particular video for distribution. Fr. Bob consigned the tape to the Peluso family].[5]

We flew into the Rome airport where Fr. Bob rented a van for traveling. We drove first to the little village of Pietrelcina, the birthplace and early childhood home of Francesco Forgione (Padre Pio), and where after his Ordination as a Capuchin priest, he was assigned from 1910 until 1916.

The village of Pietrelcina is built on the side of a mountain, on the ruins of an ancient fortress, which had fallen into decay over the centuries. All the homes of the village were built on the crumbled walls of the old castle, utilizing all of its loose stones. This accounts for the houses' entrances being at different levels and the streets being uneven, narrow and steep.

The village had no industries or employment, making all residents' survival totally dependent on having a little garden or a small farm. Many of the villagers migrated to North and South America for survival. If one of them were fortunate, they owned one or two sheep and a donkey, which helped with the hauling of field branches used for their daily cooking, for winter fuel, and to help cultivate the garden.

When the four of us arrived at Pietrelcina, the Capuchin priests invited us to be their guests at their monastery for our stay. This monastery is the one that Mary Pyle built in fulfillment of the prophecy Francesco Forgione made as a very young boy, to Padre Pannullo, that "he could hear the Angels singing and that one day a monastery would be built on that very spot." In Pietrelcina, Mary purchased the

Forgione homes and their little farm, leaving them to the Church to be preserved for posterity.

Brother John, the cameraman, recorded many scenes in the village: the homes and birthplace of Francesco, and the little church high up on the castle wall where he was baptized and served Mass as an altar boy [the Church of St. Anne.] This little church underwent a complete restoration by Fr. Bob's Padre Pio Foundation, and has been completely restored to the exact condition it was in 1887 when Francesco Forgione was baptized there—not one single detail has been omitted.

We drove to the outskirts of the village to the Forgione's little farm known as "Piana Romana." It was here at this farm, when Padre Pio was praying under a tree, that a snake crawled over his habit and he spoke to the snake, "Even here you won't let me alone!"—referring to the snake as Satan. Suddenly his hands, feet and side began to burn as if hit by a bolt of fire. It was then that he received the invisible stigmata, which later manifested themselves in 1918 at the monastery choir in San Giovanni Rotondo as the outward marks of Our Lord Crucified. The tree at the farm is preserved in a little chapel, in a room behind the altar, encased in a heavy steel cage, to preserve it from the relic seekers who had reduced the tree to a large trunk.

After lunch on Saturday, March 12, we thanked the priests and brothers and said good-bye. The four of us boarded our van, and with Brother John at the wheel, we headed via the superhighways to San Giovanni Rotondo, arriving there between 5:00 and 5:30 p.m. The weather was very cold and the streets were covered with snow.

My return to San Giovanni Rotondo, the place I have always considered my second home, was the fulfillment of a dream come true for me—to again be able to visit the little monastery of my past, to kneel at the crypt of my dear friend Padre Pio, and to visit with my adopted family, Pia and Mario.

Fr. Bob, Brother John, and Joe Peterson checked in at the local hotel. After they were unpacked and settled, we drove along the street to the bottom of a very steep hill below the monastery. It was here on a third floor apartment that Pia and Mario lived (Padre Pio's niece and her husband).

It was 6:00 p.m. when we arrived at Mario and Pia's, who were anxiously awaiting with open arms my return home after 43 years absence. Pia, who had a case of crippling arthritis, stood on the third floor balcony waving as Mario ran down the steep stairway to greet and embrace. It was a beautiful reunion, a memory I shall always cherish.

For the following three days I lived in their home, as we recalled the many beautiful memories we shared together in our earlier years.

In the remainder of Joe Peluso's first letter from the Coble manuscript, we gain more insight into the closeness of his relationship with Padre Pio. As a rule, Padre Pio did not deliver sermons during his Masses at Our Lady of Grace Friary; but in this account there is a brief mention of a sermon given by him at a very special Mass.

As the four of us, Pia, Mario, myself, and Padre Joseph Pius, sat in the living room by the warm fireplace, we relived the most beautiful and vivid memories with laughter and joy, of that day of

May 25, 1945. It was Padre Pio's 58th birthday, and the day Padre Pio united his niece and her fiancé in Holy Matrimony.

The story begins with Padre Agostino, my very dear and close friend. He and I met on my very first visit to Padre Pio. At that time, he was the Superior General of the southern dioceses of the Capuchins, which covered approximately one fourth of Italy. He was Padre Pio's closest and dearest friend, was his spiritual director from the early days of the seminary in the year 1903 until 1922, and again was appointed his spiritual director from 1933 until his death in 1963. He knew Padre Pio better than anyone, and was with him in so many of those special events that took place in the life of the Saint.

Often Padre Agostino invited me to dine with the priests and brothers at the Friary. This is unheard of, since lay persons are not permitted in the dining room, but he was the superior and he could make the rules as well as change them, as he did so often for me. He invited me to dine with them this day, and to attend their little surprise party for Padre Pio's birthday.

At the dinner table, I was always seated next to Padre Pio, on his right side. They always served him the same portions as the others, even though he would only eat very little of the servings. He never ate meat, and only a little piece of fresh fish on rare occasions. His total intake of food each day would only fill the cup of his hand.

When he was sick, the doctor advised him to eat to get better. With his sense of humor he replied, "If I eat I lose weight, and if I diet I gain weight," which was factual. His broad shoulders made him look like he weighed 200 pounds or more, but his actual weight was from 160 to 165 pounds.

When I finished my servings, Padre Pio would take the food from his dish, place it on my dish, and say, "Dear Giuseppe, eat up!" And when my wine glass became empty he would refill it from his bottle of wine, saying aloud while saluting me, "Drink up, dear Giuseppe!" All of the priests and brothers enjoyed my appetite for good food, instead of the "C" and "K" rations I was living on.

At the dinner table, Padre Pio always kept the priests and brothers in stitches and tears from laughter with his fantastic sense of humor. Some had to excuse themselves and leave the room to stop their sides from hurting with laughter.

After the dinner, we celebrated Padre Pio's 58th birthday. When the party ended, he and I left the dining room, arm in arm. As we entered the hallway, approaching were a group of about six American soldiers with a cake and burning candles singing "Happy Birthday" to Padre Pio.

After a little while I left the group of soldiers and Padre Pio, excusing myself, stating that Mike [Padre Pio's brother Michele] was looking for me. I hurried down to the Forgione home, arriving there later than I expected. Mike and Pia were waiting at the door for me. They had held up their little private family party until I got there. It was Mike's party for the newly-weds-to-be. They forgave me for being late. Laughing, they said they didn't blame me for staying with Padre Pio for as long as I did.

After our little family party, three of us, No-No (Padre Pio's father), Mike (who was a widower) and myself went up to the monastery. We sat together while attending the wedding of Mike's daughter Pia to Mario, with the ceremony being performed by Mike's brother Padre Pio. This is the only Mass I ever attended of Padre Pio's where he gave a homily.

After the wedding and the traditional ride in the carriage, another wedding party took place in a home in the village, for the families and friends of the newlyweds. After they left that party, what looked like a perfect day took a turn for what seemed like disaster, but it ended up in a hilarious day of laughter.

The fellows from my army unit were to drive the bride and groom down the mountain-side to the little farm Mario's father had given them as a wedding gift for the honeymoon retreat. Our jeep, "the honeymoon express," developed motor trouble and refused to run. John Winn finally got it to run. The newlyweds boarded it, but after a short distance it quit running again, and was stuck in a rain-filled hole. It was raining very hard that afternoon.

We contacted my army base 37 miles away, and the only vehicle available was a giant sized two-and-a-half ton truck. After a long wait, the truck finally arrived. The bride and groom got in the back of the truck. With the rain pouring in the back of the open truck as it flew down the mountain roads to their honeymoon retreat, they were wringing wet—which didn't matter, for they were so happy and it was to be part of a beautiful memory to behold. The marriage was rewarded with eight healthy children, six of whom settled in the immediate area.

So ends Joe Peluso's description of the events of May 25, 1945, as four old friends sat in Mario and Pia's living room in 1988 laughingly reliving that day. It is interesting to note that Padre Pio usually told newlywed couples, "May you have eight children!"[6]

Chapter 20

Three American Spiritual Children

MRS. Rita Peluso relates that her husband first found out about Padre Pio when he was hospitalized during the War for a wounded leg.[1] The bed next to him was occupied by the nephew of actress Irene Dunne, who told him about a priest with the stigmata. When Joe returned to his unit, he asked the chaplain, Fr. Walter Junk, if he knew about this priest, and where he was located. Fr. Junk told Joe to turn around and look at those hills in the distance, which were cloud-covered that day. "Behind those clouds on that mountain is where you can find this priest, who is called Padre Pio," Fr. Junk announced.

The very next day Joe Peluso borrowed a car, and rounded up a group of GI buddies, including Art Lucchesi and Ray Bunten, for the journey up the mountain. On that initial trip, they encountered many people associated with Padre Pio, such as Count Telfener and his wife the Countess. The couple had moved to San Giovanni from England after the Count's conversion to Catholicism. They also met Padre Pio's brother Michele (Mike), and his Dad Orazio (Grazio) Forgione. Orazio was a grandfather, which is *Nonno* in Italian, and this became the nickname that his American friends called him—slightly anglicized to "No-No." At noon that first day, Padre Pio distributed Holy Communion for the people who could not make the early Mass. As they were receiving the Sacrament, Joe and the other soldiers were pleasantly surprised when the Padre also draped a medal over their heads.

On one of his later visits, he asked Padre Pio if he could be accepted as his spiritual child. Padre Pio consented, and presented Joe with another medal. He said that this medal would keep him free from all harm. He also accepted Joe's wife Rita and their daughter as spiritual children under his protection. Joe frequently served Padre Pio's Mass, standing at the "Epistle" side of the altar. He was so close to Padre Pio that he could see right through the wounds on the friar's hands. Joe said it would have been possible to read the words in the Mass book that was situated on the other side of his stigmatized hands.

During the War, he took movies of Padre Pio with a camera that his older brother Frank had mailed to him. The films were of fragile quality, wound on a cardboard reel. Some were taken during Mass, and they showed Padre Pio crying. Back in the United States, Joe used to show the movies during talks he gave on Padre Pio. As would be expected, the attendees were deeply touched and would often ask to have the movie stopped at certain frames. The unfortunate result was that these frames began to burn out. Today many sections of the movies showing Padre Pio are now in very poor quality. Attempts by the Peluso family to restore the films have been only partially successful, and the originals are no longer shown because of their delicate condition.

One year, as cold weather was fast approaching, Padre Pio said he needed a new winter habit to replace his worn-out older one. What follows is the charming episode of Joe Peluso's involvement in procuring the Padre's new winter habit, as written by Mrs. Rita Peluso.[2]

Joe was with the friars and Fr. Pio when they were discussing the need for a new habit for the good Padre. In wartime, money and resources were very scarce, and the Capuchins could not obtain the material that was required. Joe spoke up and said, "I think I can get exactly what you need!" This was no idle statement, since Joe was the son of a tailor and the owner of a men's clothing store before the War.

He wanted to measure Padre Pio for a perfect fit, but the humble, yet always good-humored stigmatic, laughingly said, "Dear Giuseppe, I need a pocket here and one here and another pocket there and . . ." So after Padre Pio indicated the many special considerations that he wanted for his new attire, this task befell another.

Joe went back to camp and asked his lieutenant if he would accept a large package mailed from home, since officers were afforded that privilege. Securing the needed permissions, Joe wrote his brother and business partner Frank, back in New Brighton, Pennsylvania. Joe was familiar with the St. Fidelis Capuchin Seminary, about 40 miles from his hometown, where members of his wife's family had studied for the priesthood. At Joe's instruction, Frank went to their monastery in Herman, Pennsylvania, where he explained the unique request. The friar there cheerfully tendered all the materials needed for their famous stigmatic brother's new habit and cloak.

Frank immediately shipped them to Joe's lieutenant at the camp in Foggia. Upon the parcel's arrival, the officer gave it to Joe, who asked him if he wanted to see what was sent. The officer declined, so Joe excitedly got a jeep and took the package to San Giovanni Rotondo. The friars and Padre Pio were overwhelmed and grateful.

And that is how Padre Pio received his much needed new habit and cloak for the winter. Joe never did say who actually made the habit, but it surely was done by a tailor in Italy who did these things for the friars.

Joe Peluso and Padre Pio were extremely close, and Joe spent as much time as possible with him during the War. Their friendship was such that the Capuchin Provincial Padre Agostino, once told Joe, "Giuseppe! Giuseppe! Padre Pio loves everyone, but he especially loves you!" Apparently, Peluso was even given the keys to the monastery, and essentially had free access to Padre Pio.[3] Upon his suggestion, Padre Pio changed the time of his Mass from 5:00 a.m. to 9:00 a.m. during the American occupation, so that the GIs would be able to attend.[4] Padre Pio would also send Joe as a trusted messenger to his sister Pia, who was a cloistered nun in Rome, and to high-ranking Church officials.

During Joe's final illness, while he was in chemotherapy, his beloved friend appeared to him many times. Padre Pio would always tenderly rub Joe's head and then hit him a little tap on the nose, before disappearing.

Let us continue with the letters—written around 1990—from Bob Coble's manuscript. In this account, Padre Pio's spiritual child, Joe Peluso, writes about two other American spiritual children of the Padre's, Mary Pyle and Fr. Joseph Pius.

The famous hostess at San Giovanni Rotondo was the American lady Mary Pyle, who was born to one of the wealthiest families in New York City. The McAlpin Pyles were strict Presbyterians, but Mary was never satisfied with the Presbyterian faith. She was always reading and searching for a faith to satisfy her needs, even while traveling and teaching with Dr. Maria Montessori.

In 1918 she ended her search, and was converted
and baptized a Catholic in Barcelona, Spain. Mary
was very devoted to her new-found Faith. So extraordinary was her life that the Church authorities have
been collecting information on all the events of her
life, for the process of her future beatification and
canonization.

Mary told me that she had no desire whatsoever
to meet Padre Pio, and went there only because her
traveling companion wanted to meet him. In 1925
Mary built a large home located three houses from
the monastery at the bottom of a steep hill. The
exterior of her home was constructed of "pink
bricks" and the local villagers always referred to
Mary as the "The American Lady in the Pink Castle." Mary's home was open to all visitors. In her
large kitchen was a long table where her guests
were entertained. The table was capable of seating
15 to 20 guests comfortably.

Mary served all of her guests a cup of coffee, American style, and a light lunch of cooked greens, as she
spoke and answered all questions concerning Padre
Pio, and did this masterfully. Her house guests were
from all stations in life—soldiers, civilians, peasants,
kings, queens, royal families, heads of countries,
movie stars, and so on. She showed no favoritism or
partiality. Each guest was treated with the same
respect and cordiality, as they sat at her kitchen table
listening to the perfect hostess, speaking with the
warmth and knowledge of her favorite subject, as she
shared Padre Pio with them.

She could talk endlessly for hours, keeping everyone on the edge of their chairs, spellbound—listening
to her every word, watching her radiant face and

beautiful smile as her eyes danced and twinkled with joy as she spoke of Padre Pio.

Mary wrote to Rita and I, before she returned to America in 1948, asking us if she could come and visit with us here in Pennsylvania. This was the one and only time she ever left Italy for the United States after meeting Padre Pio back in 1923. She said the purpose of her trip was to put her papers in final order and to visit with and bid farewell to her immediate family.

Rita and I were honored by having Mary as our guest for one week. In that week Mary and Rita became inseparable in the years to follow. Rita said to me, after Mary returned to Italy, that she now realized the full impact Mary must have had on her guests in the Pink Castle, as they listened to her telling beautiful stories on the life of Padre Pio.

That week our house was filled every night with friends, who came to meet the lady who dressed in the brown habit of the Third Order of St. Francis, to hear her speak and learn more of our beloved Padre Pio. Each night I had to call a halt to the evening when the time got around to 3:00 a.m. Our guests were so spellbound by Mary they wanted to stay longer and hear more.

Those who were at our home those nights back in 1948 still speak of Mary, and how they enjoyed her conversation, saying they still remember those many wonderful things she spoke of, and how she made Padre Pio become part of their lives from that night on.

Those of us who have personal articles and relics of Padre Pio are very fortunate and blessed. These articles are not supposed to be available to the public since Padre Pio has not yet been canonized [as of 1990]. I have always referred to these special articles I possessed as "my black market relics of Padre Pio." It was Mary Pyle who gave me the "part of a glove" that Padre Pio wore over his open hand wound, and a "handkerchief" that Padre Pio used to wipe the tears he shed when he said Holy Mass. At each Mass he always shed tears, especially at the Consecration, as he relived the pain and suffering of Our Lord.

Joe now writes about special gifts he included with his letter to Bob Coble.

Enclosed is a picture card of Padre Pio, with a few threads from his glove and handkerchief. Accept this as "a gift from Mary Pyle to you," for it was she who made this possible. Over the years the glove and handkerchief have diminished considerably, making it difficult to share them as I would like.

I regret that there could not have been more threads for you. Even though they are few, Rita and I hope you will appreciate, treasure and benefit from these special personal articles of Padre Pio, as we have.

Joe proceeds to introduce another of Padre Pio's spiritual children from America, Fr. Joseph Pius.

An American, William Martin, after his first meeting with Padre Pio, wished he could remain near him, and Padre Pio had the same desire. His dream became a reality, and he was to become Padre Pio's constant companion. He was with Padre Pio during the final years of his life, assisting the Saint right up to his final moments. After the death of Padre Pio, William realized his calling to the priesthood. Entering the seminary, in due time he was ordained a Capuchin priest, taking the name of Fr. Joseph Pius. Fr. Joseph Pius is a very close and dear friend of Rita's and mine, being drawn together as members of Padre Pio's spiritual family. When a spiritual child meets another spiritual child of Padre Pio's, that unexplainable force draws these people together as if they had known one another all of their lives. This is the bond that unites all of Padre Pio's spiritual children as one big family.

When I was visiting the monastery in 1988, Fr. Joseph Pius was discussing the relics and personal articles that belonged to Padre Pio. He said, "Joe, all these articles we have, will in the future become irreplaceable. All the articles and relics of Padre Pio are under lock and key by orders of the Church authority, and will remain that way until after Padre Pio's canonization. Even then the articles will be given out on a limited basis."

I jokingly asked him what his future plans were. With that big beautiful smile he is so famous for, his face glowing with sheer joy, he replied, "Joe, I have no desire to return home to America. I am totally content here and will remain here for the rest of my natural life." See how similar he and Mary Pyle felt about living here. This feeling and his love for San Giovanni Rotondo is a wonderful feeling which I can appreciate and understand.

Fr. Joseph Pius passed away unexpectedly at the age of 61 on May 3, 2000, to the great grief of all. He had been host to English-speaking pilgrims at the Friary for over 20 years.

Chapter 31, "Brother Bill," presents more of his life at San Giovanni Rotondo. Joe Peluso's narrative continues:

In my days during World War II, San Giovanni Rotondo was a little village of about 14,000 people. Located a mile-and-a-half from the monastery was a German fortress that was to protect the valley below and the city of Foggia. Today that little village has extended itself up to the monastery, and has become a large metropolitan city of hotels, restaurants, gift shops, etc.

The "mercenaries" have moved in like they have at all shrines, but once you enter the monastery these mercenaries and their wares are left behind, as you join the hundreds of people like yourself inside the Friary who came to be near Padre Pio. You can still feel Padre Pio's presence and his warmth, reaching out to everyone who comes to him.

Padre Pio loved everyone, regardless of race or religion. He always managed to find time from his heavy, daily schedule of 18 to 20 hours, to greet visitors with open arms. With a big beautiful smile, his conversation with each one was overflowing with love, tenderness, laughter and humor.

I have always said, "One day Padre Pio will be honored, loved and considered the greatest Saint that ever lived." And to think of the great privilege we enjoy being part of him, and a member of his spiritual family, as we remember what he said so often, "I shall never enter the gates of Heaven until all of my spiritual children have entered in."

I could go on telling you of Padre Pio and his spiritual children of America, and his conversation with me concerning all America, how they can become his spiritual children, and the rules they must follow [see Appendix], but I have rambled on too long already. I must end this letter saying thank you for your patience and bearing with me for such a long time.

May Padre Pio bless you and yours in endless ways, now and for all the days of your life.

Always your friend in Padre Pio,
Joe and Rita.

Chapter 21

Mission of the Medals

IN his second letter to Bob Coble, Joe Peluso describes his role in one of the "missions" that Padre Pio entrusted to him. This letter also contains a first-hand account of the biblically based phenomenon of speaking and interpreting in tongues, one of the many spiritual gifts manifested by Padre Pio.

Padre Pio liked to personally bless each visitor and present them with a religious medal that he had also blessed. These religious articles were very scarce and almost impossible to obtain in Italy, due to the war crisis and shortages of materials. Mary Pyle was very sad when she found that Padre Pio's supplies of medals and rosaries were completely exhausted. She knew how he felt not having these little gifts for those who traveled up the mountain to San Giovanni Rotondo to meet and visit with him.

John Winn and I obtained a furlough from December 5 through December 10, 1944, to travel to Rome, a distance of 220 miles from our camp. Our trip to Rome was solely with three objectives: to deliver two letters and to obtain some religious medals and rosaries. Count John Telfener asked me to deliver a letter to his sister "The Countess of Marilino," who lived in Rome, and Padre Pio had asked me to take his personal letter to his baby sister, "Sister Pia," who was a cloistered nun in the order of "The Five Precious Wounds," located in the heart of Rome.

After delivering the letters and visiting with the Countess and Sister Pia, John Winn and I went in search of a supply of medals and rosaries. As we were driving through Rome, and we approached the bottom of one of the seven hills, for some unknown reason I said to John, "Let's drive to the top of this hill." At the top of the hill we had a grand view that overlooked the entire city of Rome, with a beautiful view of Vatican City. At the very top was a large building which was the cloistered Mother House Convent of the Benedictine Nuns. This was ironic, for Padre Pio's favorite medal was the Benedictine medal.

I went over to the convent and pulled the chain that rang the inner bell. To my surprise an English-speaking voice said, "Enter please." Going inside, we stood in a small enclosed reception room, facing a closed door and a small, barred window. The little window opened and the English-speaking nun, smiling, welcomed us to the convent. I told her of my search for medals and rosaries. Sister replied that she had a supply and would gladly share them with me. She gave me a large quantity of medals and one or two dozen rosaries. Plus she gave me a relic for my wife Rita, which was an authentic relic of St. Rita with papal papers.

The following day John Winn and I went to Vatican City where our Holy Father was going to have a papal audience. With thousands of us standing in St. Peter's Square, our Holy Father Pope Pius XII appeared at his balcony overlooking the huge crowd. Over the speaker system our Holy Father spoke to us. After his speech he blessed all of us. He then said, "If you have any religious articles you want blessed please hold them up." I held up all of my medals, rosaries, and the relic of St. Rita. Our Holy Father placed his papal blessing on all of these articles.

On the following Sunday, December 17, I walked and hitchhiked the 33 miles from my camp to San Giovanni Rotondo, carrying my many medals, rosaries, and Rita's relic of St. Rita. As I approached the monastery, Count John Telfener saw me and came over to me. He told me that Padre Pio had been inquiring of my whereabouts the evening (Saturday) before my arrival. John left me and disappeared into the monastery, going directly to Padre Pio to tell him I was back and was standing outside.

Next came one of those very rare occasions—Padre Pio came outside of the monastery to where I was. He was very happy and excited to see me. We greeted one another and I knelt down, and he extended his right hand for me to kiss. Then suddenly, as he had done on many other occasions, he pulled my head against his stomach and patted my face.

In the sacristy, John "The Count" did all the translating as Padre Pio and I spoke of my trip to Rome and of the visit with his baby sister, "Sister Pia." He wanted to know all that was said and all about her and her health. He said laughing, "Dear Giuseppe, were you a good boy in Rome?" As if he didn't know!

We then attended his Holy Mass. After Mass in the sacristy he took me by the arm and led me into the back room. This room was located off the sacristy, and was strictly off limits to everyone, for it was here he prayed in privacy without interruptions. Padre Pio and I were alone in this room with no one there to translate for us.

Our entire conversation, which was a very long

affair, was carried on by the "gift of tongues," since I could not speak or understand Italian, and Padre Pio could not speak or understand the American English language. Padre Pio, with the help of his Guardian Angel, made all this possible.

When this happened, Padre Pio understood everything I spoke in English, and I understood his entire conversation, as if it were spoken in perfect English in the Pittsburgh, Pennsylvania dialect of the area where I lived in America. The following conversation and events are what took place that day in the gift of tongues.

Showing Padre Pio the articles I had gotten in Rome, I asked him to bless them. When he saw how many I had, he started to laugh, saying, "Dear Giuseppe, you bought out all of Rome." He took my medals and rosaries, blessed them, and handed them back to me and we continued our conversation.

Suddenly in the middle of the conversation, he stopped and changed the subject saying, "Dear Giuseppe, may I have the medals and rosaries back. I want to bless them again. This time I want to place a very special blessing on them for you." I handed them back. He held them in his left hand, blessing them for the second time, where he placed that very special blessing on them. He then patted them with his right hand as if to say "a job well done," and handed them back to me.

I made Padre Pio very happy as I shared my many medals with him. Now he had a supply of medals to give to those who visited with him. We continued our conversation, and I never got around to asking him what the blessing was. Even today after all these years I still don't know. But one thing for sure I know is that these medals have the papal blessing of Pope Pius XII, and were personally blessed twice by Padre Pio.

I am only happy to share one of these medals with you, knowing you will treasure it as much as I do.

> Always your friend in Padre Pio,
> Joe and Rita Peluso

Chapter 22

"Ray of God's Light"

INCLUDED in Bob Coble's manuscript is a letter written by Raymond Bunten while he was stationed in Italy during the War. In it he mentions that Padre Pio was 57 at the time, which would date the letter at around 1944. Ray was part of a group of regulars from the 345th Signal Company Wing, which included Joe Peluso and Art Lucchesi, who went to see Padre Pio almost every weekend. Ray worked in the motor pool, and first found out about the "Holy Man" of the Gargano from Joe Peluso. Joe would tell Ray about Padre Pio while requisitioning vehicles for his journeys up the mountain, and finally persuaded him to go along. Here in his own words, full of reverence and awe, is the story of Ray Bunten's encounters with the man he calls the "Holy Padre."[1] (Incidentally, Ray's birthday is September 23, which is St. Pio's feast day in the Church.)

Since the year of 1918, people have been drawn to the top of the mountains known as Gargano, in Italy. The trip is dangerous, for the roads are narrow, winding and built on the edge of the mountain, ascending at a 45 degree angle. The guardrails consist of stones piled about one-and-a-half feet or two feet high and a little cement, placed only at intervals. The roads must have been built in long-forgotten streambeds, for they are full of holes. The higher you ascend, the more you pray that death will take a holiday, for the drop is about 2,000 feet, straight down.

The land on the mountainside is of no value except
for sheep raising and concealing of criminals in its
natural coverage. The small amount of soil is also val-
ueless due to the volcanic rock. After reaching the
top, you run your fingers through the clouds that
cling to the top of this famed mountain. At the very
height of the Gargano you find yourself in a little
town known as San Giovanni Rotondo, which has a
population of approximately fourteen thousand.

One-and-a-half miles up the road is the monastery
known all over the world, and people have traveled
from every country to be here. Some have come out of
devotion to see the "Ray of God's Light," others out of
curiosity. Even atheists are attracted, because in
their hearts they can't decide whether or not there is
a God. They are like St. Thomas the Apostle who said,
"Except I shall see in his hands the imprints of the
nails . . . and thrust my hand into his side, I will not
believe." Jesus Christ replied, "Blessed are they that
have not seen and yet have believed." [*John* 20:25].

In some respects all of us seem like St. Thomas,
for we can't conceive such a miracle that God has
sent down to us. But those of ideal faith believe
what God has sent down to them without question-
ing, and kneel before this chosen son of God and ask
his blessing.

The next section of the letter contains a short biography of
Padre Pio, after which the narrative continues:

The Holy Padre wears brown fingerless woolen
gloves at all times, with the exception of [when he is]
saying Holy Mass. When the Holy Padre says Mass,
"Low Mass," the services last for two hours. In those

two-hour Masses which I was very fortunate to attend, I found it to be a sublime sacrifice which uplifts souls to God. Even priests themselves remain edified. When the Holy Padre says Mass, he looks like Christ Himself, for he seems to be transfigured into a celestial being. All during Mass you can see Padre twist and move about in agony, and tears come to his eyes and roll down his cheeks.

When he offers up the Host, he doesn't look directly at the Host, but just over it into the air; and the look on his earthly face is not of this world. I wish I could tell you just how one feels during the Holy Padre's service. But I'm afraid I could never find the proper words that would describe its beauty and holiness. I would venture to say that neither Shakespeare nor Webster could ever find the proper words to describe Padre Pio's Mass.

During the Mass, Padre's hands are exposed and you can see the bloody crust around the wounds. The new blood that flows under the crusts stains the sections where there is no crust.

I happened to become a very good friend of Count John Telfener, who has spent the past six years of his life in San Giovanni Rotondo. The Count, a dear friend of the Padre, brought me over to meet the Holy Padre and introduced me to him. Padre Pio greets all visitors with a big smile and open arms. Padre Pio has a wonderful sense of humor. Even though he doesn't speak English, he knows everything you say to him.

Padre is in constant pain and agony, and tries to hide it from the public's eyes. He asks God to burden him with all the troubles of those who come to him for help. The Holy Padre is afflicted with a very bad case

of rheumatism and arthritis on the left side of his
body.

Before the services I kissed the Padre's hands (they
were covered), and as I kissed his left hand, with his
right hand he patted the side of my face and gave me
such a smile, that I'm afraid I could never describe its
beauty. I then asked him to watch over my family for
me. He nodded his head "Yes," and gave forth that
heavenly smile again.

Before Mass started, the Count asked me to serve
the Mass for the Holy Padre, and that was the happiest moment of my life. I can thank my dear Mother
for getting after me to learn my Latin, which enabled
me to serve. I was very nervous—from what I don't
know—but I was. It's too bad my education and
vocabulary is so limited, or I could try in my humble
way to relate to you the beauty and holiness of
attending and serving the Holy Padre's Mass.

After Mass we returned to the sacristy, where
quite a few people had gathered waiting to kiss the
wounds of the Holy Padre's hands. The Padre always
lets the people kiss the wounds of his hands before
covering them. Owing to the fact that I was serving,
I was fortunate enough to be one of the first to kiss
the bare wounds of his right hand. As I did so, Padre
paused for a few seconds and smiled at me with a
smile that was so beautiful that I'm afraid I could
never express it. The Padre put his other wounded
hand on my head and patted it with the gentle touch
of a mother.

Padre Pio's wounds give forth a perfume between
rose and violet flowers, which does not resemble any
artificial perfume. Many have noticed the lovely odor
either near or far away from the Holy Padre. The odor

I received is beyond description; I have smelled it before but I just can't place it.

People picture the Holy Padre completely different from other priests, but except for his wounds he is really physically normal like other human beings. Spiritually, however, he is completely different. He is a priest who receives all who come, helps them, uplifts them to God, and tears them away from Satan.

Padre always hears Confessions before Mass, and crowds flock to him. There is the story of the lady who had not seen the Holy Padre for five years, and every night she always ended her prayers by saying, "Padre Pio, watch over and guide my family." Finally, she paid a visit to the monastery at San Giovanni and went to Confession to the Padre. Automatically, after her Confession, she repeated her night prayer to him—"Padre, watch over and guide my family." Padre Pio replied, "How many times are you going to ask me for that? You have asked me that every night for the past five years!"

Due to Padre's health, he is requested to rest during the day, but he does it only to please his superiors. Often during those rest periods he goes into the choir with his fellow brothers and prays constantly for those who ask him for help.

For a man of 57 he still gets around rather well, though his steps are quite slow. The wounds on his feet are very painful; yet he walks the monastery garden that is covered with stones and gravel, forgetting his own suffering, and praying for the poor souls. He eats very little, one meal a day, and it consists of a few vegetables and greens and a little wine. He eats no meat whatsoever, and will occasionally eat a little

fish if it comes from the waters of the Gulf of Manfredonia.

Padre really doesn't eat enough to keep a baby
going. Sometimes in the afternoon or evening he will
drink a little lemonade or beer. It seems impossible
for a human being to eat so little, one meal a day, then
to work so hard and suffer the way he does; to constantly lose blood from his five Holy Wounds, to take
so little care of himself, and to carry on as he does.
Sometimes the Holy Padre has to stay in bed for one
or two days, when he has a high fever, which goes up
to 48 degrees centigrade (118.4 Fahrenheit). Even
physically he is superior, and obtains his strength
from Holy Communion.

The town of San Giovanni has grown due to the
fact that his faithful followers have moved here just
to be near this holy "Ray of God's Light." Also living
here is an American woman whose name is Maria
Pyle, who has traveled all over the world. For the past
twenty years she has settled down here, and told me
she would rather be here than any other place in the
world. Her parents are living in Morristown, New
Jersey, at present. Maria Pyle takes care of making
the altar linens and works around the altar. Incidentally, she too has been converted to the Catholic
Faith. She is also a member of the Third Order of the
Capuchins.

And that is the story of the stigmatic priest who is
a beacon of the "Ray of God's Light," which will continue to cast its light over the world for all eternity.

Ray Bunten
Somewhere in Italy

Chapter 23

More Visitors from the 345th

THE 345th Signal Company Wing based in the Foggia area, was a relatively small outfit composed of about 200 men and a few officers. Consequently, once some of them started visiting the "Holy Man" on the Gargano, word quickly spread throughout the Wing, and many others soon made the journey up the mountain. After the War, the entire Wing returned home safely on a Liberty Ship. Not one person had even been injured. The main task of the 345th was to provide communications support for the 49th Bomb Wing of the 15th Air Force (Army Air Corps). The communications that were handled by the Wing included radio, teletype, courier service, line work and related activities. They were responsible for three Foggia-area airfields.

Art Lucchesi[1] was one of the members of the original cadre from the 345th that visited Padre Pio. Not surprisingly, it was Joe Peluso who got him interested in making the trip the first time. Art made numerous other visits to Our Lady of Grace Church and was permitted to be a server at Padre Pio's Mass each time he went. He has a small collection of photos of himself and Ray Bunten serving Mass together, on the altar with Padre Pio. He was fully absorbed in Padre Pio's Mass, which "passed without consideration of time," and he recalls that "at the Consecration Padre Pio appeared to be looking at something above and beyond the Host. His body shivered and shook like he was going through the Agony of the Cross." In the sacristy, he was able to kiss Padre Pio's wounds before the Saint donned his fingerless cloth

179

gloves. Art describes the scabs as being about three inches across, and in their center was "live blood."

Remembering Padre Pio as a "marvelous" person, Art shares a few personal thoughts about his encounters with him:

> Some of those who had visited Padre Pio did observe the sweet odor when he was, or seemed to be, near them. I never did, and have always felt that for some reason I was not worthy. Just my feeling.
>
> In many ways I consider myself to be a very practical person. There are many things of faith which I just accept as truth, and they are real for me. Such were the things I knew and heard about Padre Pio. I had then, and have to this day, felt that whatever I heard or saw for myself about him, must be true. I believe, that in my privilege of being near him, Padre Pio was and is saintly.

Art Luchessi, Joe Peluso, John Winn, Ray Bunten, and a few other GIs were able to make a visit to Pietrelcina during the War. They were invited to share a light meal at the home of some of Padre Pio's relatives, where they were joined by two of the Saint's nieces, Pia and Tetina.

First Lieutenant Ray Luichinger[2] was another GI who made the trip to San Giovanni a few times with the men of the 345th Wing. But since Ray was an officer, he did not have many opportunities to visit Our Lady of Grace. He could only make the journey when the weather was bad, since fair skies meant there was flight activity at the base, and he had to remain there on duty. Ray was from Indiana, and he has often wondered why he, a "hoosier boy" and a Catholic, was assigned of all places to this spot in Italy, just a few miles from Padre Pio's monastery. To Ray there must have been a reason for this in God's plan. He was not only able to visit San Giovanni Rotondo, but also made many trips to Rome.

Whenever he entered the Friary before Mass, the locals would recognize that he was an officer, and would announce, *"Ufficiale! Ufficiale!"*—making sure he got a seat up front. Ray had been an altar boy up until High School, but he never saw a priest who was on such a spiritual plane as Padre Pio. "He was so engrossed in the Mass that he was in another world; it was just at another level . . . his holiness." When Padre Pio raised his arms during Mass, Ray noticed that at the edges of the scabs on his hands were little droplets of blood, and it seemed to him that, when they dried, they would become part of the scab.

Red Cross workers at Foggia were the first ones to tell the 345th's Dan Lemon about the Saint living on the mountain.[3] He soon joined the small groups of three or four GIs that took a jeep or a command car to attend Padre Pio's Mass. He went many times, and like the other soldiers, was seated right on the altar, although Dan never actually was a server at the Mass. This is Dan's description of Padre Pio and his experiences at San Giovanni Rotondo:

> When you met him, you felt you already knew him. During the Mass you knew he was suffering by the expression on his face. It took him a long time even to kneel, and the Mass lasted about an hour-and-a-half. He definitely changed my life. I can't put my finger on it exactly; I just know that something happened. I still feel protected every day by him, even now.
>
> The villagers were happy to see the American soldiers; they would even hug us. We would bring chocolates and American beer from the post exchange for Padre Pio. There was a little box in the church for donations to the future hospital, and the soldiers

were as generous as they could be. Padre Pio loved the American people.

Some of the soldiers that went back home told Fiorello La Guardia [Mayor of New York City, 1934-1945] about Padre Pio. After the War, a lot of the GI's returned to Foggia to see him. He became well-known in America after the War because of the soldiers' reports.

When Dan Lemon kissed Padre Pio's gloved hand, he detected a faint odor of orange blossom. Even though he did not speak Italian, he was allowed to confess to Padre Pio in English. He felt that the Padre knew what he was confessing, since he would occasionally nod his head, but he did not speak to Dan in English. He also reports that Padre Pio did not like to have his picture taken.

The poverty of the Capuchins made a strong impression on Dan Lemon. He wrote back home asking his family to include some articles of clothing for the monks, such as socks or undergarments, along with the packages of chocolates and cookies they would send him. On one visit to the Friary, a young Capuchin invited Dan and a few other GIs to see Padre Pio's cell, since he was not there just then. Dan was shocked at the bare simplicity of it. The bed was made with a wooden frame, and ropes stretched from side to side to support a very thin mattress. There was a wash stand with a bowl and pitcher, and a chair; otherwise, there was little other real furniture. He had the distinct feeling that Padre Pio was in the cell with them. Dan remembers the crucifix on the wall, and it made him realize that "They were so poor, their main purpose in life was to pray for others."

Dan was able to meet with Mary Pyle and Count Telfener and found them both to be enjoyable, generous people. The Count would invite him to Mary's for tea, and told Dan that he was a convert to the Catholic Faith. To the young Dan, who was only about 19 or 20, Mary Pyle seemed youthful looking too, "maybe in her 30's." She was actually in her mid-50's!

Chapter 24

"The Only Piece of Heaven that I Have Ever Known"

ANOTHER American serviceman who became one of Padre Pio's close friends is Mario Avignone,[1] who resides in the historic Pullman community in the Chicago area. In fact, he was one of the leaders in the successful effort to save Pullman from the wrecker's ball, and have the area designated instead as a national historic site. The list of this octogenarian's civic accomplishments and awards is long and impressive, and he credits everything to meeting Padre Pio during the War. This is what he says of his life before he met the Saint of the Gargano: "As I look back on my youth, I was just nothing." But, since befriending the stigmatized Friar, "Everything I do and have done was to have Padre Pio be proud of me as one of his many spiritual sons . . . I want Padre Pio to be proud of me."

Mario served almost two years in Italy with the 15th Air Force in Cerignola, as a member of the 304th Bomb Wing. Upon coming home after the War, he was so enthusiastic over meeting Padre Pio, and of being personally accepted as a spiritual son, that he could not stop talking about him. Perhaps he overdid it, because a few of his friends thought he had become something of a religious fanatic. Finally, when someone suggested that he should think about becoming a priest, he decided to tone down his rhetoric. Unfortunately, he went to the opposite extreme: "I felt very foolish, and decided never again to talk about Padre Pio."

This situation continued for over 25 years, until he began writing for a monthly newspaper *Fra Noi*, published for Italian-Americans in the Chicago area. In one of his columns for the paper, he wrote that he had personally met Padre Pio during World War II. He was pleasantly surprised at the great level of interest shown by his readers in just this brief mention of the Saint. He soon published an entire article about his experiences and friendship with Padre Pio in the same monthly newspaper. He followed that up with some articles for *The Voice of Padre Pio* magazine, published by the Friary in San Giovanni Rotondo. Finally, he wrote the complete story of his encounters with the Saint in a manuscript entitled *Padre Pio: My Friend and Spiritual Father*,[2] which he distributes to interested friends and acquaintances. Mario has generously consented to allow excerpts of his unpublished manuscript to appear in the present book, thereby making available a valuable first-hand account of that historic era. The selection below is presented with only minor editing. Here is the story of Mario Avignone's first encounter with the Saint of the Gargano:

> After two days and nights aboard a Liberty ship in Naples harbor, where we came under German air bombardment, we were taken to Bari, Italy, for a few days. Then on to Cerignola, near Foggia, where we were assigned to the Headquarters Squadron of the 304th Bomb Wing. Our sleeping quarters were in a school that the army had taken over. I was very happy to be assigned to Cerignola, and right in town. The city was miraculously spared by our Allied air and ground troops, so the town was pretty much intact. The people of Cerignola were friendly to the Allied soldiers, especially to the American GIs. They were born as farmers, and because of the War they

were hungry and in need of practically everything, including medicine. I did all I could to help them, securing medicine for the sick and food for the hungry. I could only speak a few Italian words, barely enough to get along. But with the waving of my arms and trying to say Italian words, I did okay.

Shabbily dressed little children would stand on the other side of the fence of the mess hall, holding tin cups or cans out to us and pleading, "Me hungry, Joe, give me food." Our hearts went out to them. We began to take more food than we needed at meals and brought it out to the children. Whoever said that "war is hell" knew what he was saying; the poor, the old and children are the ones who suffered the most.

It was here in Cerignola that I became close friends with the late Joe Asterita and Leo Fanning, both from New York. All three of us were assigned to the same outfit. We all had something in common—we had compassion for the unfortunate Italians, and all three of us were Catholics. However, I must admit I wasn't a good Catholic. I went to church on Sundays because of my wife Peggy, but did not have my heart in the prayers or the Mass.

On many evenings after our office work was done, Joe, Leo and I would attend Benediction services at the nearby Capuchin church in Cerignola. Because the American soldiers were at war and in a war zone, we were permitted to receive Holy Communion at any time during the day. So, after Benediction, we would receive Holy Communion, and then accept the invitation of the monks to visit with them in the cloister, which was their living quarters. Several times we dined with them. They were friendly and we learned to love them.

One of these Capuchin monks was to be the key for us to personally meet Padre Pio, and begin a beautiful and never to be forgotten adventure which changed my spiritual life. He was Padre Paolino of Casacalenda, and he was the Provincial Superior of the Capuchins in that area. He was heavy set, about five-and-a-half feet tall, had a short gray beard, and sparkling Italian eyes. He was very friendly, full of fun, with a good sense of humor. Sometimes during our visits he would tell us about Padre Pio of San Giovanni Rotondo, who had the five wounds of Christ. I had never heard of Padre Pio before, and the stories Padre Paolino told us fascinated me. Something in me said that I must get to know more about Padre Pio.

One evening, after Benediction and Holy Communion, we were invited to the cloister as before. It was winter and rather cold, so the monks and brothers sat around a large round container of burning charcoal. The church, like most buildings in southern Italy, had no stoves or central heating furnaces. We passed around American cigarettes to everyone as we listened to Padre Paolino, who spoke fairly good English, tell us about his visits to America. As always, his talk led to the topic of Padre Pio. "How would you like to go to San Giovanni Rotondo and meet Padre Pio?" he asked. Without a moment's hesitation, we answered "YES!" Padre Paolino looked at us and laughed, along with the monks and brothers. In broken English, Padre Paolino said, "Okay, you furnish the transportation, and next week we go to meet Padre Pio in San Giovanni Rotondo together."

You just can't imagine how excited we were. We were going to see and meet Padre Pio, the saintly monk that everyone was talking about! The appointed day finally arrived, but Leo Fanning was not able to go with us this first time. Joe Asterita and I woke up at 3:30 a.m., went to the motor pool, and signed out for a jeep, which happened to belong to our Chaplain. We drove to the Capuchin monastery to pick up Padre Paolino, who was waiting for us. It was a cold, dark morning as we drove to Foggia on the lonely highway. We passed a number of farmers going to their fields in small carts drawn by a horse or mule, moving slowly along the highway. In most cases, the farmer on the cart was asleep, so apparently the mule or horse knew where to go. We also saw men and women walking to their fields, carrying tools or baskets on their heads.

Padre Paolino, Joe and I talked about different things, but our thoughts were on what was in store for us—meeting Padre Pio in person. Soon we forgot about the cold morning. From Cerignola we had to drive through Foggia, and we were surprised how large a city it was, with a population of 120,000. We saw many buildings destroyed by our American and British planes. Passing through Foggia, we went on the highway that led to San Giovanni. We arrived at the foot of the Gargano mountains and began to climb the winding road leading to the top, until we came to the sleepy little village of San Giovanni Rotondo.

On the edge of the city were the church and monastery of Our Lady of Grace. We drove our jeep to the rear of the monastery, where a bearded brother came out and guided our jeep to a barn, where we parked next to sleeping mules. At 5:30 a.m., people had already gathered at the doors of the church to wait for them to be unlocked. The doors were soon opened, and the people rushed to be in front of the church for the best seats, to be close to the altar and Padre Pio. In a few minutes the church was full. You must remember that Italy was at war and was being defeated, and all transportation was knocked out, preventing people from travelling to San Giovanni. The ones there that morning must have walked for miles and hours to get there.

Padre Paolino, Joe, and myself were led into the cloister. Since Padre Paolino was the Provincial, he gave us special privileges to roam around the monastery and cloister. We were treated royally because we were the friends and guests of Padre Paolino. We went into the sacristy to await Padre Pio's arrival to prepare for Mass. Finally he walked into the sacristy. My heart began to beat double-time and I thought that it would burst. Padre Paolino introduced Padre Pio to Joe and me. We knelt down and kissed the palm of his hand; I was edified, speechless, and filled with indescribable joy. Joe was invited to serve his Mass, and I was allowed to sit next to the altar.

The Mass lasted almost two hours. It was a Mass that I could not describe, nor could I describe the feeling that came to me as I knelt at the side of the altar near Padre Pio. The Mass was beautiful, and although it was long, time stood still for us. We were in the presence of a living saint. The area around the altar was filled with an invisible halo of sweet smelling flowers, the perfume of sanctity is what they call it.

I could see the suffering on Padre Pio's face as he celebrated Mass. It is said that during Mass, and we could see this, Padre Pio is with Christ, and is living the Passion of Christ when He hung on the Cross almost 2,000 years ago. His feet, hands, and body would quiver as if he, along with Christ, were being nailed to the cross. Padre never once looked at the people in the church. His mind, heart and soul were with Jesus at Calvary. I could see that physically he was with us, but spiritually he was with Christ on the Cross. At times he wept, with tears running down his cheeks. When he raised his arms, we could see the painful blood-soaked wounds in the palms of his hands. The only words that came to my mouth when I saw the wounds on Padre Pio's hands were "My Lord and my God."

At 1:00 p.m., Padre Paolino invited Joe and myself to join the monks and brothers in the refectory (dining room) for lunch. The Superior of the Friary and Padre Paolino sat at the head table—Padre Pio had not yet arrived. The others sat along the walls facing one another on both sides of the room. Everyone stood up as the prayers before meals were said, and then they sat down again. All were silent as one of the friars read from the Bible. When he finished we were then permitted to talk.

It was funny to see the many monks and brothers sitting in a row. As I looked down, I could see their beards, all different colors and sizes, going up and down as they ate. All of them were friendly to us. Joe Asterita, whose parents were born near Naples, could speak their Italian dialect well enough to translate for me what was being said. Joe and I were anxiously awaiting the arrival of Padre Pio in the dining room. One of the monks told us that Padre Pio hardly eats anything, and they often wonder how he can stay alive.

Finally, Padre Pio arrived at the dining room.

Everyone except the Superior and Padre Paolino stood up in respect. He walked slowly to the front of the dining room to where the two were sitting. He seemed to be limping slightly because of the pain from the wounds on his feet. He went down on his knees and bowed, then kissed the sandals of the Superior and Padre Paolino. I couldn't see too well, so it could have been that Padre Pio kissed the floor in front of them. I can't remember because I was so excited to think that we were allowed to dine with the monks and Padre Pio. I was so thrilled . . . so very happy.

Padre Paolino knew Joe and I would be so glad if we sat near Padre Pio, so he arranged to have me sit on one side of the Padre and Joe on the other. Padre Pio hardly ate anything. He talked to Joe and I, and Joe translated for me. Padre Pio is known to be a great kidder, so he kidded Joe and I, much to the amusement of all the brothers and monks in the dining room. Again I must repeat how thrilled and fortunate we were. I thought, "There are millions of people who would give anything to be in our shoes today."

When lunch was over, the Superior gave a signal and everyone stood up, and recited prayers together. They left for more prayers in the church, and then retired for their afternoon nap. Joe and I were permitted to roam around the 400-year-old monastery. We went to the monastery garden where Padre Pio loved to visit and take evening walks. It was beautiful in the garden and so very quiet. We sat against the building in the sun, and the sun felt good . . . warm. We closed our eyes to maybe take a ten-minute nap or relax. It was so peaceful in this piece of heaven on earth. The chickens were the only ones making any noise, but they cackled very quietly as if not to wake Padre Pio.

We then decided to visit Maria Pyle, who lived a few yards away from the monastery. After we introduced ourselves, she received us very cordially and immediately made some American coffee for us. "You are Americans, and I must not forget that I was an American, and I still do not like Italian coffee called espresso," said Maria. "But, after all these many years here at San Giovanni Rotondo, I am getting used to it."

Maria introduced us to Orazio Forgione, the 84-year-old father of Padre Pio. He lived in the house with Maria, and she took care of him at the request of Padre Pio. Maria also took care of his mother in her house until she died. Joe and I went to the back yard with Orazio, where we sat and visited. Joe did all the translating, although Orazio did speak a few words of English. "I lived in Brook-a-lino a long time ago," he said, meaning that he once lived and worked in Brooklyn years ago to help pay for Padre Pio's education. After bidding Maria Pyle and Orazio good-bye, and promising that we would be back again soon, we went back to the monastery to pick up Padre Paolino.

It was getting dark as we hurried to Padre Pio's room to bid him good-bye. We talked again for a few minutes, until we received word from one of the brothers that Padre Paolino was ready and anxious to get back to Cerignola. As we said good-bye to Padre Pio, we again noticed that whenever he was in the room with us, the room had a heavenly and indescribable perfume odor that came from his wounds. We knelt down to kiss the wound on his hand. He pulled us up and put his arms around Joe and I. He kissed me on both cheeks and said, "God bless you Mario, and your family. Come back again soon and see me." Then off we went in our jeep down the dark highway back to Cerignola.

At first none of us spoke. We rode in complete silence, each of us reflecting on the wonderful day we had. A day that we would be able to tell our families about . . . if we survived this war. Finally we began to carry on a conversation. We talked about Padre Pio, Maria Pyle, and Padre Pio's father. The words that Padre Pio said to me as we bid him good-bye: "Mario, God bless you and your family," kept coming back to my mind, as we continued to drive that night along the highway from San Giovanni Rotondo, the only piece of heaven that I have ever known.

After the War, and his return to the Chicago area, Mario began to correspond with Mary Pyle. In 1949, the pastor of Mario's parish made a trip to Italy during which he met Padre Pio and Miss Pyle at San Giovanni Rotondo. Via his pastor, Mario received the following letter from Mary, in which she refers to that visit, and also to a certain chain letter about Pietrelcina:

> Dear Mario plus wife and babies, all of whom I hope to know some day,
>
> You cannot imagine how I have enjoyed meeting the good Father who brought me news of you, Mario, and who has told me what a very fine wife you have; God bless you all! If I mention Joe or Leo to Padre Pio he adds, "And Mario?" He remembers his children!
>
> One of the big mistakes in my trip to America was that I did not look you up, or give you a chance of

looking me up. I had no idea that I was going even in the direction of Chicago, and when I found that I changed trains there on my way to Springfield, Ill., where I gave a lecture on Padre Pio, I had no address book at hand. Never mind, I remember you just as much as I do the others whom I saw while I was in America and feel just as close to you in prayer, because we are members of the same spiritual family, being children of the same Father, Padre Pio. I am chiefly sorry that I did not have the chance of knowing your wife and children, it will have to be for another time.

I am asking Father to take you this letter with a photo which I am sure you will like. Thank you for your last letter which I had not yet answered, and please ask Joe Asterita to send you the long, very badly typed letter which I sent to several, to pass on to others. In it I speak of the monastery in Pietrelcina.

Affectionate greetings to all,
Maria

Chapter 25

William Carrigan and Joe Peterson

WILLIAM Carrigan, a devout Catholic, was the director of the American Red Cross Field Office in Foggia, where he had been assigned to support the 15th Air Force. Carrigan was one of many GIs who heard the accounts of a holy priest on the Gargano, and of an American woman who greeted the soldiers. The stories he heard were originally spread by some GIs who had been searching for fresh eggs on the mountain, as reported in C. Bernard Ruffin's classic *Padre Pio: The True Story.*[1] In a previous chapter, it was noted that Joe De Santis had in fact been on such a food-gathering mission to San Giovanni Rotondo. Joe and Ray Ewen then met Mary Pyle, who told them about the stigmatized priest, and the two brought back the tale of a "Holy Man" to the Cerignola air base near Foggia. It is quite possible, then, that the pair had originated the stories that William Carrigan heard. At any rate, when some of the troops stationed with Carrigan wanted to visit Padre Pio, they asked him if he could provide transportation up the mountain. He agreed, and on a snowy day in the winter of 1943-44, he and about 20 GI's made the trek to Our Lady of Grace Friary.

By the time the group arrived at the church, Padre Pio's Mass had already begun. Carrigan was struck by the Friar's profound holiness, his intense suffering during the Mass, and the way he seemed to be directly communing with God. When the Mass was over, the Americans were received warmly by Padre Pio in the sacristy. Padre Pio reportedly told Carrigan that these were the first American soldiers he had met so far during the war.[2] More importantly, at that very first meeting with Padre Pio, William Carrigan conceived the desire to make Padre Pio known back in the United States. "I knew we had a destiny together. I sensed that I wanted to help make him known in America."[3]

Over the next year-and-a-half, the Red Cross Director furnished transportation for hundreds of soldiers who wished to attend Padre Pio's Mass. He witnessed a transformation in the lives of many of these GIs, and some were even called to the priesthood. Carrigan was on such good terms with Padre Pio and the friars that they often allowed him to stay overnight in the Friary. He was also permitted to dine with them in the refectory. Once, he asked Padre Pio what he thought of the gift of his stigmata, and without hesitating Padre Pio replied, "I find them very embarrassing to have, but I deem it a great privilege to suffer with Christ."[4] As for their personal friendship, Carrigan regarded Padre Pio as "someone you could have gone fishing with."[5] Even when he went to Confession to him, he experienced it as a normal Confession, just like any other.

In 1944, the Allied Military Governor for the Foggia area, Colonel John Laboon, asked Carrigan to write an essay about Padre Pio that could be distributed to the English-speaking Catholic world.[6] Carrigan composed his essay in the form of a letter to LaBoon, and it was subsequently circulated in a wide variety of Catholic publications. It was probably the first time many Catholics, especially in America, had ever heard of Padre Pio.

This ground-breaking epistle is dated Ascension Thursday, May 18, 1944. In the letter he begins by describing Padre Pio's stigmata and his Mass. To the soldiers and to Carrigan, his Mass ". . . eclipses anything we have experienced in this theater of war." The message of love and forgiveness transmitted through Padre Pio is the antithesis of the hateful war still raging. He outlines Padre Pio's day, which consists of early morning Mass, Confessions, a scant meal, more Confessions, prayer, and then just a few hours of sleep.

The letter further describes Padre Pio's Mass, especially the Consecration, where "he is literally on the Cross with Christ." His pain is so severe that it is difficult for him to say the words of the Consecration; sometimes he has to say them in between pauses. At the elevation of the Host, "he seems lost to the world," as he prays for his spiritual children. He spends a long time with Christ at this juncture, since Padre Pio "never forgets a person who seeks his spiritual counsel."

After Mass, he will greet the soldiers in the sacristy while he is unvesting, and allows them to kiss his wounded hands. He is always patient and kind, and often gives a consoling pat on the cheek to the men. "His engaging smile and simple humility draw everyone to him." Often the soldiers are taken separately to a side room, where Padre Pio blesses their rosaries and other objects, and answers questions through interpreters.

On the way back to the base, the soldiers seem like changed men. The initial general silence is followed by conversation about Padre Pio and what they have just experienced. Once at the camp, they continue to think and talk about him, and spread the word to their buddies, who now also want to meet him. Spiritual values are taking root, and many of the men turn from their carefree attitude, and begin soberly to consider their future responsibilities and relationship with God.

William Carrigan concludes the letter with a plea for people to take advantage of the opportunity to meet and receive direction from ". . . a favored son of God" who bears with him the miracle of the stigmata. He is our ". . . ambassador to the

Throne of God," a guide of souls, a representative who can plead our case at the Court of Christ. God has given him the special gift of "designing" souls. "Would you not like to have your soul designed by so great a spiritual artist? Think about it."

After his return to the United States at the end of the War, Carrigan began to fulfill his calling to make Padre Pio known in America, while at the same time pursuing a full-time career in real estate. In one of the speeches he gave about the Saint's spirituality, he explained that Padre Pio's ". . . spiritual family numbers thousands and is open to all. To join is by will alone. He told me that if anyone wishes to join, 'I will know and they will know.'"[7]*

Another soldier stationed in southern Italy, who also launched a ministry to acquaint Americans with the Saint of the Gargano, was Joseph Peterson. Joe was based in Bari, which is about 70 miles from San Giovanni Rotondo. After he first heard about Padre Pio from another soldier, he wanted to see the "Holy Man" for himself, but was discouraged from making the visit by his military chaplain. However, with persistence he was able to obtain the address of another chaplain, Fr. John St. John, who was based further north, in Foggia. Chaplain St. John replied to a letter Peterson wrote, and included in the reply were directions to San Giovanni Rotondo. Encouraged by Fr. St. John's letter, Joe and three other GIs hitchhiked from Bari all the way to San Giovanni Rotondo. Upon their arrival, they succeeded in arranging a brief meeting with Padre Pio. Even though this first encounter lasted only a few minutes, the impact of Padre Pio's sanctity made a lasting impression on Joe Peterson,

---

*A website dedicated to William Carrigan's memory, and to his efforts at making Americans aware of Padre Pio, can be accessed at www.padrepio.net.

and he returned to Our Lady of Grace many times during the War and afterward.[8]

On his return visits, Joe was often invited to serve at Padre Pio's Mass. He described certain moments during the service when Padre Pio could be seen moving his lips; he was speaking words that were not audible, as if he were conversing with invisible beings. "Those weren't the prescribed prayers of the Mass."[9] Joe's experience as he assisted at Padre Pio's Mass was profound: "My knees were knocking. You felt you were at Calvary. You could see the great suffering he went through."[10]

He described the arrival of the American GIs at Foggia, and their subsequent discovery of Padre Pio, in an article he wrote in 1963:

> In 1943 the American forces entered the picture of Padre Pio's life. Our soldiers took over the vital air base at Foggia from the Germans and they soon learned of the Padre on the top of the mountain. The friendly people of Foggia were happy to see the Americans, although they had to do great damage to their city. Soon Mount Gargano began to become a place of pilgrimage for the GIs. Father John D. St. John, S. J., the chaplain, and his assistant, Joe Asterita of the Bronx, and Lt. Ray Ewen of Glendale, Long Island, helped many an American boy to meet Padre Pio. I was very privileged to be one of them. After the War the boys came back to America with the story of Padre Pio and his idea to one day, God willing, have a hospital on the top of the mountain.[11]

When the War ended, Peterson returned to his home in Yonkers, New York, where he gave talks and slide show presentations on Padre Pio to parish groups. His lecture min-

istry was approved by the Archdiocese of New York, yet he
would give his talks anywhere in the country for those interested in finding out about the stigmatized priest. All proceeds or donations received were duly sent to Padre Pio for
the building of his new hospital. He also became active in the
Franciscan Third Order and was elected Prefect of his local
fraternity. Eventually, he moved to Cromwell, Connecticut,
at the request of Fr. Bob McQueeney, and served on the
board of directors of the Padre Pio Foundation of America,
while continuing to give his presentations.

Joe's position with the post office allowed him to spend a
month each summer at San Giovanni Rotondo, alongside
Padre Pio. The local residents easily recognized the tall
American when he returned every year, and ". . . one would
see him continually receiving a wave or a greeting from the
local inhabitants with a, 'Ciao Joe!'" [12] During these summer
sojourns, he collaborated with Mary Pyle in helping tourists
and pilgrims on their visits. In 1963 Dorothy Day journeyed
to San Giovanni, and wrote about the:

> . . . young Americans who go to San Giovanni on
> their vacations in order to help pilgrims and tourists
> on their excursions to get the full value of their trip.
> One such young man was Joe Peterson, a former
> mailman of the Bronx, who gave me much help and
> information while I was there. He has been coming to
> San Giovanni ever since his service days in the Sec-
> ond World War . . . Joe Peterson and his little group
> reminded me very much of St. Catherine of Siena's
> "Little Company" in their devotion to Padre Pio and
> their helping him. Mary Pyle one might say is the
> center of this little company, and I enjoyed visiting
> her down the mountain-side in the big old house

which was like a house of hospitality to all the guests who came.[13]

Joe Peterson and Padre Pio had one important quality in common, a good sense of humor. Joe, who was about 6' 4" tall and weighed 230 pounds, once let himself be wrestled to the floor by Padre Pio—all 5' 6" and 170 pounds of him. Joe pretended he was hurt badly and soundly beaten, and Padre Pio was laughingly declared the victor and champion by the friars present. It was all in good fun as part of a birthday party for Joe, given by the friars during one of his vacations at San Giovanni Rotondo.

In the early 1960's, on a return visit to San Giovanni Rotondo, Joe Peterson presented Padre Pio with an autographed picture of President John F. Kennedy. The Capuchin, who was an admirer of America's first Catholic President, blessed the picture and had it placed in his hospital, the House for the Relief of Suffering. Padre Pio requested that the hospital correspondent write a letter to President Kennedy, thanking him for the picture and expressing how happy they were to receive it.[14]

Joe, who was born in 1923, died on March 12, 1992, only a few days after giving one of his presentations on Padre Pio. During his talks, he would show a collection of about 100 slides that were personally blessed by the Saint. The slides were taken by Friederic Abresch of San Giovanni Rotondo, who was Padre Pio's unofficial photographer. After Joe's passing, Fr. McQueeny of the Padre Pio Foundation asked Joe's close friend, Bill Accousti, to carry the torch and continue with the presentations. Bill, who gives talks on Padre Pio to this day, using a copy of the original slides, says his friend Joe Peterson was a "man of God, a special person."[15]

Chapter 26

The Flying Monk

NORMAN Lewis was a British Intelligence Officer temporarily assigned to the American Fifth Army in Naples during 1943-44. He kept a diary of his observations of the suffering and poverty of the war-ravaged populace, which was published in 1978 as "Naples '44."[1] There is a curious entry for March 29, 1944, in which he presented the tale of a "flying monk" at Pomigliano who bore the stigmata. During an aerial dogfight, the monk soared into the sky to catch in his arms the pilot of a downed Italian plane, and carry him safely back to earth. Lewis asserted that many educated Italians firmly believe this story. The author added a footnote, not part of the original diary, saying that this man was ". . . the celebrated Padre Pio." Pomigliano d'Arco is a town in the Naples vicinity.

The significance of this diary entry rests in the fact that it may be the only contemporary written account of Padre Pio's exploits as the "flying monk." It lends credence to the stories that emerged after the War, and proves that they were not just post-war fabrications by some of Padre Pio's devotees with overactive imaginations.

The complete story of "The Flying Monk" goes well beyond Norman Lewis' account. It encompasses one of the most spectacular and incredible tales associated with the Second World War. This story also concerns American servicemen who came to Our Lady of Grace Friary to see Padre Pio, but the circumstances were quite unlike those of the previous chapters.

During the battle for southern Italy, in all likelihood many attempts were made by Allied air forces to bomb the small town of San Giovanni Rotondo, the city whose only boast was the monastery where Padre Pio resided. Intelligence data spoke of a cache of German munitions in the area. The correspondence of the American soldier Joe Peluso mentioned that a German fortress was located about a mile-and-a-half from the monastery. Placing such a fortification on the high cliffs of the Gargano, overlooking the whole *Tavoliere* below from Manfredonia to Foggia, would make sense strategically.

Padre Pio had often prophesied that San Giovanni Rotondo would remain unscathed by the War and that not a bomb would fall on it. The people of the town were quite concerned because they were so close to the major air base at Foggia, and the Saint assured them that their city would be spared.[2] The fears of the *Sangiovanese* were legitimate, since Foggia, considered an Italo-German enemy stronghold, sustained heavy damage during the Allied bombardments, resulting in the tragic loss of over 20,000 civilian lives.

In contrast, none of the Allied planes sent to bomb the San Giovanni Rotondo area were able to complete their missions successfully. There were often mysterious malfunctions, causing the bombs to drop harmlessly in the fields, or mechanical failures which caused the planes to veer off course. But the real story is told by the pilots who did make it near to the city—they reported that they were beckoned to turn back by an apparition in the skies—a vision of a "flying monk" who waved them away. Most of the airmen were afraid to mention any of this until after the War, when many groups of American and British soldiers came to pay their respects to the famous Friar. It was then that he was identified as that very same "flying monk" by those who had seen him in the sky!

It is interesting to see just how the story of the "flying monk" developed over the years, to the point where it has become an integral part of the Padre Pio folklore. There are three traditional elements to the tale. The first is the apparition witnessed by the pilot or crew; the second is the inability to drop any bombs; and the third, the witnesses' visit to San Giovanni Rotondo and their recognizing Padre Pio as the monk in the sky.

Possibly the earliest published account of an apparition of Padre Pio to Allied pilots appeared in an obscure Italian biography of Padre Pio written in 1950 by Piera Sessa.[3] This account is cited in the well-known 1952 Padre Pio biography by Pascal Parente, *A City on a Mountain*, in only two brief sentences: "It is reported that when certain Allied fliers were about to drop bombs on San Giovanni Rotondo, they saw the figure of a friar with protecting arms extended over it. This vision so unnerved the airmen that they flew on without releasing any bombs." In this short anecdote, the first two traditional elements of the "flying monk" scenario are presented, the vision of the friar, and the failure to drop any bombs.[4]

The same 1950 Sessa biography was also referenced in another early Padre Pio classic, Malachy Gerard Carroll's *Padre Pio*,[5] printed in Ireland in 1953. However, Carroll instead cites a story that is similar to the Norman Lewis account of a downed pilot being saved. Here, the parachute of the Italian pilot would not open, and a "Capuchin" saved him from plunging to his death. The pilot himself was not a devotee of Padre Pio, but rather, it was his mother who had been praying to Padre Pio for her son's safety. After the War, she insisted that her reluctant son visit San Giovanni Rotondo to thank the Saint in person for rescuing him. As soon as the skeptical pilot saw Padre Pio for the first time, he was down on his knees thanking the man he recognized

—PHOTO SECTION—

Our Lady of Grace Friary

Our Lady of Grace Friary

Above: Maria Giuseppa, Padre Pio's mother. Immensely devoted to his mother, the Padre was so heartbroken at her death that he could not bring himself to attend her funeral.

Right: Grazio Forgione, Padre Pio's father, who had emigrated to the U.S. as a young man, working as a laborer in "Brook-a-lino" and Pennsylvania to earn money for his son's education. In San Giovanni Rotondo, Grazio was affectionately known to visiting GIs as "No No"—an Americanization of the Italian word *Nonno*, "Grandfather."

Our Lady of Grace Friary

The young Padre Pio bearing the stigmata, the wounds of Christ, which he had received on September 20, 1918. When asked whether the wounds hurt, he would reply: "Do you think the good Lord gave them to me for a decoration?"

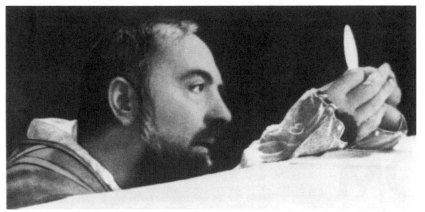

Our Lady of Grace Friary

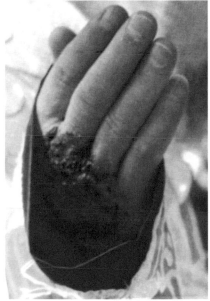

Our Lady of Grace Friary

Above: Padre Pio offering Mass. Pilgrims all testified that attending Mass offered by Padre Pio was an unforgettable experience, since the priest was united so visibly with Christ on the Cross.

Left: Wound in the hand of Padre Pio. For the 50 years that he bore the wounds of Christ, they neither healed nor became infected. Science could offer no explanation.

Our Lady of Grace Friary

A beautiful photo of Padre Pio vested in the Roman chasuble worn for offering the Traditional Latin Mass.

204-4

Our Lady of Grace Friary

Padre Pio was a friend to all. For over 50 years, pilgrims flocked by the thousands to visit him and go to Confession to him at the remote Monastery of Our Lady of Grace in San Giovanni Rotondo, Italy.

Our Lady of Grace Friary

Padre Pio got along famously with Americans, including GIs during World War II. Nevertheless, it is reliably claimed that he appeared in the sky to wave American bombers away from San Giovanni Rotondo. Padre Pio often stated that he wanted all Americans to become his Spiritual Children.

National Centre for Padre Pio

Vera Calandra, founder of the National Centre for Padre Pio (now in Barto, PA), with her husband Harry and Pope John Paul II.

Frank Rega

Part of the *Casa Sollievo della Sofferenza*—the "House for the Relief of Suffering." A substantial portion of the funding for this huge hospital came from American donors.

Our Lady of Grace Friary

Padre Pio had a wonderful sense of humor. Sometimes his fellow
monks had to leave the refectory at meal time because their sides
ached from laughing at his jokes and funny stories.

204-8

Padre Pio Foundation of America

Above: Joe Peterson *(right)*, who served Padre Pio's Mass on his annual trips to see his personal friend and spiritual advisor.
Below: Fr. Joseph Pius *(left)* and Fr. Alessio Parente with other pilgrims in the "English" visitors' room of the Friary of Our Lady of Grace.

Frank Rega

204-9

Our Lady of Grace Friary

Above: Photos of Mary Pyle —known as *"l'Americana"*— just after receiving the Third Order Franciscan habit and near the end of her life.

Right: The "Pink Castle." Mary Pyle and her Pink Castle were a tremendous blessing to thousands of American pilgrims during her 43 years in San Giovanni Rotondo.

Frank Rega

Our Lady of Grace Friary

Padre Pio wearing his brown half-gloves to cover the stigmata.

Our Lady of Grace Friary

Above: Padre Pio being escorted from a voting station to a waiting car which would be covered with flowers as it passed through the town.
Below: Padre Pio with Padre Pellegrino, who would assist him in the hour of his death.

Rocky Falatico

An aged Padre Pio being helped by Charles Mandina of California. *(Grateful acknowledgement to Rocky Falatico, Charles' nephew, for this photo.)*

Our Lady of Grace Friary

A famous portrait of Padre Pio in his later years.

Our Lady of Grace Friary

Padre Pio in death. He went to his reward on September 23, 1968. The Bishop of the diocese, Msgr. Andrea Cesarano, is shown next to the bier. When visiting Padre Pio, this prelate, instead of imparting his own blessing, used to take hold of Padre Pio's hand and raise it in blessing.

Our Lady of Grace Friary

The beginning of Padre Pio's funeral procession, which took about four hours to wind its way past some 100,000 mourners who had gathered from around the world.

Those left on earth are consoled by Padre Pio's promises to help them after his death. He frequently said: "In the tomb I will be more alive than ever!"

as the one who had saved his life. This account, while it does not mention attempts to bomb San Giovanni Rotondo, contains the third traditional component of the flying monk episode, the airman visits San Giovanni Rotondo and recognizes Padre Pio.

One of the earliest full-blown "flying monk" stories was presented in John McCaffery's 1978 book *The Friar of San Giovanni*.[6] However, this is a fourth-hand account, since it was written by McCaffery, who heard it from a friend, who heard it from another friend, who heard it from the American pilot himself. Since McCaffery is a reliable author, and one of the 'friends' was an English Lord, there should be a strong element of reliability to the narrative.

The American pilot who told the story was the squadron-leader. Their bombing mission was a target "close to Foggia," which meant it could have been San Giovanni Rotondo. Suddenly, the pilot saw in front of his plane the image of a monk in the sky, gesturing with his arms and hands for the plane to turn back. The shocked pilot did just that, and jettisoned his bombs elsewhere. When he returned to the base and told his story, his commanding officer decided it was best to put this pilot in a hospital under observation for mission-fatigue.

At the hospital, an Italian orderly heard of the pilot's tale, came to him, and revealed that there might be something to his story of a friar in the sky. He proceeded to tell the pilot about a monk living in that region who was said to have miraculous powers. This greatly relieved the pilot, who had been bewildered about the whole episode.

After the War the pilot made a number of inquiries, which led him to make a visit to the monastery at San Giovanni Rotondo. He recognized in Padre Pio that same monk in the sky, and "had the veracity of the account admitted to him." At the time that he told this whole story to McCaffery's "friend of a friend," Lord Eldon, the unnamed pilot and his wife were on the train to Foggia, in order to pay their respects to the monk with miraculous powers.

Biographies of Mary Pyle relate that she often told the flying monk story to visitors who came to see her, because she had heard it herself first-hand.[7,8] After the war in Southern Italy was over, a group of American airmen visited her at the "pink castle." This group was part of a squadron that had embarked on a raid on July 26, 1943, in order to destroy German munitions supposedly stored in a school building in San Giovanni Rotondo. As the planes approached the target, they saw a strange white cloud, and in the cloud were images of a monk with a beard, a woman holding a child, and a young man carrying a sword dripping with blood. The planes were unable to release their load of bombs because of a malfunction in the release mechanism. They made a second pass with the same negative result.

Mary took the group of GIs to see Padre Pio, and a number of the men remarked that this was the bearded monk they had seen in the sky. Then she took them into the church, and when they saw the picture of Our Lady of Grace, they said this was the same image they had seen in the cloud. Finally, she accompanied them to the sanctuary of St. Michael, a few miles outside the city, and upon seeing Sansovino's famous statue of the Archangel, they exclaimed that this was the young man with a sword they had seen.

Were it not for the reliability of the sources that report that Mary Pyle herself told this story, it would seem difficult to accept that not one, but three, images appeared in the sky to prevent San Giovanni Rotondo from being bombed. It appears that this is a completely different incident from the earlier story of the hospitalized squadron leader. However, if the initial efforts to bomb San Giovanni Rotondo did not prove successful, it is reasonable to assume that further attempts would have been made.

The Mary Pyle story apparently has been confirmed by Padre Paolo Covino, a Capuchin who was living at a friary in Cerignola during the War. In 1994, he told a reporter for an Italian magazine that he had personally spoken with an American machine-gunner based in Cerignola, who had seen the three images in the sky on a bombing mission in the summer of 1943.[9] The GI reported that there was a mechanical failure of the bomb-release apparatus, causing the bombs to fall accidentally on an uninhabited area a few kilometers from San Giovanni Rotondo. A year later, the airman and some of his colleagues, including Protestant soldiers, visited the monastery. After they recognized Padre Pio and the image of Our Lady of Grace as the figures they saw in the sky, some of the Protestants later became Catholic converts. Covino said the gunner returned with his family to San Giovanni Rotondo in 1952 to pray at the monastery. As of this writing, Padre Paolo Covino resides in the infirmary of Our Lady of Grace Friary, and is the same priest that Fr. Leo Fanning had once befriended in Cerignola.

Another rendition of the "flying monk" episode was told by Dr. Bernardo Rosini, an Italian Air Force General, who said he heard it from several American officers while he was stationed at Bari. The pilot and squadron leader of the group of planes headed for San Giovanni Rotondo was an American General. As they neared the target, the vision of the monk appeared, and the bombs dropped of their own accord and fell in the woods. After the War, this American General and some of the other pilots visited Padre Pio, having heard that this monk performed miracles. They recognized him as the one from the vision, and Padre Pio went over to the General and said to him, "Ah! So you are the one who wanted to kill us all!"[10] The Padre spoke in Italian dialect, but the officer heard him in English. He was won over by the kindliness of Padre Pio, and the two became good friends. The General eventually converted to Catholicism.

The Rosini version of the story was told to the Italian writer Renzo Allegri, and shows up in at least two different books he published, in 1993[11] and 2000.[12] However, except for the mention of Doctor Rosini as the source, it is almost identical to an account published in Fr. Charles Mortimer Carty's famous book, *Padre Pio: The Stigmatist*.[13] Further, according to C. Bernard Ruffin, the Carty account itself stems from an unpublished "circular letter" written by Padre Pio's secretary, Fr. Dominic Meyer, in 1949.[14]

There is also a variation of Rosini's story, which holds that there were many attempts out of Bari to bomb San Giovanni Rotondo, not just one, and all ended in failure because of the "flying monk." The pilots were allegedly of various nationalities, including American, British, Polish, and Palestinian, and of different religions (Catholic, Orthodox, Moslem, Protestant, Jewish).[15] Their stories were laughed at on the base as tall tales, but the incidents kept recurring. Finally, the American General decided to lead the squadron himself, because he wanted to find out if these stories of a monk in the sky were true.[16]

But in none of these anecdotes do we have the identity of someone who actually saw the Friar in the sky. The only account that provides even a partial name was told by someone who overheard a conversation that a fighter pilot named "Pope," who was killed during the War, saw the apparition.[17] There is an impressive list of people who talked to the witnesses, such as Mary Pyle, Lord Eldon, Padre Covino, and Dr. Bernardo Rosini, but they supply no names of the eyewitnesses themselves. Fr. Armand Dasseville was another Capuchin Priest who once met a witness. While in Rome, he had spoken to a former American bombardier who had been unable to release his bombs over San Giovanni Rotondo; but, as usual, the name of the airman is not given.[18]

However, upon the death of Padre Pio in 1968, one person did come forward, who had kept his experience to himself for over 20 years. His name is Gaetano Pavone, an American airman, gunner and flight engineer during the war. A very brief mention of his experience was reported in one Padre Pio biography,[19] and he had also written a letter about it for *The Sign*, a Catholic magazine that is no longer published. The present author was able to locate Mr. Pavone, and obtain the account which follows.

Gaetano's plane was returning from a bombing mission, and was heading south over the Adriatic Sea towards the Gargano, on the way to the base in Cerignola. As an engineer, he manned the top turret of his B-24 Liberator bomber, and this gave him a very clear view of the heavens. While nearing the twin lakes Varano and Lesino in the northern part of the Gargano peninsula, he saw in the sky, in a break in the clouds, an image of Padre Pio. The image of him was from the shoulders on up, and he had a short beard and was young looking. It was a three-quarters view of his face, and it had colors—the beard was dark brown—it was not just a cloud formation. Gaetano understandably did not say anything about it to his fellow crew members, and does not know if they saw the vision also.

The timeframe was somewhere between June and October of 1944. Gaetano tries to be objective about what he saw. As with any other flyer during the War, there was constant stress and uncertainty over what each day or mission would bring, and he was always praying. He observes, "I don't know if it was my imagination, or from hoping." He recalls that the image was not in motion, and Padre Pio did not wave his arms or give a blessing.

Gaetano explains that as flight engineer, it was his job to monitor various systems and check on the condition of the B-24. The plane was flying high enough (over 10,000 feet) that the crew needed to be hooked up to oxygen. But in order to check the various systems prior to landing, Gaetano would briefly have to unhook from the oxygen supply. He believes it was after he had made his check of the plane and had just re-hooked to the oxygen supply that he saw the image. Trying to cover all possible explanations, Gaetano entertains the possibility that he might have suffered a brief period of oxygen deprivation (anoxia) at that time. The fact that he is so objective about this lends credence to the conclusion that he definitely saw something unusual in the skies over the Gargano.

Gaetano adds:

> Shortly after my letter to *The Sign* magazine, I was contacted by phone with some official of the Church that was investigating these sightings. After a few minutes it was his opinion that the story was not worthy of belief. I let the matter drop. If Padre Pio was to be canonized a saint, it would have to be without my help. He was, so it all ended well.[20]

A final intriguing note to the "flying monk" mystery is added by American GI Bob Coble, whom we met in a previous chapter. Bob had done some microfilm searches of the records of the Second Bomb Group, based in Northern Africa. He found an anomalous report of airborne activity within a day or two of July 26, 1943. This is the date given for the "flying monk" sighting in the Mary Pyle reports, in which the planes were unable to drop their cargo of bombs. Twenty-one B-17 planes took off from Ain M'Lila, Algeria, headed for Foggia/San Nicola Air Depot. The records show that the squadron flew for six hours and forty minutes, and no bombs were dropped from any of the planes. "0 planes returned early, 21 planes dropped 0 bombs, at 0 time from 0 altitude." Bob remarked that "Most of the reports of that nature tell about the type of bombs carried, the time they reached the target, weather over the target, flak encountered, things observed, and enemy aircraft report of some kind. And this one says—NADA, nothing."[21]

Chapter 27

Postwar, and the "Work of Padre Pio"

A T THE close of the War in Italy, the Allied armies remained in the country as an occupying military force. Providentially, a Padre Pio devotee from Pittsburgh, Colonel John F. Laboon, was appointed Allied Military Governor for the Foggia region.[1] Although he had known about Padre Pio for many years, he had never met him in person. Laboon was overjoyed with his assignment to Foggia, and immediately befriended its Bishop, Msgr. Farina, and also the Vicar General, Padre Renato Luisi. Within a few days of his arrival in Foggia, he made his first trip to San Giovanni Rotondo, accompanied by Padre Luisi, who would act as his interpreter. When they were greeted by Padre Pio, it seemed to Luisi that he was actually expecting their arrival, in view of the warm welcome the Colonel received. Padre Pio and the officer engaged in a long conversation, which ended with the Padre embracing Laboon and inviting him for a return visit.

In his brief 40-day tenure as Governor of Foggia, Laboon won the love, respect, and admiration of the local populace. He immediately set to work rebuilding the area's infrastructure, focusing first of all on restoring public sanitation and health services. He directed the distribution of food and medicine from America, giving preference to hospital patients, babies, and the needy. He personally visited many neighboring towns, and attended a Mass for the repose of the souls of eleven *partigiani,* Italian freedom fighters, who had lost their lives fighting the Nazis.

But what endeared Laboon most to the people of Foggia was his restoration of the annual Corpus Christi Procession through the streets of the city. This traditional ceremony had been suspended since the War's beginning. Many citizens had advised against holding the event, because the streets were so badly damaged and cluttered from the Allied bombings. However, Colonel Laboon had the American troops repair all the roads on the planned route, removing tons of debris and filling in the holes and bomb craters. To Vicar General Luisi, it seemed as if ". . . these fine young fellows felt they had to make reparation for those other squads of their own Air Force who had unloaded their bombs on our city and reduced it to dismal ruins."[2] On the day of the procession, Colonel Laboon, in full military dress, walked immediately behind the canopied Sacred Host. Onlookers and marchers alike remarked at the sincere and devout demeanor of the Colonel. The event came to an end at the Piazza Venti Settembre. The colorful closing ceremonies at the Piazza, the final Benediction, and the procession itself, all combined to uplift the spirits of the war-weary citizens of Foggia, giving them new hope that their city would rise again from the ruins of war.

Whenever he had a spare moment, Laboon would send for the Vicar General, and the pair would bounce along in an army jeep over unpaved roads, to visit Padre Pio at San Giovanni Rotondo. On one such visit, the Colonel confided to the Saint his anxiety over the safety of his oldest son John. He was an officer in the United States Navy, assigned to the Far East, where the War was still raging. Padre Pio assured the Colonel of his prayers. But this was not enough to allay Laboon's worries, and he persisted in voicing his fears to Padre Pio. Finally, the Saint decided to put an end to the Colonel's anguish. "That's enough!" he said sharply. "Your son will come back and he'll become a priest." Not only did the Colonel's son John become a priest after the War, he became Chief Chaplain to the U. S. Atlantic fleet. He served with such distinction that in 1995 the Navy commissioned a guided missile destroyer named in his honor, the "Laboon." John was not the only child of Colonel Laboon to enter religion; another son also became a priest, and three of his daughters became Sisters of Mercy. The three nuns were honored guests at the commissioning of the "Laboon."

As the War wound down in the summer of 1945, Laboon and the occupying forces gradually departed from Italy, and the visits of the Allied soldiers to San Giovanni Rotondo slowed to a trickle. But the ebbing flow of GIs would soon be replaced by a flood of pilgrims, many coming from abroad after hearing about Padre Pio from returning veterans. The advent of peacetime also signaled a massive effort to rebuild the war-ravaged Italian peninsula. It enabled Padre Pio and his friends to begin anew the project of building a great hospital on the Gargano to serve the whole region. On October 5, 1946, the juridical standing of the hospital was established by creating a shareholding company to raise one million Lire. One thousand shares, worth one thousand Lire each, were to be distributed among a thousand shareholders, each one renouncing any personal profit.

Sadly, on that same October day, Padre Pio was at Mary Pyle's home, attending to his father Grazio, now 86, who was approaching death. Grazio had been living at Mary's house since 1938, except for a short stay in Pietrelcina during the War. Mary had been taking care of him in her "pink castle" as if he were her own father. He had chosen to live in the same room and sleep on the same bed where his wife, Mamma Peppa, had died in 1929.

Grazio, who was also known affectionately as Zi'Orazio (*Zio* means uncle), had spent many hours sitting on the stone bench that encircled the elm tree in front of the monastery. Here he would chat with pilgrims, friends and GIs about his special son and entertain them with colorful stories and anecdotes. As he became older and had difficulty climbing the hill that led from Mary's house to the Friary, his friends gave him a donkey to ride, so that he would not have to miss his son's morning Mass. But sometime in early 1946, he fell down the steep flight of stairs that led to his upstairs room at Mary's house. Some said it was a miracle that he survived the accident. When he complained of the pain, Padre Pio said he should instead thank his Guardian Angel for putting a pillow on each step for him!

Unfortunately, the fall took its toll on Padre Pio's aging father. He became bedridden, and by October he was in serious condition. His son obtained special permission from the Superior, Padre Raffaele, to remain at Grazio's bedside during his final days. Padre Pio had to climb that same steep stairway his father had fallen on, and for two nights he slept on a plank bed in a room near Grazio. This was the same bed that Mary Pyle normally used, and Padre Pio remarked to her, "My daughter, what a hard bed you have!"[3]

Padre Pio spoon-fed Grazio, and Holy Communion was brought for both men from the Friary. Finally, the son administered the Last Rites to his father. Grazio died in his son's arms on the evening of October 7, 1946. Padre Pio's grief was intense, and it took a week after the funeral for him to recover fully and to return to his ministry.[4] When some of the friars tried to comfort him, Padre Pio whispered, "It is a father I have lost."[5]

It was just two days before Grazio's death that the shareholding company for the hospital had been established. On that day, two of the founders, including Dr. Sanguinetti, who was to be the medical director, arrived at Mary Pyle's home, where Padre Pio was tending to his dying father. They presented him the documents that defined the legal corporation, and Padre Pio gave the contract his blessing. The institution would be known as the *Casa Sollievo della Sofferenza*, the House for the Relief of Suffering. Padre Pio spoke these prayerful words: "May it be as God has wanted. May it grow. May it heal bodies and sanctify souls." As for the collaborators, he added: ". . . may the good Lord reward them a hundred times over in this life, and with eternal life in the next."[6]

The hospital would be built right into the side of the mountain, adjacent to Our Lady of Grace Friary, on property that had been donated for it. A road was needed, and land had to be cleared and blasted away to create a level foundation for the edifice. Even though the available funds were meager, the digging began in May of 1947. The difficulties to surmount were enormous, since there was no infrastructure to provide supplies, materials, or labor. Even basic services such as water and electricity were minimal. It would take an Herculean effort to bring the project to fruition, but Padre Pio found the man who could do it.

His name was Angelo Lupi, whose architectural plan for the building was the one selected to be used. Lupi was a rugged, self-taught man who in fact had no degree in architecture or anything else. But Padre Pio recognized in him the talent, ingenuity, and energy that would be needed to make the *Casa* a reality, and he chose him to be not only the architect, but also the builder and general supervisor of the entire project.[7] One of Lupi's first tasks was to recruit and train a small army of laborers and construction workers, enlisting hardy men from the ranks of the returning soldiers and the area farmhands.

To solve the water problem, he tied in with the regional aqueduct, and erected great cisterns to collect rainwater. For electricity, he built a diesel-generated power plant. Making use of the natural resources of the mountain itself, Lupi constructed a kiln to extract lime for plaster. The stone and bedrock from the Gargano provided the material for tiles, sinks, tubs, bowls and artificial marble. Scaffolding and left-over wood were used for fabricating sturdy furniture. Even the iron beds were made on site by farmers, whom Lupi had transformed into craftsmen.[8] In addition, there was the massive building itself, which gradually emerged from the barren hillside, to the amazement of the naysayers. When it was finally completed ten years later, other architects, the ones who actually had degrees, called it a "genuine miracle."[9]

Lack of financial resources had almost brought the enterprise to an early end. A year after work began, Sanguinetti and Lupi were facing the fact that not enough donations were arriving to allow a project of this scope to be completed. Padre Pio would not seek bank loans, and insisted upon relying on Divine Providence. His approach was to let the pace of the work be determined by the amount of money available; if necessary, construction would stop until more funds were raised. But a nearly empty treasury, and the slow pace of the undertaking, signaled that work on the *Casa* was in serious trouble not long after it had begun.

Padre Pio's faith in Providence would be answered in a remarkable way, because it took an act of Congress (literally) and an apparent miracle to garner the additional funding. In the Autumn of 1947, British journalist Barbara Ward was on assignment in Italy for *The Economist* magazine, reporting on the postwar reconstruction of the country. She was especially interested in the work being done by the United Nations Relief and Rehabilitation Administration (UNRRA), an organization set up to aid the recovery of war-torn Europe, most especially the restoration of health services. Her fiancé, Commander Robert Jackson, was a deputy director of the organization.

Miss Ward, a Catholic, was well-acquainted with one of the

original shareholders of the hospital, who invited her to visit Padre Pio in San Giovanni Rotondo. Upon her arrival, she examined the work in progress at the hospital site, asking information about the cost and financing of the project. She discussed the possibility of an UNRRA grant with Dr. Sanguinetti, who explained the importance of building the hospital in the cooler clime of the mountain.[10] This was preferable to locating it in a large city on the sun-baked plain of the *Tavoliere*.

She also attended Padre Pio's Mass, and later was able to talk with him. During their conversation, she found him fascinating and gathered the courage to ask the Saint for a grace. Her fiancé, Commander Jackson, was not a Catholic, and she asked Padre Pio to pray for his conversion. Padre Pio answered that if God willed it, her fiancé would be converted. Miss Ward then asked him when this would occur. "If God wills, right now," Padre Pio replied.[11] This answer did little to reassure her, since it seemed that Padre Pio was just making casual statements.

When her writing assignment in Italy was over and she returned to London, she was amazed to learn that the very day that she had asked Padre Pio for his prayers, her fiancé had been converted to the Catholic Faith! He had been passing by a Jesuit Church on that particular day, and felt inspired to go in and visit the rectory, where he asked if he could begin to receive instructions in the Faith.[12] The overjoyed Barbara lost no time in prevailing upon Robert Jackson to enlist the help of UNRRA in financing the hospital.

Subsequently, the Commander asked UNRRA to award four hundred million Lire for construction of the *Casa*. The grant would be in memory of the late Fiorello La Guardia, former mayor of New York City, and former Director General of UNRRA. Appropriately, La Guardia's family was originally from Foggia. The proposal was also actively supported by La Guardia's widow. Since the United States was the primary source of UNRRA funds, the proposal was presented to the U. S. Congress, which gave its approval on June 21, 1948.[13] At this point, the Italian state bureaucracy kicked in, with the result that much of the grant was earmarked for other causes. In the end, the *Casa* received two hundred and fifty million lire, which was still an immense sum at that time. Publicity surrounding the UNRRA award stimulated the flow of donations from other sources, and the work moved ahead at a fast pace. Angelo Lupi was able to hire a work force of 350 people, and by 1950 most of the outer structure was in place.

Everyone realized that Barbara Ward was the inspiration behind the critical UNRRA award, and Angelo Lupi conceived of a unique way to honor her. He commissioned a special stained glass window of the Madonna in the hospital chapel. When Barbara returned in the autumn of 1950 for a visit, she was overwhelmed to see that the face of the Blessed Virgin on the glass was her own.

A great part of the donations for the hospital were from Americans, and one gift in particular touched Padre Pio deeply. Mario Gambino, a poor maintenance worker at Hunter College in New York City, sent in five dollars. A few days later, he mailed another donation of ten dollars, one for each of his ten children. This inspired Padre Pio to begin a fund for the poor, who could not afford to pay for their stay at the hospital. It became known as the "Mario Gambino Fund," and Gambino was able to collect large donations for the fund from the United States.[14,15] In appreciation for the generosity and support of the Americans, to this day the United States flag flies next to the flag of Italy along the roof of the hospital, where the flags of all the nations that contributed to the *Casa* are displayed.

The hospital was inaugurated on May 5, 1956 (Padre Pio's name day—the feast of Pope St. Pius V) before a crowd of 15,000 people, including dignitaries of the Italian government and the Church. Visitors were impressed by the beauty of the structure, its light and cheerful rooms, the faux marble walls, and by the up-to-date medical equipment. Even the grounds were carefully manicured, to provide a welcome and pleasant environment for patients. The barren hillside around the building had been transformed into a sea of greenery, thanks to the efforts of Dr. Sanguinetti, who had thousands of trees planted along the rocky slopes.

In a speech that day, Padre Pio outlined his vision for the *Casa*. It would be ". . . a place of prayer and science where human beings should meet one another in Christ . . ."—so that the suffering of both body and soul would be alleviated. He encouraged the continued generosity of its supporters so that the work would grow into a great ". . . hospital city that can cope with the most demanding medical needs . . ."[16]

As part of the inaugural events, the *Casa* hosted an international cardiology symposium, attended by some of the world's greatest heart specialists. Two noted Americans were in attendance, including Dr. Paul Dudley White, who was President Eisenhower's personal physician. After the ceremonies, Padre Pio was able to meet with the doctors, and later Dr. White expressed his great admiration for Padre Pio's vision. He remarked, "This clinic, more than any other in the world, seems to me to be more adapted to the study of the relationship which runs between the spirit and the sickness."[17]

One of the subsequent Health Directors of the hospital, Dr. Giuseppe Gusso, expounded on the way the *Casa* must approach this relation between "the spirit and the sickness." Everyone connected with the hospital, from Chaplains and doctors, to the nurses and visitors, should be imbued with the spirit of Padre Pio, and view each patient as a sacred brother in need. The sick person should not be considered as just a case, a number, or a bed. "The work of the doctor in particular should be detached from narrow and cold professionalism and has to take into account the sick person in his entirety, since mostly he needs to be cured in the body and at the same time in the spirit."[18]

Only two years after its opening, construction on the first major addition to the original structure was started. The hospital has grown steadily since then, and by the new millennium was admitting over 60,000 patients a year, and treating hundreds of thousands of out-patients. While the *Casa* initially boasted 300 beds, today the complex provides well over 1200 beds. In addition, the "hospital city" maintains farms and orchards that supply olive oil, meat, and dairy products, not only for its own use, but also for the commercial market. Although now owned and operated under Vatican auspices, the *Casa* is also a regional hospital in the Italian health system and is eligible for government funding.[19]

The House for the Relief of Suffering itself is but the core of what is known as the "Work of Padre Pio," which encompasses the whole hospital city effort. Included are homes for spastic and retarded children, orphanages, homes for the aged, nurseries, retreat centers, medical research centers, and professional schools. International conferences are frequently hosted, attracting learned scientists and world-famous doctors. Satellite centers of the *Casa* have been opened in other cities of the region, including San Severo, Rodi Garganico and Vieste. Truly, the Work of Padre Pio continues to grow as he envisioned it, and perhaps even more so. Americans can be proud of the role they played—and continue to play—in making Padre Pio's dream of a hospital that cares for the whole person, body and soul, a concrete reality.

Chapter 28

Padre Pio Prayer Groups

THE worldwide phenomenon of the Padre Pio Prayer Groups has its origins as far back as Padre Pio's 1916 sojourn at St. Anne's Friary in Foggia, when he formed an informal prayer group comprised of some of his first spiritual daughters. Later that year, after his arrival at nearby San Giovanni Rotondo, the Foggia prayer group was re-established at Our Lady of Grace Friary. The impetus for a larger movement, that would extend well beyond San Giovanni Rotondo, came many years later, as the Second World War was raging. Realizing the desperate need for prayer in those trying times, Pope Pius XII made an urgent plea for people everywhere to join together in prayer for peace in the world. He observed that, "Groups of faithful will fully and openly live Christian lives, as His Holiness wishes, if they are first groups of people who pray together."[1]

Padre Pio's response was immediate. To a group of spiritual children who had gathered in his cell, he said, "Let's do something about it. Let's roll up our sleeves and be the first to respond to the appeal of our Roman Pontiff."[2] The news of Padre Pio's wishes spread by word of mouth among his devotees, and soon informal prayer meetings sprang up in many parts of Italy. There were no formal rules or requirements, and initially no real structure. People simply met once or twice a month in churches to pray the Rosary and attend Mass. In Padre Pio's words, "I have not organized groups; I invited souls to pray together, as Jesus wants."[3]

The prayer meetings continued informally after the War

222

until, providentially, they came to be associated with Padre Pio's new hospital. As construction progressed on the *Casa Sollievo della Sofferenza*, it became evident that the hospital's supporters should receive news updates on the course of the work. This resulted in the publication in 1949 of a biweekly informational bulletin, which was given the same name as the hospital. This publication also began to carry news of some of the gatherings of Padre Pio devotees that were praying together according to his wishes. In short order, these prayer meetings spontaneously spread all over Italy and beyond, and the hospital bulletin quickly became the source for announcements of their locations and activities. In 1950, Dr. Sanguinetti, the medical director of the *Casa*, for the first time used the formal designation "Prayer Group" in the bulletin.

Padre Pio and the hospital's directors realized that the spiritual benefits of the prayer groups would complement the physical treatments of the medical doctors, in a synthesis of prayer and action. This balance between the hospital and the prayer groups would be underscored more than half a century later by Pope John Paul II. In a letter addressed to Archbishop Domenico D'Ambrosio, the current Vatican administrator for the Works of Padre Pio, the Holy Father wrote:

> The spiritual movement inspired by the charism of St. Pio of Pietrelcina did not end with his earthly death; on the contrary, it has continued to grow, becoming significantly important to the life of the entire Church . . . He was able to recognize the Suffering Christ not only in the interior colloquium of prayer, but also in his encounters with people visited by illness, and he strove to bring them comfort. He thus became a moving example of human sensitivity,

presenting anew in himself two characteristics pecu-
liar to the Franciscan and Capuchin tradition: con-
templative prayer and effective charity. The Prayer
Groups he founded are an expression of the former;
the *Casa Sollievo della Sofferenza* is a rare witness to
the latter.[4]

By 1951, Dr. Sanguinetti had codified the regulations for
the prayer groups, with Padre Pio's guidance. The hospital
had now become the *de facto* center for prayer group activities. As put forth in a book published by the hospital in 1986,
"It was the ever present impetus of the *Casa* to promote,
develop and organize the prayer groups as the other face of
the relief of suffering, in a Christian sense."[5] As the number
of groups grew, and expanded to other countries, conventions
were held on regional, national and finally international levels. An International Convention of Prayer Groups was held
in honor of the 50th anniversary of Padre Pio's stigmata,
September 20, 1968. At that time the apostolate had grown
to over 700 groups, with 68,000 members in 15 countries. By
the turn of the century, there were a phenomenal half a million members in 3,000 groups worldwide.

The official, Vatican-approved statute for the groups was
implemented in May of 1986. It defines the overall purpose
of the groups, which is ". . . to promote the spreading of the
Kingdom of God, according to the teaching of Christ, who
repeatedly insisted on the necessity of prayer."[6] Completely
loyal to the Catholic Faith, and organized under the hierarchy, groups normally meet monthly for Mass and
prayers, under the guidance of a spiritual director nomi-
nated by the local bishop. Groups pray primarily for the
Church and for the Holy Father. Other prayer intentions
include: ". . . the conversion of sinners and of atheists, the
sick, especially the incurable, the old and other intentions,

which include the needs of the Church and society at any particular time."[7] Members are also encouraged to engage in concrete works of charity, especially for the sick, the old and the marginalized.

A Padre Pio Prayer Group is not initiated by the Church hierarchy; it is generally the result of a grass-roots movement by some of the faithful in a local area who wish to pray together in the spirit of Padre Pio. It is necessary to find a priest willing to be the spiritual director, together with a suitable meeting place, which should be a church or oratory, used with the permission of the pastor. The approval of the local bishop is needed before the group can be officially recognized. The formal organization of each group is minimal, with the primary officer being a group leader who assists the spiritual director. Ideally, the spiritual director is present at prayer meetings, which should be held before the Blessed Sacrament.

In the United States there are about 100 groups, reporting to the current National Director, Fr. Francis Sariego, a Capuchin. Fr. Sariego has instituted a web site* that will be a permanent reference source for announcements and contact information. He feels that the Padre Pio Prayer Groups can be a powerful force in the United States. In essence, they are a strong Catholic Action body, whereby the laity become well-grounded in their Faith, based on devotion to the Eucharist, Our Lady, and the Holy Father and Magisterium. Bound together as a group, each member is helped to live out the Gospel in the spirit of Padre Pio and is called to provide assistance on a material level where needed.[8]

Many of the groups in North America have been started with the help of some of Padre Pio's special spiritual children who have a calling to assist others in the creation of his

---

* The address of the site is www.pppg.org

prayer groups. On the West coast, Charles Mandina, who was a close friend of Padre Pio and is mentioned in many articles and books about the Saint, has helped start a large number of them.[9] Since 1968, he has assisted in the foundation of fourteen in the Los Angeles area, and three in Mexico—two of these are in Mexico City and one is in Monterrey. Charles also helped start groups in Oregon, New York, Hawaii, and the Philippines, and most recently helped a new prayer group get started in West Covino, California. Charles notes that in the 1960's it was very difficult to establish prayer groups on the West Coast, for the simple reason that very few people knew who Padre Pio was at that time.

The type of support and counsel provided by Charles Mandina for the groups he works with is spiritually based, as well as organizational. He emphasizes that each person must first of all be grounded in humility and prayer. The essential purpose of a group is to bring its members closer to God, within an atmosphere of sincere and humble prayer. Such love of God silently leads to loving concern for others' needs, through Padre Pio's intercession. Charles views the groups as providing a valuable means of spiritual growth for countless people.

Charles began his prayer group ministry as the result of his personal friendship with Padre Pio, who inspired him to undertake this important mission. Charles Mandina's visits to San Giovanni Rotondo began in the early 1960's, and he would remain there for two or three weeks at a time. Then, in 1966, Padre Pio asked him to stay longer and help Fr. Alessio Parente and William Martin (the future Fr. Joseph Pius) in assisting the English-speaking pilgrims who were flocking to the monastery. Charles spent the next six months working in the Friary and was privileged to see Padre Pio every day and attend his morning Mass. For five of those months, Mass started at 5:00 a.m.; but during one month,

Padre Pio felt that more reparation had to be offered to the Lord, so he started the Mass at 4:00 a.m.! One of Padre Pio's biographers and confreres, Padre Ripabottoni, commented about those early-morning Masses: "He celebrates Mass at an extremely early hour, 4:00 a.m., in the presence of many people who wait for more than an hour in front of the church and who compete with one another in order to obtain seats nearest the altar."[10]

English-speaking pilgrims wishing to talk to the Padre often came to Charles Mandina first, and when possible, he would bring them to the Saint and act as an interpreter. At certain times he could smell the supernatural perfume of flowers associated with Padre Pio and his stigmata. He recounts an incident when a skeptical doctor from overseas came to the monastery full of doubts about Padre Pio and his sanctity. But when the Padre permitted this man to experience, with unusual intensity, this mystical perfume, the doctor immediately dropped to his knees before the Saint. Mandina observes, "Curiosity might bring people to him, but once you had seen Padre Pio, you couldn't explain it, but you were changed."[11]

In the evenings, Charles would often stop at Mary Pyle's home for a visit. This "very intelligent and humble woman" was now in her seventies and in poor health. Charles, along with any others who happened to be at the Pink House, would gather around her bedside and listen to her relate stories of life alongside Padre Pio. She suggested to Charles that he join the Third Order of St. Francis, the same lay person's order of which she was a member. A few years later, after both Padre Pio and Mary Pyle had passed on, Charles was accepted into the Third Order at the monastery in San Giovanni Rotondo by Fr. Alessio and Fr. Joseph. (To Americans, these two well-liked Capuchins were often known as "Father" rather than "Padre.")

Charles says the prayer groups were very close to Padre Pio's heart. He was able to speak to him in Confession just four days before Padre Pio's death in 1968, during which the Saint promised his blessing for the groups. Charles was in San Giovanni Rotondo that week to attend the International Convention of Prayer Groups, which coincided with the 50th anniversary of Padre Pio's reception of the stigmata. He had the privilege of attending the last Mass the Saint celebrated, a solemn High Mass which was sung on September 22, 1968, the day prior to Padre Pio's death.

Charles continued to assist the newly-formed prayer group in Monterrey, Mexico. The group's leader and founder, Magneli Villanueva, says that Charles Mandina's help was especially needed and appreciated in order successfully to establish the Monterrey group, which began in 2003.[12] According to Villanueva, ". . . Padre Pio is well known in the USA, since many soldiers met him or heard about him during the War, but this does not happen here at Monterrey . . . you have to work hard to make him known . . ." During meetings, the 80-member group prays the Rosary while the Blessed Sacrament is exposed; this is followed by Mass, and afterwards a small talk is given on the spirituality of Padre Pio. The talk tries to communicate on a personal, meaningful level the ways that Padre Pio's life, teachings and powerful intercession lead one closer to the Lord. It may touch on those areas dear to the Padre, such as the Madonna, Guardian Angels, or the souls in Purgatory.

Villanueva notes that ". . . people begin to transform their souls when they become spiritual children of Padre through the prayer group." She adds that Charles ". . . has been of great help through his counsel, advice, prayers and ideas. He is always interested in how the group is doing. Prayer groups are a core issue of his life . . . he keeps you on track and always makes it clear that we of ourselves are nothing, the ones who are really at work in a prayer group are Jesus, the Madonna, and Padre." In addition to receiving support from Charles, she also was generously assisted by Amos Miller from a Chicago area prayer group, especially regarding leadership and practical considerations. As this edition was being prepared for publication, we learned that Charles Mandina passed away on April 3, 2005, Divine Mercy Sunday, at the very hour of Mercy, 3:00 p.m.

One of the most active Americans in promoting the prayer groups has been Mario Bruschi of New York City.[13] Mario first encountered Padre Pio in the summer of 1957, and like so many others had a life-changing experience. On a pilgrimage to San Giovanni Rotondo with his mother, the restless young Bruschi reluctantly went to Confession to Padre Pio at her request. Padre Pio calmed the nervous penitent, but at the conclusion of his Confession, instead of reciting the formula of absolution, he gave Mario his blessing only. Mario did not realize this until later that day, when he described his experience to a friar he had befriended. This friar then took him to a private room in the monastery, heard Mario's Confession, and gave him sacramental absolution. Following this, the friar accompanied him to Padre Pio's cell, and encouraged Mario to ask Padre Pio for absolution. Again, the Saint would only give him a blessing.[14]

Mario ". . . slowly walked out of the monastery, experiencing loneliness, sadness, bewilderment, and a contrite state of mind."[15] But the events of that day made him realize the necessity of turning his life toward God and to the Sacraments of the Church. Mario says that this "spiritually overwhelming" experience was the greatest thing that ever happened to him. Once a lukewarm Catholic, he now fervently practices his Faith—attending daily Mass and going to Confession every two weeks, in addition to praying the Rosary and other devotions. In gratitude to Padre Pio, he has spent over 40 years in a myriad of activities dedicated to making the Saint known and loved throughout the United States and overseas.

Mario soon founded a Padre Pio Prayer Group in New York City, and also helped start one in Cleveland. He subsequently became regional head of the New York area groups, and in 1979 convened a meeting of the leaders of all of the prayer groups in the country, where they could share their experiences and encourage one another. At about this time, he was contacted by a religious Sister from the Shrine of the Blue Army of Our Lady of Fatima in Washington, New Jersey. The Sister asked him to coordinate a Padre Pio Day of Prayer at the Shrine, since Padre Pio is the spiritual patron of the Blue Army. Thus, in 1980, Bruschi organized the first Day of Prayer, which attracted 400 prayer group members and other Padre Pio devotees from the greater New York area. The event has been held annually ever since. The number of participants has grown to over 3,000, including many priests and bishops, with attendees arriving from as far away as California and Florida. In addition to talks and presentations about Padre Pio, there is an outdoor Mass.

In 1989, Mario invited the then Vatican administrator for the International Prayer Groups, Monsignor Riccardo Ruotolo, to New York to say Mass for his group. Shortly thereafter, Monsignor Ruotolo appointed Mario as National Coordinator for the prayer groups in the United States. Mario Bruschi held this position for seven years, providing guidance to existing groups and helping to start many new ones. He tried to ensure that groups conformed to the intentions of the Prayer Group Statutes, meeting monthly in a church or oratory, with a priest for a spiritual director. He says that, ideally, meetings should consist of the Rosary, Mass and, if possible, a Holy Hour before the Blessed Sacrament, with a social afterwards. He adds, "Joining a Padre Pio Prayer Group makes one a spiritual child of Padre Pio, provided we don't make him lose face."

Mario is also the founder and director of the National Office of the Devotees of Padre Pio, an organization started with the permission of John Cardinal O'Connor and the Archdiocese of New York. The purpose of the National Office is to spread knowledge of Padre Pio and what he represents, which is devotion to Christ through the altar and the confessional. The National Office promotes the annual Padre Pio Day of Prayer at the Blue Army Fatima Shrine, provides information on how to begin a prayer group, holds conferences, and shows films about the Saint. During conferences Mario Bruschi often presents the personal testimony of his 1957 encounter with Padre Pio. After his talks, individuals frequently approach him, including fallen-away nuns and priests, attesting that the story of Padre Pio has touched them so profoundly that they have decided to return to the Church and to the Sacraments.

Bruschi has given many hundreds of presentations on Padre Pio, not only in North America, but also in India and Sri Lanka. He met his Sri Lankan wife, Sarojini, in New York, when she attended one of his prayer group meetings. Married in 1972, they have been blessed with four children. His biggest audience was in India, where 16,000,000 people watched his televised talk and film on the Saint. Mario is currently helping the Archbishop of Sri Lanka raise funds for the construction of a Padre Pio shrine church near the city of Colombo. It will be the first such church dedicated to the Saint in that part of the world, where there are mostly Buddhists and Moslems.

Currently he leads two Padre Pio Prayer Groups in New York City. In addition to his Padre Pio activities, since 1970

he has coordinated First Friday all-night vigils in honor of
the Sacred and Immaculate Hearts of Jesus and Mary. The
vigils, which include Mass, Rosary, and devotional prayers,
are held at Our Lady of Peace Church on East 62nd Street
in New York City.*

*Mario Bruschi can be contacted by phone at 212-838-6549, or by writing
to him at 1154 First Avenue, New York, NY 10021.

Chapter 29

The Last Decade

THE opening of the Hospital in May of 1956, and the dedication of a large new church three years later, signaled a period of flourishing activity for the ancient town of San Giovanni Rotondo and the Friary. The new church building was adjacent to the tiny, original chapel of Our Lady of Grace, and it could accommodate a thousand worshippers. In 1958, on only the second anniversary of the hospital, work commenced on a new wing of the *Casa*, that would house a nursing school and residence, and provide additional services for the sick. The expanding Hospital and the new church, and of course Padre Pio himself, attracted ever increasing numbers of people to the area. Pilgrims, curiosity-seekers, medical professionals, patients seeking treatment at the *Casa*, or perhaps hoping for a miraculous cure from the Saint, all flocked to the city on the mountain. The local economy of San Giovanni Rotondo thrived from the influx of guests and their money, leading to the construction of sorely-needed hotels and restaurants, and improvements in the roads and services. A new 20th-century quarter of the city arose along the former mule trail which had connected the Friary with the old town center of San Giovanni Rotondo.

It might be expected that the last decade of Padre Pio's life would be a time of peaceful, tranquil enjoyment of the fruits of his long and arduous ministry. He had gained international fame for his stigmata, his miracles and his works. San Giovanni Rotondo, and even Pietrelcina, were now under a spotlight, and it seemed as if the earlier suppressions of his ministry were destined to be an historical footnote. But then, on October 9, 1958, Pope Pius XII passed away.

This Pope, who inspired Padre Pio to begin his prayer groups, had supported him in his work and pastoral activities for the past twenty years. Padre Pio was relatively free of harassment from Church authorities during that time, except for some minor difficulties in the early 1950's. Beginning in 1951, the Holy Office and Capuchin officials resumed some of their visitations and investigations, due to the usual charges of fanaticism and confusion surrounding the activities at the Friary. In order to stem the enthusiastic tide of Padre Pio's devotees, the Capuchin Minister General urged that pilgrimages to San Giovanni Rotondo not be promoted by the clergy and that writings and photos of him should not be distributed.[1]

The most serious development during this period was the condemnation by the Vatican of eight books written about him, because the authors had not obtained ecclesiastical approval before printing them. Ironically, some of these works, which were placed on the *Index* of forbidden books, are now considered historical sources for information on the Saint. It was true that there were often "pious exaggerations," if not outright fabrications, of miraculous occurrences attributed to Padre Pio that were occasionally published. Mary Pyle used to wryly refer to these publications as "Third Editions." Padre Pio would say to her, "Don't worry, it's going to get worse!"[2]

However, in spite of the restrictions and visitations, there had been no real suppression of Padre Pio's ministry that was comparable to the events of the early 1920's and the "imprisonment" of the 1930's. But the passing of Pope Pius XII, the "sweet Christ on earth" as Padre Pio referred to him,[3] and the election of John XXIII to the seat of Peter, marked the beginning of a long period of severe trials for him. In many ways, because of his advanced age, and the stature and level of respect he had attained throughout the world, this final cross was his biggest. What occurred was not just a suppression of his ministry, but a personal humiliation of the man—if not outright persecution.

The very success of his hospital was one reason for Padre Pio's difficulties. The steady stream of contributions for the *Casa* that came pouring into the Friary became a source of contention and quarrels, in the wake of financial problems within the Capuchin Order in Italy. The Capuchins had fallen prey to a financial wheeler-dealer named Giambattista Giuffre. He had concocted a pyramid-like investment scheme, whereby he would pay very high interest rates *in advance* on sums consigned to him. The rates that "God's Banker" offered have been reported to be from 30% interest,[4] to as high as 90%.[5] Many Church organizations, including the Capuchins, rushed to invest large sums of money with Giuffre. The success of his scheme depended on constantly finding new buyers, who would provide the capital for the high interest payments to the existing investors.

The Capuchins were hoping they would be able to make a significant return on their shares, enabling them to complete the rebuilding of their war-ravaged monasteries. Several Capuchin superiors asked their monks to approach friends and relatives for loans and donations, so that the monks could then invest that money with Giuffre.[6] Capuchin functionaries also approached Padre Pio and asked him to invest some of the funds arriving for the hospital with "God's Banker," so that the whole Capuchin Order could benefit from the high interest rates. After examining the necessary documents, Padre Pio sensed something was wrong, and refused to turn over any money earmarked for the hospital. He had ultimate administrative control over the hospital and its funds,[7] and had even been dispensed from his vow of poverty in so far as it affected accepting donations for the *Casa*. But with his refusal to invest with Giuffre, the first rumblings of discontent over his control of the hospital were heard, in spite of the *Casa's* great success.

In the summer of 1958, "God's Banker," Giambattista Giuffre, declared bankruptcy. The financial blow to the Church was so severe that the Vatican was forced to set up a commission of Cardinals to engage in damage-control. The commission ordered that religious orders had to make full restitution to everyone they had borrowed money from, which had been invested with Giuffre. The Capuchins were especially hard hit, and they faced an economic disaster.[8] Capuchin officials approached Padre Pio once again, this time to seek loans from the hospital donations to repay those who were cheated in the Giuffre scheme. And once again, Padre Pio refused to part with the hospital's money, saying that it did not belong to him but to the *Casa*. This second refusal further aroused the resentments and jealousies harbored by Padre Pio's detractors, and the old accusations of improprieties surrounding Padre Pio's ministry were made with renewed vigor. A primary motive behind the allegations was an attempt to take control of the hospital from him. There were even reports that the Minister General of the Capuchins had denounced him to Pope John XXIII himself, as being a poor administrator, disobedient and morally unfit.[9]

In the spring of 1960, shocking rumors surfaced that various areas of the Friary were being bugged with tape recorders and microphones, in order to spy on Padre Pio. According to the reports, listening devices had been installed in the Friary guest room where Padre Pio met with visitors. Supposedly, recorders were also placed in his own cell, and even in his confessional. The exact facts are hard to determine, although many years later, in 1989, the Capuchins admitted that the Friary parlor had been bugged, but denied knowledge of any other locations.[10] The reason given for making the recordings was that the Superior of the monastery at that time, Padre Emilio of Matrice, wanted to obtain proof that nothing irregular was occurring between Padre Pio and his spiritual daughters.

Whether his confessional and cell were secretly rigged with listening devices, and who did it, are still matters of speculation. Emmanuele Brunatto published evidence he had gathered, in an attempt to prove that secret microphones were indeed placed in Padre Pio's cell. On the other hand, the Vatican newspaper *L'Osservatore Romano* printed a denial that his confessional was ever bugged.[11] However, a recent biography asserts that Padre Pio himself discovered tape recorders in his confessional, and tearfully reported it to the Archbishop of Manfredonia.[12] When news of the bugging incidents was reported in the secular press, they did their best to sensationalize the story, adding further to the cloud of confusion and intrigue swirling around Padre Pio.

Finally, the Vatican decided it was time to act, but it was not in defense of the Saint. At the request of the Capuchin Minister General, Pope John XXIII appointed Msgr. Carlo Maccari as an official apostolic visitor to Our Lady of Grace Friary. The investigation lasted from July through October of 1960. The visit began during planning for a grand celebration in honor of the 50th anniversary of Padre Pio's Ordination, on August 10th. As a harbinger of the final report that he would issue, Maccari ordered a curtailment of the ceremonies, prohibiting any special speeches. He also suspended a special edition of the magazine published by the *Casa*, that was to commemorate the anniversary.[13] Maccari's assistant began to oversee the opening of Padre Pio's mail in order to verify that donations were being properly handled.

He even followed the mail carriers to make sure all letters were delivered to their intended recipients and soon started opening the mail himself.[14] Maccari interviewed only a few of the friars, instead spending most of his time talking to Padre Pio's detractors among the local clergy, including those who had made accusations as far back as the 1920's.

When he finally got around to talking to Padre Pio himself, it is reported that he deeply hurt the Saint with his criticism of the hospital. He is said to have told Padre Pio that the hospital would likely have to close its doors upon his death because he failed to locate it in a major city.[15] Apparently, Maccari was one of those who subscribed to the notion that San Giovanni Rotondo would become a ghost town with Padre Pio's passing. His denigration of the hospital hinted at the secret agenda apparently underlying the whole visitation, which was to wrest control of the *Casa* and its finances from Padre Pio's hands. In the history of the hospital published by the *Casa* itself, Padre Pio's humiliation during the investigation was aptly described: "These were bitter days and months. For Padre Pio it was the start of a long agony. His time of joy was ended."[16]

Only one day after Maccari completed his "inquisition," a new superior arrived at Our Lady of Grace Friary. He was Padre Rosario of Aliminusa, a Sicilian and a strict disciplinarian. Soon afterwards, the Provincial Minister was replaced, and then Padre Pio's friend of so many years, Padre Raffaele, was assigned to another monastery. Other transfers of friars who had been Padre Pio's close friends soon followed. On January 31, 1961, the prefect of the Holy Office, Alfredo Cardinal Ottaviani, sent a long report to Padre Rosario, outlining the restrictions to be placed on Padre Pio, in order to insure that no special "cult" revolved around him.

From now on the time of his daily Mass would be varied, and the duration of the celebration could not exceed 40 minutes. Other priests or bishops were no longer allowed to assist on the altar at his Masses. Penitents were to be given a maximum of three minutes in order to make their Confession to him. The faithful were prohibited from congregating near his confessional, the sacristy and even the friary garden. This was done to prevent attempts by anyone to speak with him. Under no circumstances could he receive or talk to women alone. He was prohibited from conducting weddings or Baptisms. Railings were to be erected around the womens' confessionals to prevent eavesdropping or interruptions. Furthermore, two iron gates were to be erected in the hallway connecting the old church with the new one, as an impediment to gaining access to him. Understandably, the gates and railings sent an ominous message to his outraged devotees: Padre Pio was a prisoner in his own monastery.[17,18,19]

In addition to these directives from the Vatican, the new superior, Padre Rosario, added some of his own, that only further offended the faithful. He erected signs in the church warning people not to talk to Padre Pio outside of the confessional. He prohibited the friars from showing any kind of special respect for him, and they were even prevented from helping the stigmatized Friar climb up and down the stairs. He was not allowed to visit the sick in his own hospital. There were no longer to be special Masses for the pilgrims who would come to celebrate with Padre Pio on major feast days, such as Easter and Christmas. Incredibly, it is reported that he actually told Padre Pio that he could no longer weep while he was saying Mass.[20]

The oppression did not end here. On November 17, 1961, the Capuchin Minister General arrived in person to have Padre Pio sign the papers which would end his administration of the *Casa* and its finances, and turn over control of the hospital to the Vatican. In response to those who wanted to protest this humiliation by holding back their financial support of the hospital, Padre Pio dissuaded them with this reminder: "But I am still the founder of what is God's Work."[21]

Through all this, Padre Pio's defenders and friends were not sitting by passively. The town mayor, Francesco Morcaldi (yes, he was back as mayor after all these years), contacted the Vatican Secretary of State on behalf of the citizenry, imploring him to lift the restrictions. The townspeople demonstrated, and held up signs calling for the punishment of Padre Pio's "jailers."[22] But it was Padre Pio's old friend and confidant Emmanuele Brunatto who took the boldest steps. He returned from France to Rome, where he met with Padre Pio's supporters to devise a strategy for his liberation.

In mid-1962, he formed the "International Association for the Defense of Padre Pio." He prepared a "White Paper" for delivery to the United Nations, documenting that Padre Pio's basic human rights and dignity were being violated by the Capuchins and the Vatican. The paper was ready by the next June. Before it was formally presented, copies were sent to the newly elected Pope Paul VI, the UN Secretary General, the President of Italy, and all of the Bishops attending the Second Vatican Council, which was then in session. In the spring of 1964, Brunatto scheduled a highly publicized conference for the press and international dignitaries in Geneva, Switzerland, in order to go public with the "White Paper." However, ten days before the conference was to take place, Brunatto received an urgent message from Padre Pio asking him to call off the entire effort. Brunatto was upset and confused at the unexpected request, but he dutifully obeyed his spiritual father.[23]

Padre Pio's rescuer this time was not to be Brunatto, but the Vatican itself, in the person of the newly elected pontiff, Pope Paul VI. Pope Paul informed Cardinal Ottaviani of his desire that Padre Pio should be allowed to carry out his ministry in complete freedom, instead of being treated "like a criminal."[24,25] Apparently, this good news had reached Padre Pio in time for him to call off Brunatto's distribution of the "White Paper," with its devastating criticism of Church authorities for their maltreatment of him.

Before becoming Pope, Cardinal Giovanni Montini had been a great admirer of Padre Pio and was convinced of his sanctity and of the value of his ministry. In fact, on the occasion of the 50th anniversary of Padre Pio's Ordination (the very celebration which Msgr. Maccari had restricted), Padre Pio received a congratulatory letter from Cardinal Montini, who was then the Archbishop of Milan. In the letter, the Cardinal expressed his ". . . congratulations for the immense graces that have been bestowed upon you, and which have been dispensed by you." He commended Padre Pio for a priesthood ". . . which was favored by so many gifts and so much fecundity."[26]

There are many stories about Padre Pio's ability to predict future popes, and the case of Cardinal Montini was no exception. In 1958, he had asked a confrere to convey to the Archbishop of Milan the message that he would one day be Pope and that he should be prepared. He made the same prediction right after the death of John XXIII, in response to the repeated entreaties of his fellow friars, curious to know what the result of the papal conclave would be.[27]

Though he could now resume his ministry as before, the last few years of his life were not kind to Padre Pio. The dissent within the Church that resulted from the implementation of Vatican II saddened him, as did the general moral decline that occurred in the 1960's. What made matters worse were a long series of deaths that occurred among his close friends and people dear to him. In May of 1963, his oldest friend and former spiritual director, Padre Agostino, passed on. In November, the assassination of America's first Catholic President, John F. Kennedy, deeply grieved him. The next year another beloved friend, Padre Paolino, died. Then it was the turn of Emmanuele Brunatto. In 1967, his brother Michele Forgione passed away. In 1968, shortly before his own death, Padre Pio's close spiritual daughter and collaborator of 45 years, Mary Pyle, expired peacefully in her hospital bed at the *Casa*.

L'Americana, afflicted by high blood pressure and crippling arthritis, had suffered a series of strokes and also had a heart condition. In November of 1964, when she was 76, she became seriously ill, and never fully regained her health for the remaining three-and-a-half years of her life. The onset of her illness was so severe that in that same month she composed her final will and spiritual testament. In it she thanked God for enabling her to survive the initial crisis, which she now regarded as a warning that her passing might be soon. "From now on, I shall accept Sister Death on any day, at any hour that is pleasing to God . . ." In death she wished to be clothed in the Franciscan habit, with cord and sandals, and desired to be interred in the Capuchin's burial chapel, located in the San Giovanni Rotondo town cemetery. She bequeathed all her possessions to the Capuchin Fathers of the Foggia province; this included her own "Pink Castle" at San Giovanni Rotondo. The two Forgione family homes that she had purchased in Pietrelcina were also entrusted to the Capuchins ". . . so that they may preserve them for posterity as a remembrance of . . . Padre Pio of Pietrelcina and of his simple and humble parents, Uncle Orazio and Aunt Maria Giuseppa."[28]

Eventually, as age and illness took their toll, she found it ever more difficult to attend Padre Pio's daily 5:00 a.m. Mass. To arrive at the Friary, she had to navigate a steep iron stairway that had been built into the side of the hill that led from her home to the monastery. Even within her house, in order to reach her tiny bedroom, she had to climb the long, treacherous flight of stairs upon which Padre Pio's father Grazio had tripped and fallen. Heeding Padre Pio's advice, she had a small elevator built in the "pink castle"—at least her worries over one set of stairs would be eliminated. Eventually, her personal physician told her that she should stop going to the Friary for Mass altogether. Her reply was, "I prefer to die rather than give up Holy Mass!"[29] Instead, she had a taxi cab drive her there for Mass and Confession. In the end, Padre Pio himself had to tell her to attend Mass only on Sundays and Holy Days; the other days someone from the Friary would bring Holy Communion to her at home. The time had arrived for her to accept the fact that her health no longer allowed her to attend daily Mass, and she obediently bowed to the wishes of her spiritual father.

Padre Pio had once told Mary that she would be the first to die and that he would follow soon after. Her view was that, "Without Padre Pio, I do not wish to stay, neither on earth or in heaven."[30] During the last few months of her life, she was visited by many of her American relatives, including in-laws, nieces, nephews and even grand-nephews. The joy and consolation she received from their presence did not cause Mary to overlook her role as Padre Pio's collaborator. The visitors responded to her suggestion that they support the Pietrelcina Friary she had endowed, by donating funds for a new heating system and gymnasium.

During Easter week of 1968 her condition worsened, and on the morning of her 80th birthday, April 17, she was admitted to Padre Pio's hospital. Initially she had resisted going, insisting she wanted to die in her own home, on her own hard bed. But when she found out that Padre Pio agreed with her doctor that she should be taken to the hospital, she complied—on the condition that her nurse would be Maria

Salvatori, an old friend. She only survived for nine days following her admission to the *Casa*. When the end was near, a friar approached Padre Pio in the monastery to ask him if he would like to see her at the hospital. Padre Pio, who himself was weak and ailing, was pained on hearing she had another stroke, and could only reply, "I shall pray to the Lord that He greet her in Paradise with the angels." After some moments he reflected, "She can finally listen to the Heavenly melodies without having to play the organ . . ."[31]

Maria Salvatori was with her on the evening of April 25, trying to cheer her by talking about the impending visit in June of some of her relatives, in honor of her recent birthday. Then, seeing that Mary was rapidly failing, she put in an urgent call for the doctor. At 11:00 p.m., as she was assuring her patient that she would be well enough to see her relatives, Mary Pyle's head fell back, and it was over. Maria Salvatori rang a bell, and as soon as a nurse arrived, asked her to hurry and fetch a priest to administer the Sacrament of the Last Rites. When the doctor finally entered the room, Mary's face and lips had already paled. Realizing that it was too late to do anything for Mary, he appeared annoyed that he had been summoned, in spite of Maria Salvatori's explanation that she had called for him while Mary Pyle was still alive. Another 20 minutes passed before the priest arrived.

What happened next was one of those mysterious, unexplainable events that one associates with the lives of holy persons. As soon as the prayers of the Last Rites (Extreme Unction) were begun by the priest, color returned to Mary's face and lips, her mouth opened, and Maria Salvatori verified that she could feel her pulse. It appeared that she had returned to life in order to receive the Last Rites of the Church! As the prayers of the Sacrament were intoned, Mary quietly uttered the words, as if to herself, "Even this is needed!"[32] When the ritual was over, Mary's body ceased to function once again, and her soul took its definitive flight. Maria Salvatori would later state, "I am willing to swear, even on my deathbed, before God and Our Lady, before anyone, that she was dead and returned to life in order to receive the Sacrament of Extreme Unction. . . ." Maria Salvatori added: ". . . her heart had stopped; yet without any stimulant whatever, without injections, it began to beat again."[33]

The funeral in Our Lady of Grace Church was attended by a large crowd of friars and townspeople, including 80 seminarians from the Pietrelcina monastery that she had founded. Friars from many other locations in the province also attended, since, in the words of the eulogist Padre Carmelo di Donato, "There is no monastery that has not received some gift from her, some token of her charity . . ." The eulogy praised Mary for being concerned for everyone who came to her, and who found ". . . in her a mother who did without in order to help others."[34]

Padre Pio was too ill and weak to participate actively in the ceremony, but he watched it from the gallery of the church. As she had requested, Mary was laid out in the Capuchin habit, and her remains were to be placed in the Capuchin Chapel of the village cemetery. The cortege made its way from Our Lady of Grace across town to her final resting place, passing a long line of mourners. A woman in the crowd impulsively cried out words that expressed why Mary was so dear to the people of San Giovanni Rotondo: "I thank you Miss Pyle, for that bread that you always gave me! I shall always pray for you. Thank you! Thank you!"[35] Her body was placed in the same Capuchin Chapel where both of Padre Pio's parents, who had died in her home, were interred. On her tomb inscribed in gold letters are the words:

Adelia Mary Pyle
Full of charity and of seraphic virtue
May you remain eternally in the memory
Of Pietrelcina to which you donated a monastery
Of San Giovanni Rotondo,
where you were admired for nine lustra,
docile spiritual daughter of Padre Pio,
from the Capuchin Fathers who wanted you to
rest in this chapel.[36]

In addition to a voluminous correspondence with people throughout the world, and in many languages, Mary left behind a notebook written in Italian. It contained many sayings of Padre Pio, stories of graces received, and various anecdotes and vignettes.[37] There were also three large guestbooks, containing thousands of entries, with addresses, signatures, and declarations of gratitude by her visitors. In a final act of charity, she had many of her papers destroyed, particularly those which recorded those who owed her money, or would cause discomfort to someone after her passing.[38]

Only a few days after Mary's death, Fr. Alessio Parente asked Padre Pio about the current state of her soul. He immediately replied that she was in Purgatory. Alessio was surprised, and reminded him of all the good she had done. Padre Pio's response to that observation was, "Yes . . . but that which she failed to do before."[39] However, not long after this incident, one of Padre Pio's spiritual daughters had a dream about Mary Pyle. In the dream, Mary told her that she was now in Heaven, having entered on May 5, the feast of St. Pius V (in the Traditional calendar). When Padre Pio was informed about the dream and asked if it was true, he gave a reply which implied that Mary was in fact now in Heaven: "She was always a good religious, and the Lord knows how to give a *just reward* to those who deserve it."[40] Evidence of Padre Pio's fondness and appreciation of *l'Americana* can be seen to this day. On the wall of his tiny cell he had placed the *In memoriam* card from her funeral, which carries her picture. It accompanies the photos of his parents and of others very dear to him—Dr. Sanguinetti, Angelo Lupi, and Pope Paul VI.[41]

Chapter 30

Final Weekend . . .
Joy Turned to Mourning

THE events of the past decade had taken an exacting toll on Padre Pio, not only on his physical health, but also on his mental outlook and well-being. He was almost continually ill during the last few years of his life, and felt he was becoming a burden to the community. Friars were assigned in turns to watch over him day and night; an intercom system was installed in his cell and was always kept on. His asthma, bronchitis and coughing were depriving him of even the little sleep that he had normally enjoyed. By the time of his 80th birthday in 1967, he could no longer get out of bed or bathe without someone helping him. He groaned, "I am reduced to a state of helplessness. May the Lord call me now because I am no longer permitted to be of any use to my brethren."[1] When people would ask him how he was feeling, his answer was often, "I am lacking only one thing: the grave."[2]

Another characteristic of his last years was his almost complete silence. He spoke very little and even then only in monosyllables. He was often alone and engaged in prayer. He cut back on the number of Confessions he heard, and frequently was too ill to say Mass. On many days, he would spend the whole time in his room. Yet, at other times he was afraid to be alone, or appeared to be confused. One day, his confrere, Padre D'Apolito, spent an hour speaking quietly with him, and when he was about to leave, Padre Pio exclaimed, "Where are you going? Do not leave me alone!" On another occasion he complained to Padre D'Apolito, "Lord, so much suffering! They have all betrayed me!" Padre D'Apolito did not have the courage to ask him to whom he was referring. During his last months, though he sought death and had begged his superior to give him the obedience to die, he experienced a holy fear at the thought of meeting the Lord. He was heard to say, "Pray for me: I am afraid to meet Christ. I have not corresponded to His love and to His infinite graces."[3]

Padre Pio had predicted the time of his own death on many occasions. When the new friary church at San Giovanni was opened in 1959, work had only just begun on its crypt area. At that time, he accurately foretold to a woman from Naples that he would not die until the final blessing of the crypt; this took place nine years later, on the very eve of his passing. He had also correctly predicted to his blind friend Pietruccio that he would die during his eighty-second year.[4] Approximately two years before his 1968 death, Padre Pio's niece, Pia Forgione Pennelli, had asked him about the outcome of some sensitive family matters. He replied that they would be resolved within two years, but ". . . I will no longer be here. I'll be dead and a lot of things will change." He seemed so certain of his words that she wrote them out and recorded them with a notary.[5] Apparently, Padre Pio had confided to some of his spiritual children that he was given a revelation about his death as early as 1918, shortly after he received the stigmata. He had been praying to Jesus to take away the embarrassing external signs of the stigmata, while still allowing him to feel all of their pain. He heard the Lord reply, "You will bear them for 50 years, and then you will see Me."[6]

In the summer of 1968, Padre D'Apolito received a request from a family in northern Italy, asking that their daughter be allowed to receive her First Holy Communion from Padre Pio. The date was set for the last weekend of August, at which time the family was to make the trip to San Giovanni Rotondo for the ceremony. Then Padre D'Apolito received a letter from them asking to have the ceremony postponed until the next spring, since certain problems would prevent their arrival that summer. Padre Pio told him, "Let them know that they must come, at any cost, on the date set: if they delay, they will no longer find me." Padre D'Apolito informed the family of Padre Pio's ominous words. Fortunately, they were able to overcome their difficulties, allowing their daughter to receive her First Communion at the hands of Padre Pio on August 24, a month before he died.[7]

In another incident involving Padre D'Apolito, a woman making her Confession to him in September of 1968, asked to be allowed to kiss Padre Pio's hand. Padre D'Apolito told her it would be impossible because of the large crowds, but if she came back the next day he would arrange it. The woman began to cry, explaining that she was very poor and had to borrow the money to make the trip from Sicily, and could not afford to stay overnight in a hotel. All her life she had wanted to meet Padre Pio, and a few days ago he had appeared to her in a dream, saying that she should come to San Giovanni Rotondo right away, ". . . because in a few days I am going to die." Moved with compassion upon hearing the woman's story, Padre D'Apolito took her with him to the sacristy, telling her exactly where to stand and wait. A short time later the overjoyed and grateful woman returned to thank Padre D'Apolito. Padre Pio had passed by the very spot where she was standing. Greeting the woman, Padre Pio had placed his hand on her head in blessing, addressing gentle words of comfort to her. She left that evening for Sicily, and two weeks later heard the news that the Saint had died.[8]

The 50th anniversary of Padre Pio's stigmata was on Friday, September 20, 1968. That weekend, an International Congress of the Padre Pio Prayer Groups was scheduled to meet in San Giovanni Rotondo. The Capuchins planned a big celebration to honor Padre Pio on this important anniversary, but they decided to hold the celebrations on Sunday the 22nd, in order to better accommodate the expected flood of pilgrims and prayer group attendees. Thus, the actual anniversary on Friday was scheduled to be just a normal day for Padre Pio, since no commemorative festivities had been arranged. Yet, 2,000 people jammed the 1,000-seat church as he celebrated the early morning Mass at 5:00 a.m. that Friday. The worshippers, perhaps sobered by Padre Pio's frailty and obvious suffering, and seeing him surrounded by priests who had to help him move about, did not applaud or shout when it was over.[9] Afterward, he heard Confessions, and then withdrew for prayer. In the afternoon, he joined in the recitation of the Rosary and the Benediction of the Blessed Sacrament. Other than the crowds, the only outward indication that this day was the anniversary of his stigmata were the 50 vases of red roses donated by his devotees, which decorated the church and the altar. The large crucifix that faces the choir loft, before which he was praying when he received the stigmata, was surrounded by vases of flowers, as was the picture of Our Lady of Grace near the altar.

That evening, a tremendous candlelight procession (*fiaccolata*), complete with marching band and led by the Mayor and town council, made its way through San Giovanni Rotondo and up the hill to the monastery. Almost the entire town, joined by the pilgrims and prayer group members, overflowed the *sagrato* in front of the church. They gathered in large numbers beneath the window of Padre Pio's cell, shouting "*Viva Padre Pio!*"—"Long live Padre Pio!"—hoping he would show himself and impart his blessing. But the

Saint did not appear; he was lying restlessly in bed, exhausted by the events of the day. He did not even witness the impressive fireworks display shot off that night in his honor.

The next morning, Saturday the 21st, he was scheduled to celebrate his 5:00 a.m. Mass as usual. But, while still in his cell preparing for the ceremony, he suffered a severe asthma attack, along with a racing heart and chest pains. His doctor, Giuseppe Sala, was quickly summoned, and he feared the worst. The monastery superior and many of the friars kept vigil in the room until the attack appeared over. Padre Pio himself kept repeating, "It's the end. It's the end."[10] Although unable to appear for Mass, he made a slow recovery during the course of the morning. With help, he managed to attend evening prayers seated in the gallery of the church, where he imparted his blessing on the large assembly of prayer groups gathered below.

Sunday, September 22nd finally arrived, the day set for the grand celebration to honor the 50 years Padre Pio had borne the stigmata. Countless thousands, including representatives of hundreds of prayer groups, were in San Giovanni Rotondo. All the hotels and inns had been booked three months previous. The *Casa* was festooned with lights and banners. A large platform for the featured speakers stood in the church square, and a huge wooden cross was erected overlooking the plaza. Everyone was in a festive mood except the humble Padre himself, who said to his superior, "I am so confused that I should like to run and hide."[11]

Although still very weak, he was feeling a little better that morning, and entered the sacristy at 4:30 a.m. to prepare for the 5:00 Mass. But he was to receive a surprise: the superior of the monastery, Padre Carmelo, asked him to *sing* a solemn High Mass in honor of the Prayer Group convention. Padre Pio complained that it would be too tiring for him, but he resigned himself to obey when Padre Carmelo insisted: "Those are the orders."[12] Soon the doors of the church were opened, and an immense crowd surged forward. People were packed into every corner, and those who could not gain entrance were forced to stand outside in the piazza. According to the Friary chronicles for that day, "The crowd seemed to be delirious with joy on seeing him and on celebrating his feast day, and silence and order was obtained not with a little difficulty."[13] Two priests helped him to the altar, and he was seated facing the worshippers as he began the Mass. Most Catholic Masses by this time were now being said in a new format, and in the native tongue instead of Latin. However, Padre Pio had a dispensation to perform the ceremony in the traditional Latin Tridentine Rite that he had used throughout his life, with the exception that he was to face the people instead of the altar. As a concession to his age and frailty, he was permitted to offer the Mass seated.

As he sang the High Mass, film and television crews recorded the event for future generations. Even the BBC had flown in a crew from England to make a documentary feature about him.[14] His voice was shaky and tired, and at one point he simply spoke the words, because he was too exhausted to chant. At other times it seemed he was confused and needed prompting by the assistants. Yet, at the Consecration of the bread and wine into the Body and Blood of Christ, he was completely absorbed in the Mystery that was unfolding. During the ceremony, two girls and a boy came forward to receive their First Holy Communion from his hands.[15]

When the solemn High Mass was over, the church was transformed into a chamber of joyful cheering. The Friary annals recorded the ". . . deafening and never-ending applause with sincere cries of 'Viva Padre Pio!', 'Best wishes, Padre!'" that greeted him as he descended the altar.[16] But suddenly the crowd gasped in horror, as the Padre teetered and stumbled on the altar stairway, and began to fall backwards. Nearby priests rushed to assist him. The young American, Brother Bill Martin, dashed about 20 feet from where he was standing, and cradled Padre Pio in his arms to prevent his falling. Padre Pio was eased into a hastily procured wheelchair, and was slowly taken into the sacristy. As he passed by the congregation for what would be the last time, he raised his hand in blessing, lovingly repeating "My Children! My Children!"

The small chapel and tomb in the crypt area below the church, where Padre Pio was to be laid to rest some day, had recently been completed. At 10:00 a.m. on the 22nd, Padre Clemente, a Capuchin official from Rome, gave the official blessing to the tomb. No one suspected how soon it would be occupied. At 10:30 Padre Pio made an unexpected appearance at the choir window in the old church to give his personal blessing to the crowd below. He had planned to give a greeting at noon, but he was extremely tired and wanted to appear sooner, so that he could then rest for awhile. He came to the window assisted by two friars, and waved his handkerchief to the cheers and excited applause of the assembled pilgrims. Later that evening, at 6:00, the prayer groups gathered in the church for the evening Mass. Padre Pio watched from the balcony in his wheelchair, and at the conclusion he tried to rise and bless the expectant congregation. But he was too weak to stand and needed help in lifting his right arm to bless his spiritual children. He was then wheeled back to his cell, where a short time later he managed to appear at his window to impart his blessing once more to the joyful throng gathered below. It would be his last. The annals of the Friary re-create those bittersweet moments:

In the space beyond the wall of the cloister, a good

number of Prayer Group members holding lighted
torches and candles, waited for Padre Pio's evening
greeting; a spectacle similar to that of the twentieth.
After repeated greetings and shouts of "eviva!," "best
wishes!," "goodnight, Padre!," the window of Padre
Pio's cell closed forever; shutting behind it the vision
and memory of a man whom everyone, after having
met him, had learned to call "Father."[17]

The evening of the 22nd, Padre Pellegrino Funicelli
checked up on Padre Pio at 9:00 p.m., as he had done for the
past few years. He found Padre Pio already in bed, and then
he went to his own room, where an intercom was always on,
so that he could hear any sounds from Padre Pio's cell. From
9:00 until midnight, Padre Pio called Padre Pellegrino into
his cell about a half dozen times. He would ask what time it
was, and since his eyes were red from weeping, Padre Pellegrino would dab away the tears. At midnight, Padre Pio
asked him to remain in the room with him, and grabbed his
hands like a frightened child. For the next hour, he continued to ask what the time was, and asked Padre Pellegrino to
say Mass for him that morning. Padre Pellegrino later
recounted, "It seemed like he had an appointment, and that
he was impatiently waiting for the time to come."[18]
    Padre Pio then asked his confrere to hear his Confession.
While not his regular confessor, Padre Pellegrino had sometimes heard Padre Pio's Confession during his evening
watches. When they finished, the Saint indicated that he
wished to renew his religious vows. At this, Padre Pellegrino
was taken aback. "His request made me shudder because it's
our custom, as monks, to do so on our deathbed."[19] After
renewing his vows of poverty, chastity and obedience, Padre
Pio asked a favor of Padre Pellegrino: "My Son, if the Lord
calls me today, ask pardon for me from the confreres for all

the bother I have given them and ask them and my spiritual children to pray for my soul."[20] Padre Pellegrino assured him that he still had a long life ahead of him, and he made a request of Padre Pio that turned out to be prophetic. "Just in case you should be right, may I ask you to give your last blessing to your fellow priests, your spiritual children, and your patients?"[21] Padre Pio proceeded to bless them all, and expressed his wishes that the Father Guardian also impart this last blessing for him.

A few moments later, he asked Padre Pellegrino to help him get out of bed. He got dressed, washed his face, and sat down for a moment in the armchair. Then, saying he wanted to see the stars outside on the veranda, he got up from the chair unassisted, which amazed his confrere. Another surprise awaited Padre Pellegrino when Padre Pio stood up completely straight, which he had not been able to do in years, and walked briskly out to the balcony as if he were a young man. They remained standing outside under the night sky for a few minutes, then Padre Pio sat down and appeared to be staring at a part of the veranda. The spot at which he was staring was the precise location where the friars would shortly place his body, until he could be laid out in the church.

After a few minutes, his face beginning to pale, he asked to be taken back to his cell. Now, however, he could barely stand, and Padre Pellegrino hurried to fetch a wheelchair. Once back in his room, Padre Pio sat in his armchair, and continued to grow paler. He kept repeating "Jesus . . . Mary," as his lips turned purple and it became difficult for him to breathe. The worried and frightened Padre Pellegrino started to leave the room to call for help, but Padre Pio stopped him, saying that he did not want to disturb anyone. He stayed with the failing Padre a few minutes longer; then, in spite of Padre Pio's protests, he strode out the door to find help. Noticing that Brother Bill Martin's door was open, he went in, turned on the light, and exclaimed, "Padre Pio is dying!"[22] While Brother Bill ran to Padre Pio's cell, Padre Pellegrino grabbed a telephone and called Dr. Sala, then he dashed off to arouse the superior and other friars.

Within ten minutes, Dr. Sala was at Padre Pio's bedside, and a short time later Dr. Gusso, Director of the *Casa*, arrived with an assistant. Padre Pio continued to pray quietly, "Jesus ... Mary," while the doctors administered oxygen and injected heart stimulants. Padre Pio's eyes were closing and his breathing was labored, as he slumped in his armchair. He seemed to be oblivious of his surroundings, paying no attention to the instructions of the doctors. The superior had Padre Paolo administer the Last Rites, and those friars present joined in the prayers. Finally, Padre Pio sighed weakly, and leaning his head against the arm of one of the doctors, he quietly expired. Dr. Gusso remarked that the clinical signs of death were "... the most peaceful and sweet I have ever seen."[23] The time was 2:30 a.m. on Monday, September 23, 1968.

In the months preceding his death, the wounds of the stigmata had begun to close, and had slowly stopped bleeding. As his body was being prepared for the wake, the friars and Dr. Sala observed that the lesions on his hands, feet and chest were now completely healed. The skin over the spots where the stigmata had been open and bleeding for 50 years, was now as smooth as a baby's, without even a trace of a scar. Deep open wounds, that had been bleeding for 50 years, had perfectly healed! Dr. Sala concluded that this was a miracle in itself, and even greater than the stigmata, because it meant that dead tissue had been regenerated.[24] Within an hour of his death, one of the friars photographed the places where the wounds had been, in order to document the phenomenon. However, it was decided to put the fingerless mittens on Padre Pio's hands for the viewing, in order to avoid confusion and hasty interpretations among the Faithful.

By 3:00 a.m. on the 23rd, the urgently summoned *Carabinieri* had already begun to arrive, in anticipation of the need to keep order during the wake and subsequent funeral procession. Among the first to learn the shocking news of Padre Pio's passing were the early risers for what would have normally been his 5:00 a.m. Mass. As the morning progressed, an enormous crowd, stunned and weeping, gathered on the square in front of the church. Inside Our Lady of Grace, the friars were placing the Saint's body in an open wooden coffin, surrounded by flowers and candles. Finally the preparations were completed, and sufficient police were positioned throughout the church, Friary and adjacent areas, to allow the viewing to begin. At 8:30 a.m. that Monday, the large bronze church doors were finally opened. And so began the endless crush of mourners, who would fill the church with sorrowful outcries and bitter tears for four somber days. Late on that first day, the wooden coffin was replaced by a steel casket covered with a piece of glass to protect his body, but still keep it visible.

Tens of thousands of mourners, many waiting for two or three hours, filed past the casket bearing the remains of their beloved Padre Pio. People kissed the coffin, touched personal objects to it, prayed, and paid their final respects to the man that had been their protector for over half a century. Devotees poured into the little town of San Giovanni Rotondo from all over Italy, and many foreign nations. The whole plateau upon which San Giovanni Rotondo and the nearby small towns were seated was ". . . literally jammed with people."[25] In a remarkable display of affection, the great and the small filed past the bier day and night in an endless procession, all through Tuesday, Wednesday, and into Thursday morning. Finally at noon on Thursday the 26th, the Capuchins reluctantly closed the church doors to the crowds, in order to prepare for the funeral procession and Mass.

It was a sad, yet also a triumphal procession. At 3:30 in the afternoon, the church doors opened and the coffin was placed in an open hearse. The crowd in the plaza applauded as uniformed soldiers with marching drums began the procession, while platoons of *Carabinieri* provided an honor guard. Thousands lined the streets of San Giovanni Rotondo, as the cortege made its way mile after mile through the town. From the balconies and windows, people had festooned their finest textiles, along with large pictures of their Padre. A squadron of military planes flew overhead in tribute, and police helicopters showered flowers on the crowd below. People cried, prayed, and called out to their Saint for the last time. The procession reached the village cemetery before turning back, as if to allow Padre Pio to greet his parents and many others close to him, including Mary Pyle, who were interred there. Overall, the huge crowds along the march were orderly, with few instances of hysteria. Estimates placed the number of Padre Pio's friends who gathered that memorable day at 100,000.

It was almost dark when the hearse brought Padre Pio's body back to the *sagrato* in front of the church for a 7:00 p.m. funeral Mass. Twenty-four priests concelebrated, accompanying two Bishops and the Minister General of the Capuchin Order. At the end of the Mass, a telegram from the Vatican was read, in which Pope Paul VI conferred "his Apostolic Blessing and condolences to the religious community in their sorrow, to the doctors, staff and patients of the 'Home for the Relief of Suffering,' and to the entire population of San Giovanni Rotondo."[26] Finally, the casket carrying the Saint's body was carried to the lower level of the church, for burial in the center of the crypt. A huge monolithic block of Labrador granite weighing about seven tons was lowered over the burial niche. Thus was fulfilled the wish expressed by Padre Pio in far off 1923: ". . . I express the desire to be buried in a quiet little corner of this land, provided that my Superiors are not opposed to it."[27]

Some might say that Padre Pio is now gone. However, in his old age, when people had expressed their apprehensions about his approaching death, Padre Pio would reply gruffly yet playfully:

> Silly person, I will be here in your midst, more than before. Come visit my tomb. Before, in order to speak to me, you had to wait. Then, it is I who will be waiting there. Come to my tomb and you will receive more than you did before![28]

Padre Pio frequently stated, "In the tomb I will be more alive than ever!"[29] And when one of his collaborators ventured the opinion that, with so many persons to pray for, the Padre must simply lump everyone together in one big kettle or cauldron, Padre Pio responded:

> In a cauldron is where I am going to throw *you!* I remember them and I call them one by one, and count their hairs, and then some.[30]

Publisher's Note: The complete fascinating article from which the above quotes are taken is available on the author's website: http://members.aol.com/fmrega4/Promise.htm

Chapter 31

"Brother Bill"

THROUGHOUT this book, the names of Fr. Joseph Pius and, as in the prior chapter, Brother Bill Martin, have often appeared. They are, in fact, one and the same person. Fr. Joseph Pius was born in Brooklyn (or as he called it, Flatbush), New York, on August 1, 1938, and was baptized as William Martin. As a young man of only 21, Bill had embarked on a tour of the great cities of Europe. While he was in Italy, booking tickets at the Naples train station, the agent asked him if he wanted to visit San Giovanni Rotondo to see Padre Pio. Bill casually replied, "Why not?"[1] Although he had heard about Padre Pio from a seminarian friend, he admitted that his initial motivation was merely curiosity, and he arrived at San Giovanni Rotondo as a tourist rather than a pilgrim.

A few years later, he made a second visit, and this time he decided to stay a little longer. On three separate occasions during this visit, he felt he was ready to leave, but Padre Pio always stopped him. The third time, he was packed and prepared to take the bus to Foggia the next day, when a friar arrived with the message that Padre Pio wanted him to remain at San Giovanni Rotondo. Bill responded to Padre Pio's request by making arrangements to reside permanently near the Friar of the Gargano. Padre Pio in turn accepted him as his spiritual child and guided him along the path of a religious vocation.

For the first year-and-a-half of his stay at San Giovanni Rotondo, Bill was a layman and did not live in the Friary.

Eventually, he became a Third Order Brother, and as "Brother Bill" (Fra Guglielmo to the Italians), he was given permission to live at the monastery. He spent three years alongside Padre Pio, coinciding with the final years of the Saint's life. He was one of the men chosen to assist the elderly and frail Padre Pio in his day-to-day activities, and was either nearby, or actually at his side, day and night.

On most days, from 1:00 p.m. to about 3:30 p.m., Padre Pio would sit on the veranda near his cell in order to pray the Rosary and recite his Breviary (a priest's book of daily prayers), prior to hearing the mens' Confessions later in the afternoon. He was usually accompanied by "Brother Bill" and one or two confreres. One day, when the two of them were sitting together on the veranda, Bill began to think of what a marvelous grace it was to be living in San Giovanni Rotondo and sitting here, side-by-side, with a living saint. He wondered just who had obtained this great grace for that boy from Brooklyn, William Martin; was it Padre Pio or Our Lady? He kept these thoughts and musings to himself and did not mention what he was thinking about to his companion. Then, slowly, Padre Pio turned to him and said, "It was Our Lady."[2]

On September 22, 1968, Padre Pio celebrated his last Mass before thousands of his spiritual children and prayer group members. At the end of the Mass, he collapsed from exhaustion, and Brother Bill rushed towards the ailing priest and supported him with his arms, until the Padre could be placed in his wheelchair. The dramatic scene of the tall brown-robed Franciscan Brother darting to Padre Pio's side was captured for posterity in the widely circulated films of Padre Pio's last Mass. In the early morning hours of the 23rd, when the monastery was awakened by a call for assistance from Padre Pellegrino, who was looking after Padre Pio, Brother Bill was the first on the scene. He observed that Padre Pio was bathed in a cold sweat, and he reached for a towel and began to dry him, saying, "It's all right Father . . . you'll soon come out of it."[3] Brother Bill assisted him until the end came, listening with tear-filled eyes to Padre Pio's final prayer of "Jesus . . . Mary."

Not long after Padre Pio's death, Bill Martin asked the Capuchins for permission to enter the seminary to begin his studies for the priesthood. His request was quickly granted, and in 1969 he began his novitiate at Morcone—the very friary where Padre Pio himself had been a novice in 1903. After completing his studies and formation, he was ordained a priest on August 10, 1978, which was the 68th anniversary of Padre Pio's own Ordination. He was now to be known as Padre Giuseppe Pius, but to the American pilgrims he was simply Fr. Joseph.

Fr. Joseph spent his entire priesthood serving at Our Lady of Grace Friary. He became a focal point for English-speaking visitors and groups and, along with Fr. Alessio Parente, would welcome them in the "English room" of the Friary. There the pilgrims were served American-style instant coffee and could sit and relax while thumbing through the English-language literature on Padre Pio. Afterwards, a few chosen souls would help Fr. Joseph with the clean-up, including the washing out of the coffee cups.

Fr. Joseph was appointed editor of the popular English-language edition of the Friary's magazine, *The Voice of Padre Pio*. He wrote a column for each issue called "In the Margin," giving an update of events at the Monastery. His articles often included progress reports on Padre Pio's Cause for Canonization, and the status of the newest church, being built adjacent to the first two. In his humility, he would sign the column simply "J. P."

Fr. Joseph once commented on the different aromas associated with Padre Pio and his stigmata. He said that at one time he had seen a list of fourteen different fragrances and what they signified, but he commented, "I don't hold to it." According to the list, the scent of roses or other pleasant aromas meant that a grace had been granted, or soon would be. A medicinal or acidic odor signified mortification or penance. The smell of pipe tobacco supposedly meant danger. "I think that list is fanatical," Fr. Joseph concluded.[4]

Fr. Joseph said that he never personally witnessed a miracle occur while he was in the presence of Padre Pio. However, he did know of many documented cases of cures, including spectacular cancer cures. Two years after Padre Pio's passing, Fr. Joseph met a woman from New York who was at the Friary in thanksgiving for a grace. She had been diagnosed with throat cancer, and her situation had been so critical that she was not expected to live. The bedridden woman prayed to Padre Pio, who suddenly appeared at the foot of her bed and gave her a blessing. Then he commanded her to get up; she did, and was completely cured! In the words of Fr. Joseph, "I wouldn't have believed it if I hadn't seen it."[5]

He also had heard a reliable report of an incident of bilocation from the niece of one of Padre Pio's earliest spiritual daughters, Raffaelina Russo. The niece told Fr. Joseph that one evening in the Friary guest room, Raffaelina and a few others were present, along with Padre Pio. At one point, Padre Pio stopped talking and just sat there for a long time, with his arms folded and his head bent downward, without moving a muscle. All at once, he sat up in his chair and was again present to the group. Perhaps being a little too forward, they asked him where he had been. He nonchalantly replied that he had been back home in Pietrelcina greeting his father, was in Rome seeing his sister who was in a convent there, and was with his brother Michele in Jamaica, New York![6]

Fr. Joseph witnessed some of Padre Pio's battles with the devil—not only exorcisms but actual physical encounters.

One morning he and another friar, Padre Onorato, took a break from looking after Padre Pio in his cell and went downstairs for coffee. In Padre Pio's final years, a little buzzer had been attached to his armchair, and if he needed help, he could easily press the button. For that reason, the two friars were not worried about leaving the Padre alone for a short while. But just five minutes later, Padre Onorato, who was on his way back up the stairs, heard Padre Pio yelling out for help. He rushed into the cell, and found the Padre lying on the floor of the room. In Fr. Joseph's words, "The devil had come in and started the battle, and had knocked him onto the floor." An even fiercer battle with the devil occurred shortly after Fr. Joseph's arrival at the monastery. There had been a tremendous noise during the night from Padre Pio's room, and when the Superior rushed into the cell, he found Padre Pio on the floor, cut and bleeding, with his eyes blackened. Strangely enough, there was a pillow under Padre Pio's head as he lay on the floor bruised. The Father Superior asked, "Who put the pillow under your head?" Padre Pio's reply was: "La Madonna."[7]

The Salerno sisters, Jeanette and Joan, who first met Fr. Joseph in 1966 when he was still known as Brother Bill, hail from his old neighborhood in Brooklyn. In fact, his uncle, Fr. Daniel Martin, had been their parish priest at St. Francis of Assisi Church in "Flatbush." Through the years, in all the letters, visits and phone conversations the Salernos had with Fr. Joseph, he never failed to ask, "What's happening in New York?" Surprisingly, at one time he had aspired to a career in the theater. Jeanette, who once entertained similar aspirations in her youth, relates, "In talking about it years later, we learned that we both gave up the idea because we were not spiritually in tune with the life; we were at odds with much. It just didn't seem to fit."[8] However, Fr. Joseph's former love for the theater was reflected in his splendid diction. He had a ". . . beautiful way of speaking that seemed accustomed to Shakespeare, which he loved." Jeanette Salerno, who has written often about Padre Pio, has tapes of her interviews with Fr. Joseph along with a collection of their correspondence. She is planning to write a short remembrance of him in the near future, portraying "Father Joseph's—and Brooklyn's—contribution to the legend of Padre Pio!"

One of Fr. Joseph's happiest moments was his presence in Vatican City for the Beatification ceremony of Padre Pio on May 2, 1999. He was among the select group of friars chosen to greet Pope John Paul II during the ceremony that day. No one suspected that one year and one day later, on May 3, 2000, Fr. Joseph Pius would be taken away from the friars, the community, and the pilgrims that loved him so much. He died in Padre Pio's hospital from complications caused by an infection, after undergoing a routine operation.

In a befitting eulogy, the Capuchin Provincial Minister, Padre Paolo Cuvino, spoke of Fr. Joseph's traits of kindness, his consideration for others, his simplicity and his humility. "Who could ever forget his way of speaking Italian and his typically American accent that often caused him to confuse words and meanings? He took the jokes and had a sense of humor." Padre Cuvino noted that Fr. Joseph had the opportunity to see himself as great in the eyes of the world, since he was a close friend of the Saint. He could have been a public figure, appearing in magazine and newspaper articles, with a spotlight shining on him. Instead, he chose to be hidden and did not even want to shine in the reflected light of Padre Pio's glory. "He was truly faithful to his intentions, to the life project God inspired him with, always faithful to his Spiritual Father in memory, in prayer, in his testimony, in affection and devotion."[9]

Chapter 32

Two Unique Apostolates

PRAY, *Hope and Don't Worry* is the name of the quarterly Padre Pio newsletter published by Ron and Diane Allen, of San Diego, California.[1] Their high-quality four-page bulletin is completely dedicated to stories about the Saint, and includes testimonies from those who knew him or experienced his graces. With a circulation of 7,000, it is produced under the auspices of the Padre Pio Prayer Group based at Our Lady of the Rosary Catholic Church in San Diego. The group has over 300 members, and holds devotions each month to a standing-room-only crowd.

Ron and Diane are converts to Catholicism, and their conversion was a direct result of Padre Pio's miraculous intervention in Diane's life. She was brought up as a Protestant, attending the "Church of Christ" until she was 16. A few years later, Diane became interested in the teachings of Paramahansa Yogananda, a Hindu teacher and writer. He had established a California-based church called the Self Realization Fellowship, which Diane eventually joined. She had absolutely no interest at all in Catholicism, until one day, when she was about 20 years old, a minister at her church told a brief story about Padre Pio. The minister related that someone had once asked the Saint what was the main thing missing in the world today. Padre Pio had replied that it was "the Holy Fear of God," and then he proceeded to give the questioner a gentle slap.

This little story played over and over in Diane's mind like a tape recorder. She relates that it ". . . was like a light imprinted in my mind." She thought of the story hundreds of times during the next 20 years, but made no attempt to find out more about Padre Pio or the Catholic Church. She continued her regular attendance at Self Realization Fellowship, along with her husband Ron.

Finally, when Diane was in her early forties, the day arrived when she knew it was time to find out about Padre Pio. She woke up one morning, "very, very excited," wanting to know immediately who this man was. She searched the phone book for the nearest Catholic book store, shopped there that same day, and came away with Fr. Charles Mortimer Carty's *Padre Pio: The Stigmatist*, one of the first English-language books on his life. Reading about the wonders of the Saint made Diane feel she was in Heaven, an experience familiar to those who engross themselves in books about Padre Pio. Inspired by the story of the life and miracles of the Stigmatist, she sensed a new door opening in her own life, and decided to embark on the path of becoming a Roman Catholic.

For the next two years, Diane pursued her own self-study course of the Catholic religion. Her full-time job as a data entry specialist allowed her to listen to instructional tapes while at work. She took notes and studied faithfully, but there were many areas of Catholic doctrine and practice that she could not fully accept. She made numerous attempts to complete the classes of the Rite of Christian Initiation for Adults (RCIA), given by the Church for prospective new members, but her conscience invariably caused her to drop out of the course. Diane felt she could not let herself be admitted into the Catholic Church and receive the Sacrament of Confirmation if she did not truly believe everything the Church teaches. In her own words, she was "stuck and miserable."

But once Padre Pio accepts someone as his spiritual child,

he will never forget him or allow him to be lost. It was time for him to personally enter Diane's life. One evening in 1994, she awoke in the middle of the night, opened her eyes, and saw a "flesh and blood Padre Pio" standing before her. He was suspended above the floor near her bedside, with his Capuchin hood pulled up over the top of his head. His brows were knitted, and his stern, riveting eyes pierced her soul. Not a word was said as he continued to scrutinize Diane, who felt paralyzed. Finally he disappeared, and the "striking and beautiful experience" was over.

When she awoke the next day, and as she was telling her family what had happened, she began to realize that Padre Pio's visit had resulted in a special grace—the gift of faith. Her doubts and conflicts about Catholic beliefs had simply disappeared, and she was able to accept fully the teachings of the Church. Determined to learn everything she could about Padre Pio after such a wonderful encounter, Diane and her husband Ron boarded a plane for Barto, Pennsylvania, a short time later. Barto is the home of the National Centre for Padre Pio, an extensive shrine and resource center dedicated to the Saint. At the Centre's bookstore, Diane purchased every single book on Padre Pio that was available. In addition, she was able to obtain most of the back issues of *The Voice of Padre Pio* magazine. The rest of the back issues, as well as some additional books on Padre Pio, were obtained from the Friary at San Giovanni Rotondo with the help of Fr. Alessio Parente. Fr. Alessio was one of the two English-speaking liaisons at Our Lady of Grace, the other being Fr. Joseph Pius.

Diane soon became a Catholic, while Ron continued to attend the Self Realization Fellowship Church. Diane's husband was still quite happy with the Fellowship, and she and Ron had an agreement whereby she would not try to convert him to Catholicism. But it became obvious to him that Diane had become a different person, once she started receiving the Sacraments, and the change was favorable. In fact, after her first Confession, Ron even became a little envious. Her joy and peace reflected a beautiful quality about her interior life that was missing in his. He understood that Diane enjoyed something that he did not have, and he wanted it too. Eventually, Ron Allen followed the path his wife had taken, and converted to the Catholic Faith. He became quite active in the Church and well-versed in her teachings, and soon accepted the position of Director of Religious Education for one of the largest parishes in San Diego.

Diane's extensive reading on Padre Pio made her aware of the worldwide prayer groups that the Saint had established. She wrote to the Centre in Barto asking if there were any Padre Pio prayer groups in the San Diego area. Yes, there was one in San Diego, she was told, that had been started 12 years earlier by Celina Florentino. Diane and Ron joined Celina's group, and before long the couple was asked to write and publish the group's quarterly newsletter. The elderly Celina eventually passed the leadership torch of the prayer group to the Allens in 2001.

The spiritual director of the 300-member group is an Italian priest, Fr. Louis Solcia, CRSP. Meetings are held the first Monday of each month, and include the Rosary, Mass, Benediction, and the prayers of Padre Pio. The members raise funds which benefit Padre Pio's hospital, and also the brand new church and shrine at San Giovanni Rotondo. The group's quarterly Padre Pio newsletter, *Pray, Hope and Don't Worry*, and a Padre Pio prayer packet, are available from them free of charge. The Allens have also designed an attractive and popular Padre Pio web site.*

*To obtain the newsletter, write to D. Allen, P.O. Box 191545, San Diego, CA 92159. Website: www.saintpio.org

On the opposite side of the country resides another "apostle" for Padre Pio. Many people throughout the world have come across a small booklet containing "Counsels" and "Exhortations" of Saint Padre Pio of Pietrelcina, Italy. On the upper right corner and along the bottom of the title page is written "FREE! *Not to be sold!*" Over 3,000,000 copies of the booklet are in circulation; it has been printed in four languages and distributed in 27 countries. Vincent Falco of Miami Beach, Florida, is the publisher, printer, and distributor of this collection of gems from Padre Pio's wisdom.[2]

The booklet itself is a reprint of one that he purchased in San Giovanni Rotondo in 1956. Many decades later, he came across his tattered copy tucked inside of a storage carton he was rummaging through. Finding the old pamphlet sparked his sense of mission, and he embarked on his unique ministry by setting up a printing shop in his own home in 1994, to reproduce the booklet. He had previously gained some experience with printing techniques from helping a friend set up a newspaper press.

Most of Vincent Falco's days are spent in his home, operating the machines that produce stacks of neatly folded and stapled Padre Pio booklets. He performs all the printing himself, and accepts donations only for mailing costs and expenses. Requests range from private individuals who just want one or a few copies, to religious groups, hospitals, pastoral centers, and prison ministries, who send him the postage for hundreds and even thousands of booklets. It is the only booklet that he prints.

Vincent's appreciation of Padre Pio resulted from his personal encounter with the Saint during a 1956 visit to San Giovanni Rotondo. He had been serving in the United States Army as a soldier stationed in Germany, and his term of duty was over at that time. He decided to take an "overseas separation" so he could visit his family in Naples, where he remained for a year. While there, he was moved by the plight of an ailing woman who seemed to be suffering from many problems. During his efforts to find a way to help her, someone suggested to him that Padre Pio might be able to do something. He knew very little about him, and though he rejected the idea at first, the thought kept tugging at Vincent to make a visit to see this Padre Pio. Finally, he boarded the train for Foggia, with the intention of only spending one day in San Giovanni Rotondo. But as soon the train began to head to the south of Italy, he felt a joyful transformation within himself: "I cried tears like Niagara Falls. It was beautiful."[3]

For highlights of the rest of his story, including his establishment of a foster home for the handicapped, Vincent has requested that the reader refer to *The Story Behind the "Little" Book*, printed on the inside back cover of his booklet. On the outside of the back cover, Vincent writes: "I print this booklet only in my home and give it out free as a devotion to Padre Pio, in thanksgiving to my Lord, and to my beautiful Heavenly Mother." At the bottom of the page he adds: " I pray with hope that this publication will awaken those souls who are lost in the depths of darkness and will bring them back to the Divine Light." His ministry is truly a unique tribute by an American to an equally unique Saint.*

---

*Vincent Falco's web site is www.saintpadrepio.com, and anyone desiring copies of the booklet can phone him at 305-673-8403 or write to him at: 4514 Sheridan Avenue, Miami Beach, FL 33140.

Chapter 33

Two Major Ministries

THE Padre Pio Foundation of America, located in Cromwell, Connecticut, was founded in 1977 by Marge Spada, in memory of her late husband, Joseph, and in gratitude to Padre Pio. While the Foundation has a number of goals, its primary purpose is to encourage devotion to Padre Pio by spreading his teachings and spiri tuality. The organization also fosters vocations to the priesthood and promotes spiritual and corporal works of mercy in remembrance of the Saint. The Foundation provides financial support for places associated with him in Italy and is especially interested in the preservation of the sites in Padre Pio's birthplace of Pietrelcina that played a part in his early life. The group has donated to Padre Pio's hospital, the *Casa Sollievo della Sofferenza*, and has raised funds for the construction of the brand new basilica at San Giovanni Rotondo.

Two years before the Foundation was conceived, Joe Spada had been hospitalized with terminal cancer. At the time, the Spadas had not yet heard of Padre Pio; but a friend gave Marge a book about the Saint, and she gave it to her husband to read. He was immediately captivated by the life and achievements of the stigmatized Friar, and ardently began praying to him. Joe's prayers were answered in ways that would be unusual for anyone but Padre Pio. Soon the nurses tending to Joe began to experience an unexplainable fragrance of roses coming from his room, although there were no flowers present. Joe told his wife that Padre Pio frequently appeared to him; sometimes they even walked the halls of the hospital together. Marge has proof of these visits in the form of a handkerchief that has on several occasions given off the aroma of fresh flowers. According to her husband, Padre Pio left the handkerchief behind after one of his mystical visits.

Joe Spada was not cured of his cancer, but he felt an inner peace during his final days, thanks to the comforting spiritual presence of Padre Pio. After his funeral, friends and relatives arriving at the Spada home, could smell fresh flowers outdoors, although it was a chilly autumn day. Marge still continues to be gifted on occasion with this wonderful reminder of Padre Pio, his "perfume of sanctity."

In honor of the Saint and in memory of her husband, she established the Padre Pio Foundation shortly after Joe's passing. Thanks to the Foundation's generous benefactors, the organization recently made a large donation for the construction of the Baptistery for the new church at San Giovanni Rotondo. In past years, the Foundation made possible the complete restoration of the Santa Anna Church in Pietrelcina, where Padre Pio had been baptized and confirmed. In addition, the organization helped to rebuild Padre Pio's parish church, Santa Maria degli Angeli, which had been severely damaged by an earthquake. The Foundation commissioned artists to frame the central altar with floor-to-ceiling murals of the holy Angels.

News reports of the Foundation's activities, along with stories about Padre Pio and his spiritual children, are featured in their bi-monthly publication, the *Padre Pio Gazette*.* Their web site features many inspirational "Stories of Mercy," written by the late Fr. Bob McQueeney. In addition, the site provides information on their current pilgrimages,

---

*The address and phone number of the organization is: The Padre Pio Foundation of America, 463 Main Street, Cromwell, CT 06416. Phone: 860-635-4996. Web site: www.padrepio.com

features an online gift shop and bookstore, and contains extensive information about the life of the Saint.

Another large-scale Padre Pio ministry is The National Centre for Padre Pio. Located in Barto, Pennsylvania, the organization is familiar to many North American devotees of the Saint. For many years, until the Canonization of St. Pio of Pietrelcina on June 16, 2002, it was the official center for The Cause of Padre Pio for the United States and Canada, authorized by the Capuchin Friary in San Giovanni Rotondo. Its function as an official center was primarily twofold. The first was to provide the public with accurate and reliable literature, videos and other information on Padre Pio, a service the Centre continues to perform. Secondly, it was a focal point for gathering testimonies and stories of graces received through Padre Pio's intercession. This information was forwarded to the headquarters of the Postulation for Padre Pio's Cause in Italy. Since the Cause for his Canonization has been successful, and Padre Pio now belongs to the world, the Capuchins at San Giovanni Rotondo no longer have the need for official worldwide information centers to gather information on the Saint.

However, just as the death of Padre Pio did not turn San Giovanni Rotondo into a ghost town or force his hospital to shut its doors, the end of "officialdom" for the Barto Centre has not caused it to slow down its operations. On the contrary, the Centre continues to flourish, not only as a source of information on the life of St. Pio of Pietrelcina, but also as a mecca for his devotees. Tens of thousands each year visit what has essentially become America's unofficial Padre Pio shrine, drawn to the Barto site by replicas of the buildings and places associated with the life of the Saint.

The driving force and foundress of this effort was Mrs. Vera M. Calandra, who was in charge of the National Centre from its inception in 1970 until her passing in August of 2004. It was begun in thanksgiving for a singular miracle bestowed upon her family by Padre Pio, shortly before his death. Vera had first learned about Padre Pio through reading a book and began earnestly praying to him to intercede for her two-year-old daughter, Vera Marie. Her little girl was in danger of death, due to severe congenital problems with her kidneys and urinary tract. The child had undergone almost half a dozen major operations, including one to remove her bladder. At the suggestion of a friend, Vera twice cabled Padre Pio, imploring his prayers for a miraculous cure. The second cable, sent after the removal of Vera Marie's bladder, read: "Please Padre Pio, continue your powerful prayers. Little Vera is alive, but without a bladder. Implore God's mercy that she will be given a miraculous return to good health." On the Feast of the Assumption of the Blessed Virgin Mary, August 15, 1968, Vera experienced the heavenly perfume of fresh roses often associated with Padre Pio.[1] She also sensed the Saint telling her, in an interior locution, that it was urgent that she bring her daughter to him without delay. If they arrived *immediately*, everything would turn out well.[2] Within two weeks, Vera was on her way to San Giovanni Rotondo, bringing with her the ailing Vera Marie, and also her recently born sixth child, two-week old Christina Rose.

During her four-day stay there, she managed to meet with Padre Pio twice. Placing a stigmatized hand upon their heads, he blessed the mother and her two children; on the next day, Vera gratefully kissed his wounded hand. As she looked into his eyes, Vera vowed to do whatever God wanted of her, if her rapidly failing daughter, Vera Marie, could only be restored to health. She would then let the whole world know about the greatness of Padre Pio's intercession with the Lord. Upon their return to America, and further hospital

visits, it was discovered that little Vera Marie was growing a
"rudimentary bladder" in place of the defective one that had
been surgically removed. This was medically unprecedented,
and was the miracle her family had been hoping and praying for!

Mrs. Calandra was determined to keep her promise, now
that, thanks to Padre Pio's prayers, Vera Marie was regain-
ing her health. Working off of the kitchen table of her home,
with the help of her husband Harry, she began her efforts to
make Padre Pio known in America. The Capuchin friars at
San Giovanni approved of and supported her work. They
provided photos and writings about Padre Pio, that Vera
would distribute to those interested in knowing more about
him. She also initiated a monthly Holy Hour in her church,
that attracted up to 200 of the faithful. Books, photos, magazines, and prayer cards were soon being mailed to all parts
of the country.

Before long, requests for lectures and presentations on
Padre Pio began to pour in, and Vera gave the first of her
thousands of talks on the miracle-worker of San Giovanni
Rotondo. She accepted speaking engagements that required
her to fly throughout the United States and even abroad.
Often, Padre Pio Prayer Groups in distant parts of the country invited her for extended visits, and she would spend a
week at a time lecturing at a particular locale. One publication commented: "A naturally gifted speaker, she can hold an
audience's attention for literally hours."[3] She also made
numerous return visits to San Giovanni Rotondo, praying in
thanksgiving before the tomb of the Saint.

As the ministry grew, her husband, children and an eager
volunteer staff assisted in responding to the endless
requests for books and information about Padre Pio. Soon a
separate office was added to the back of her Norristown,
Pennsylvania home, and The Cause of Padre Pio, Inc., was

born. In a short time, with the blessing of the Capuchins of San Giovanni Rotondo, it grew into the official National Centre for Padre Pio, Inc. The Centre sponsored the first monument and statue of Padre Pio in the United States, dedicated in October, 1977, in a courtyard adjacent to Holy Savior Church in Norristown.[4]

The Calandra apostolate continued to experience phenomenal growth, and eventually moved to Barto, in rural Pennsylvania. Among its many activities, the Centre organizes annual pilgrimages to Italy, so that devotees may visit the cities and places associated with Padre Pio. Guidance is also provided for those who wish to start Padre Pio Prayer Groups, or become spiritual children of Padre Pio. The organization continues to collaborate closely with the Capuchins at San Giovanni Rotondo, and is a point of contact for subscribers to the Friary's magazine, *The Voice of Padre Pio*. Anyone wishing to contribute financial support to the work of the Capuchins at Our Lady of Grace Friary or for Padre Pio's hospital can do so through the Centre.

At the hundred-acre Barto facility, a number of structures have been erected that re-create the Padre Pio shrine in San Giovanni Rotondo, including the medieval chapel of Our Lady of Grace. Astonishingly similar to the original in Italy, the Barto edifice is complete even to the side altars, replicas of paintings, and the choir loft. A magnificent crucifix, similar to the one before which Padre Pio was praying when he received the stigmata, crowns the interior domes and arches. Placed in one of the side altars is an actual confessional that was used by Padre Pio in his ministry of reconciling souls to God. Viewed from the grounds outside, it almost seems as if the cream-colored stucco chapel had been magically transported from its site in Italy.

Adjacent to the chapel is a 6,000 square foot Padre Pio Spirituality Center. Equipped with hand-carved Portuguese benches and kneelers, the Center is beautifully decorated with numerous works of religious art and sculpture. Behind the main altar and directly beneath a stained glass window, a larger than life-sized statue of Padre Pio raises its hand in blessing. Colorful, exquisitely carved, hand-painted Stations of the Cross grace the perimeter of the room. Even the main hall leading to the Center has it share of artwork, including five imported stained-glass windows depicting scenes from the life of Padre Pio.

The newest addition to the Barto shrine is the St. Pio Museum and Cultural Center. Three times larger than the Spiritual Centre, it houses a collection of Padre Pio relics and artifacts, a library and archival area, conference center, and a book and gift shop. Also included are replicas of Padre Pio's monastery cell, his birthplace and family home in Pietrelcina, as well as the Forgione's country farm house at Piana Romana. The facility hosts speakers, symposia, cultural events, and a variety of programs serving people from every walk of life, all in the name of Padre Pio.*

Mrs. Calandra, who was a Third Order Franciscan, was recognized by the Holy See for her many accomplishments. In 1987 she was a recipient of the *Pro Ecclesia et Pontifice* award, an honor bestowed by the Holy Father for outstanding contributions to the Catholic Church. She and her husband Harry had numerous private audiences with Pope John Paul II, and attended Mass in his personal chapel many times. On May 2, 1999, during the Beatification Ceremony at St. Peter's for Padre Pio, Vera Calandra was chosen to represent the United States by giving the first Scripture reading at the solemn Papal Mass.

*The address of the Centre is: National Centre for Padre Pio, Inc., 2213 Old Route 100, Barto, PA 19504; phone: 610-845-3000. Web site: www.padrepio.org.

Chapter 34

Recent Developments

THE Canonization of St. Pio of Pietrelcina on June 16, 2002, marked the culmination of years of work and commitment by the Postulation for Padre Pio's Cause, based at the Friary, and by his loyal followers. On that day, Pope John Paul II decreed that September 23 would now be the obligatory feast of St. Pio in the Universal Church. There were also two major steps that had occurred prior to his Canonization. The first was the Vatican declaration of his heroic virtues in December of 1997, with the accompanying designation of the friar as "Venerable." Then followed his Beatification on May 2, 1999, when he joined the ranks of the Blessed. At that ceremony, almost a half million people were present at two separate locations. A huge crowd overflowed St. Peter's Square, extending all the way to the Tiber River, filling up the main avenue, Via della Conciliazione. In addition, a gathering of 100,000 devotees assembled at the square in front of St. John Lateran Basilica, where the Pope made a special appearance at the conclusion of the Beatification ceremony at St. Peter's. Thousands of American pilgrims were present at both the Canonization and Beatification ceremonies, with most also visiting San Giovanni Rotondo and Pietrelcina as part of their itinerary.

There are further developments ahead on the spiritual front regarding Padre Pio; his Canonization was not the end of efforts in this regard. A movement has been initiated to have St. Pio of Pietrelcina declared a Doctor of the Universal Church. This is merited in large part by the highly esteemed spiritual and mystical content of his collected letters, compiled in the four-volume *Epistolario*. Such an honor would entail a strict and thorough study of his writings, teachings, and thoughts by the Vatican. Padre Gerardo Di Flumeri, who was Vice-Postulator for Padre Pio's cause, has commissioned a group of scholars to lay the groundwork for such an investigation.[1] In 2,000 years of Church history, there have only been 33 men and women designated as Doctors of the Church. Padre Gerardo is also gathering another group of experts, in order to evaluate the stigmata of Padre Pio. The goal is to obtain an official declaration from the Vatican that his wounds were truly a supernatural phenomenon. This would not be unprecedented, since the Church celebrates September 17 as the Feast of the Stigmata of St. Francis of Assisi.

Following the Canonization of Padre Pio, the Vatican announced that Catholic pilgrims visiting the tomb of the Saint at San Giovanni Rotondo may obtain a plenary indulgence, on condition that they go to Confession, receive Holy Communion and pray for the Pope's intentions. In recognition of Padre Pio's long years at San Giovanni Rotondo, the Vatican authorized the name of the diocese in which the town resides to be changed from Manfredonia-Vieste to the diocese of Manfredonia-Vieste-San Giovanni Rotondo. In 2003, the Holy Father appointed Archbishop Domenico D'Ambrosio as head of the new Diocese and as Delegate for the Shrine and Institutions of Saint Pio of Pietrelcina. In the widely-circulated letter to Archbishop D'Ambrosio, made public in early 2004, Pope John Paul II wrote the following tribute to Padre Pio:

> The spiritual movement inspired by the charism of
> St. Pio of Pietrelcina did not end with his earthly
> death; on the contrary, it has continued to grow,

becoming significantly important to the life of the entire Church. The secret of these far-reaching echoes is certainly to be found in the humble Capuchin's total immersion in the mystery of the Cross. Throughout his life, Padre Pio sought to conform ever more closely to the Crucified Christ, with a clear awareness that he was called to collaborate in a very special way in the work of Redemption.

In the same letter the Holy Father commented on the "evangelizing action fostered by Padre Pio" that radiates from San Giovanni Rotondo:

> Responding to this spiritual outreach, countless people, not only from Italy and Europe, but from all the continents, come to San Giovanni Rotondo. They are not only members of the "Prayer Groups." They are also followers of other religions and sometimes also non-believers, who are drawn there by the fame of the holy Capuchin Friar.
>
> Today it can be said that the boundaries of the devotion to this humble son of St. Francis have become, as it were, the boundaries of the world. For years the Capuchin Community has cherished in its heart, like a precious pearl, the marvelous treasure of Padre Pio's holiness; with a generous impulse it has become more and more open to the universal dimension that is characteristic of the Church.[2]

As can be gathered from the Holy Father's words, one of the most significant developments since the passing of Padre Pio in 1968 has been the phenomenal growth in the number of pilgrims visiting Our Lady of Grace shrine in San Giovanni Rotondo. The millions who come each year to the tomb of the Saint rival the numbers that visit the great Marian shrines of Lourdes, Fatima, and Guadalupe. To accommodate the ever-increasing tide of pilgrims, the Capuchins commissioned the construction of a massive new church, exclusively funded by donations from Padre Pio's followers throughout the world.[3] This newest addition to the Padre Pio shrine in San Giovanni Rotondo was dedicated on July 1, 2004, exactly 45 years after the 1959 dedication of what was once also known as the "new church." Present at this latest inaugural, as guest of honor, was Pia Forgione Pennelli, the 74-year-old daughter of Padre Pio's brother Michele.

The 1959 church was built to serve 1,000 pilgrims when Padre Pio was still alive; now an edifice many times larger is needed for those making the pilgrimage after his death. Designed by internationally renowned architect Renzo Piano, this architectural wonder can hold 8,000 worshipers (over 6,000 seated). The adjacent plaza can contain an additional 40,000, who are also able to participate in the religious services. The immense sanctuary alone can accommodate 300 priests.[4] Ten years in the making, the spiral-shaped basilica is located only a few yards from the original medieval Chapel and Friary of Our Lady of Grace.

The town of San Giovanni Rotondo itself is keeping pace with the growth of the Shrine, and dozens of new hotels and restaurants have cropped up in recent years. At the time of the July 2004 opening of the new church, the city boasted 120 hotels, providing 6,500 beds. In addition, the stalwart hospital, *Casa Sollievo della Sofferenza*, is constantly expanding and remains one of the best equipped hospitals in Europe. And so the "City on a Mountain" continues to flourish, fulfilling Padre Pio's words that he would make more of a clamor after his death than when he was alive.

Epilogue

IF one looks simply at the course of his life, in terms of events and people, it is easy to understand why Padre Pio had a great affection for America. Even during his youth in Pietrelcina, Francesco Forgione was well aware of what America meant to his family and to his future. Both his father Grazio and his brother Michele emigrated to these distant shores in order to provide for their families in Pietrelcina. Much of his father's wages were used to finance the essential pre-seminary schooling for the young Francesco Forgione. Although both men eventually left America to live out the remainder of their lives in their native country, there is no record of anything but a favorable and fruitful time spent in the United States. Apparently, the only negative experience was Grazio's unproductive stay in South America, after his first journey across the ocean.

Only a few years after Padre Pio received the stigmata, Mary Pyle settled in San Giovanni to be close to her mentor, and she remained there for 45 years. A wealthy American heiress, she renounced a worldly life-style in order to embark on a spiritual journey under the guidance of a living Saint. She was the person primarily responsible for the construction of the Capuchin friary and church in Padre Pio's home town of Pietrelcina, a project greatly desired by him. Not only was she his spiritual daughter and friend, but she became a friend to those close to him, both to his relatives and to his Capuchin family. He trusted and respected this American woman to the point of allowing his mother, and later his father, to spend their dying days in her home. She was not only a member of his spiritual family, but also in a

284

sense a part of his natural family.

The close bond Padre Pio felt with the American soldiers who visited him, and the warm reception he always gave them, reflected his great affection for the United States. As we have seen, this affection was shared by other Italians, even the citizens of Foggia, a city that was left in shambles by Allied air raids. During the course of the war, Italy became an ally of the United States, and it was essentially the American military who liberated the country from the hands of the German occupiers. It is known that Padre Pio felt that Nazism was an even worse scourge than Communism. He called it ". . . the most diabolical slavery that one can imagine."[1] Like most Italians, he was deeply grateful to the Americans for ridding their country of Fascism and Nazism.

He must have been deeply touched and impressed by the large number of GIs who made the trek up the Gargano to attend his Mass and met with him afterwards. Although no accurate count is possible, it is quite probable that from 1943 to 1945, many thousands of soldiers visited him. Some, such as Joe Peluso, Mario Avignone and Joe Peterson, developed a close, personal friendship with the stigmatized friar. Others, thanks to Padre Pio's inspiration, eventually became Catholic Priests. Even the head of the benevolent post-war Allied Military Government in Foggia, Col. John Laboon, was a Padre Pio devotee.

After the war, many of these GIs made Padre Pio known in America, not only on a one-to-one basis, but by giving talks and presentations to large groups. They also spread the word about Padre Pio's dream of a great hospital to serve the needs of that neglected part of southern Italy. Contributions from Americans began to pour in for the hospital, culminating in the large UNRRA grant approved by the U.S. Congress in 1948. Many Americans, including former GIs, chose to live at San Giovanni Rotondo for extended periods of time in order to assist Padre Pio in his ministry. There is no question that Padre Pio would not be as well known in the United States as he is today, were it not for the providential "discovery" of the Saint of the Gargano by the American troops stationed in Southern Italy. It was through the GIs, who always showed him their sincerest love and respect, that Padre Pio transmitted his personal wish—that all Americans would become his spiritual children.

The other side of the coin—the attraction of Americans towards Padre Pio—can be contrasted to their affection for another son of the Italian countryside, who was also a stigmatic, St. Francis. The "poor man of Assisi" is associated with rural vistas, nature, animals, the outdoors and especially today, the environment and ecology. These associations are meaningful to a country that was until relatively recently an open-spaced frontier, and now feels a need to preserve its natural heritage. For Americans, St. Francis is often more associated with love of God and of God's creation than he is with "Catholicism." Padre Pio on the other hand was a cloistered monk, a man dedicated to the confessional and the altar. He is associated with mysticism and the Catholic priesthood. It would seem that achievement-oriented Americans would have little interest in him. To the extent that this may be true for some, it is probably due to their lack of knowledge of the Saint, if they have heard of him at all.

But it seems that once one learns even a little about the Friar of the Gargano, a hunger to find out more about his life is aroused. Some may feel an affinity with his humble beginnings, or be drawn by the wondrous miracle stories, or be fascinated by the stigmata. And how can a "practical" American not be astounded at the cloistered monk who built one of the greatest hospitals in Europe, in what was then a backward area of southern Italy?

Ultimately, however, Americans have been attracted to him as a person. Padre Pio's personality itself had a way of drawing people to him. We have seen how the GIs were struck by his kindly eyes and gentle, friendly manner. They were able to encounter this saintly man on a down-to-earth level, and were so awed and amazed by his warmth and humanity that they wanted to tell all of America about him.

His spectacular charisms make interesting reading, but they were only the outer manifestations of the inner depths of his soul. He was truly committed to God, a fact reflected in the unwavering manner of his virtuous lifestyle. His life was one of constant prayer—the Rosary, the prayers of the Holy Mass, the Divine Office, the novenas, the Benedictions, the Way of the Cross, and the countless other Catholic treasures that nourish spiritual growth. It has been said of both St. Francis of Assisi and St. Pio of Pietrelcina that they were more than men of prayer, they were men who had *become* prayer. Padre Pio was an exemplar of what a good Christian should be—one who lives out the Faith to the fullest by loving and suffering for God and others, even in the midst of persecutions.

The underlying reason for this attraction to Padre Pio as a person, then, lies in his deep spirituality. He was Christian to the point of being truly Christ-like, and the Lord confirmed this by marking him with the stigmata—the Seal, so to speak, of the Living God-Man. He was imbued with the spirit of Christ, and he radiated that spirit. To the extent that America is still largely a Christian nation, the appeal of such a man, a 20th century Saint who lived in our time, should come as no surprise. The words of the Apostle Paul to the early Christians, "But we have the mind of Christ" (*1 Corinthians* 2:16), find fulfillment in St. Padre Pio of Pietrelcina, for his Christ-like quality is the simple reason why America and the world continue to be drawn to him.

"How beautiful upon the mountains are the feet of him that bringeth good tidings, and that preacheth peace: of him that showeth forth good, that preacheth salvation, that sayeth to Sion: Thy God shall reign!" (*Isaias* 52:7).

Afterword

FORMER GIs and others who have additional information on the American soldiers who met Padre Pio during the Second World War are invited to contact the author. His email address is frankrega@earthlink.net and his mailing address is: Frank M. Rega, P.O. Box 1832, Millsboro, DE 19966.

Susan De Bartoli has been asked to gather documentation in support of Mary Pyle's Cause for Beatification, under the direction of Padre Cosimo Vicedomini of Our Lady of Grace Friary in San Giovanni Rotondo. Readers having any information related to Mary Pyle that may assist in advancing her Cause should contact Miss De Bartoli. This includes any letters or other documents pertaining to Mary Pyle's life, and especially, information regarding favors or graces received through Mary Pyle's intercession.

Susan De Bartoli's mailing address is: 145 Fieldstone Road, Staten Island, New York 10314. Her web site is www.littleflowerpilgrimages.com, and her email address is Susan@littleflowerpilgrimages.com.

Appendix

How to Become a
Spiritual Child of Padre Pio

DURING his lifetime, Padre Pio accepted countless persons as his "spiritual children." What does this mean? We can answer in Padre Pio's own words. The following quotes from him are found in many books and articles but have been conveniently gathered together on the home page of the Padre Pio Foundation of America:*

"I love my spiritual children as much as my own soul, and even more."

"Once I take a soul on, I also take on his entire family as my spiritual children."

"To my spiritual children, my prayers for you will never be lacking."

"If one of my spiritual children ever goes astray, I shall leave my flock and seek him out."

These promises are capped by the famous "Great Promise" of Padre Pio, which he repeated many times: "I will ask the Lord to let me remain at the threshold of Paradise, and I will not enter until the last of my spiritual children has entered."[1]

Even now, after Padre Pio's death, one can still become a spiritual child of Padre Pio.

*www.padrepio.com

The Friary at San Giovanni Rotondo has enumerated the following five conditions for becoming Padre Pio's spiritual child:

1. To live intensely a life of divine grace.
2. To prove your faith with words and actions, living a true Christian life.
3. To desire to remain under the protection of St. Padre Pio and to want to enjoy the fruits of his prayers and sufferings.
4. To imitate Padre Pio's virtue, particularly his love for Jesus Crucified, for the Most Blessed Sacrament, for the Madonna, for the Pope, and for the entire Church.
5. To be animated by a sincere spirit of charity towards all.

If you have not already done so, you can ask St. Padre Pio in your heart to be his spiritual child, or you can be formally enrolled. One way to do this is by requesting either the Padre Pio Foundation of America or the National Centre for Padre Pio to enroll you; see Chapter 33 for contact information.

You may also enroll by writing to the Friary directly. It is customary to enclose a small donation.

Our Lady of Grace Capuchin Friary
71013 San Giovanni Rotondo
(FG) Italy.

Chapter Notes

INTRODUCTION.

1. Bonaventura Massa, *Mary Pyle: She Lived Doing Good to All* (hereafter identified as *Massa*), San Giovanni Rotondo, 1986, p. 143.
2. *Ibid.*, p. 21.
3. Joseph Pius, *The Voice of Padre Pio*, Vol. XV, No. 3, 1985, p. 3.

Chapter 1. PIETRELCINA

1. Alessandro da Ripabottoni, *Padre Pio of Pietrelcina: Everybody's Cyrenean* (hereafter *Ripabottoni*), San Giovanni Rotondo, 1987, p. 11.
2. Alberto D'Apolito, *Padre Pio of Pietrelcina: Memories, Experiences, Testimonials* (hereafter *D'Apolito*), San Giovanni Rotondo, 1986, p. 31.
3. *Ripabottoni*, p. 11.
4. Alessandro da Ripabottoni, *Guide to Padre Pio's Pietrelcina* (hereafter *Guide*), San Giovanni Rotondo, 1987, p. 16.
5. C. Bernard Ruffin, *Padre Pio: The True Story (Revised and Expanded)* (hereafter *Ruffin*), Huntington, IN, 1991, p. 25.
6. John A. Schug, *Padre Pio* (hereafter *Schug*), Chicago, 1983, p. 15.

7. *Ripabottoni*, p. 18.
8. Fr. Stefano M. Manelli, *Padre Pio of Pietrelcina*, New Bedford, MA, 1999, p. 11.
9. *Guide*, p. 28.
10. Augustine McGregor, *Padre Pio: His Early Years* (hereafter *McGregor*), San Giovanni Rotondo, 1981, p. 83.

Chapter 2. "EMIGRATE OR STEAL . . ."

1. P. Pio Antonio Finizio, *Voce di Padre Pio* (hereafter *Finizio*), Vol. XXXIV, No. 9, 2003, p. 28.
2. *Ruffin*, p. 36.
3. Mary F. Ingoldsby, *Padre Pio: His Life and Mission*, Dublin, 1988, p. 10.
4. *Finizio*, p. 29 (present author's translation).
5. *Ibid.*
6. *Ruffin*, p. 94.
7. *Schug*, p. 22.

Chapter 3. ROAD TO THE PRIESTHOOD

1. *Schug*, p. 30.
2. Padre Pio of Pietrelcina, *Letters, Vol. III: Correspondence with His Spiritual Daughters (1915-1923)*, San Giovanni Rotondo, 1994, p. 1016.

Note: For the publishers of these works, please see the Sources (p. 304).

3. Rino Cammilleri, *La Storia di Padre Pio*, Casale Monferrato, 1995, p. 21.
4. Nesta De Robeck, *Padre Pio* (hereafter *Nesta*), Milwaukee, 1958, p. 11.
5. Jim Gallagher, *Padre Pio: The Pierced Priest* (hereafter *Gallagher*), London, 1995, p. 26.
6. *Nesta*, p. 12.
7. *Ruffin*, p. 53.
8. Maria Winowska, *The True Face of Padre Pio* (hereafter *Winowska*), London, 1961, p. 58.
9. *Ibid.*
10. *McGregor*, p. 102.
11. *Ripabottoni*, p. 40.
12. *Ibid.*, p. 41.
13. *Ibid.*, p. 41.
14. *Ruffin*, p. 54.
15. *Schug*, pp. 31-32.
16. *Gallagher*, p. 46
17. Padre Pio of Pietrelcina, *Letters, Vol. I: Correspondence with his Spiritual Directors (1910-1922)* (hereafter *Letters I*), San Giovanni Rotondo, 1980, p. 204.
18. *Guide*, p. 20.
19. Padre Pio of Pietrelcina, *Letters, Vol. I: Correspondence with his Spiritual Directors (1910-1922)*, San Giovanni Rotondo, 1980.

Chapter 4.
THE "INVISIBLE" STIGMATA

1. *Letters I*, p. 234.
2. *Ibid.*, pp. 235-236.
3. Graziella DeNunzio Mandato, *Padre Pio: Encounters with a Spiritual Daughter from Pietrelcina*, Sea Bright, NJ, 2002, p. 10.
4. *Ruffin*, p. 79.
5. *Letters I*, pp. 264-265.
6. *Ibid.*, p. 300.
7. *Ibid.*, pp. 746-747.
8. Giorgio Cruchon, *Acts of the First Congress of Studies on Padre Pio's Spirituality*, (ed. by Fr. Gerardo Di Flumeri), San Giovanni Rotondo, 1978, p. 127.

Chapter 5. FOGGIA

1. *Ruffin*, p. 85.
2. *Letters I*, p. 770.
3. Padre Pio of Pietrelcina, *Letters, Vol. II: Correspondence with Raffaelina Cerase Noblewoman (1914–1915)* (hereafter *Letters II*), San Giovanni Rotondo, 1987, p. 563.
4. *Ruffin*, p. 125.
5. *Letters II*, p. 8.
6. *Letters I*, p. 896.
7. *Ibid.*, p. 888.

Chapter 6. MARY MCALPIN PYLE

1. Dorothy M. Gaudiose, *Mary's House. Mary Pyle: Under the Spiritual Guidance of Padre Pio* (hereafter *Gaudiose*), New York, 1993, p. 37.
2. *Ruffin*, p. 212.
3. *Gaudiose*, p. 38.
4. *Ruffin*, p. 212.
5. Even if already baptized when they were Protestants, con-

verts to the Catholic Faith sometimes receive "conditional" Baptism, if there is no documentation to determine whether the original ceremony actually occurred, or was acceptable according to Catholic standards. The conditional Baptism would be valid only on the *condition* that there had been some invalidating defect in the earlier ceremony. The words used by the priest in performing a conditional Baptism would be these or similar words: "If you are not baptized, I baptize you . . ."

6. *Ruffin*, p. 213.
7. *Schug*, p. 147.
8. *Gallagher*, p. 108.
9. *Ruffin*, p. 213.
10. *Ibid.*
11. *Gaudiose*, p. 41.

Chapter 7. FROM SPIRITUAL DIRECTOR TO SOLDIER

1. Renzo Allegri, *Padre Pio: Man of Hope* (hereafter *Allegri*), Ann Arbor, 2000, p. 62.
2. *Ruffin*, p. 133.
3. Padre Pio of Pietrelcina, *Letters, Vol. III: Correspondence with His Spiritual Daughters (1915–1923)*, San Giovanni Rotondo, 1994.
4. *Letters II*, p. 291.
5. *Ripabottoni*, p. 85.
6. *Letters I*, pp. 950-951.
7. Pascal P. Parente, *A City on a Mountain: Padre Pio of Pietrel-*

cina (hereafter *Parente*), St. Meinrad, IN, 1956, p. 31.

Chapter 8. "MY GOD, MY GOD, WHY HAST THOU FORSAKEN ME?"

1. *Letters I*, p. 1139.
2. *Ibid.*, p. 1148.
3. *Ibid.*, p. 1172.
4. *Ibid.*, p. 169.
5. *Ibid.*, p. 1178.
6. *Ibid.*, p. 1180.
7. *Ibid.*, p. 1186.
8. Joan Carroll Cruz, *Mysteries, Marvels, Miracles—in the Lives of the Saints*, Rockford IL, 1997, pp. 66-68.
9. *Letters I*, p. 175.
10. *Ruffin*, p. 152.

Chapter 9. THE IMPRINT OF GOD

1. *Letters I*, pp 1217-1218.
2. *Ruffin*, p. 155.
3. Gennaro Preziuso, *The Life of Padre Pio: Between the Altar and the Confessional* (hereafter *Preziuso*), New York, 2002, pp. 108-109.
4. *Ruffin*, p. 154.
5. *Letters I*, p. 1218.
6. *Ibid.*, p. 1257.
7. *Ruffin*, p. 166.
8. Gerardo Saldutto, *Un Tormentato Settennio (1918-1925) Nella Vita di Padre Pio da Pietrelcina*, (Doctoral Dissertation, Gregorian Pontifical University, Rome; hereafter *Saldutto*), San Giovanni Rotondo, 1986, p. 223 (present author's translation).

9. *Ibid.*, pp. 223-224.
10. *Ruffin*, p. 161.
11. *Allegri*, p. 153.
12. *Ripabottoni*, p. 107.
13. *Allegri*, p. 145.
14. *Letters I*, p. 1341.

Chapter 10. The Doctors are Summoned
1. *Ripabottoni*, pp. 98-99.
2. *Ibid.*, p. 99.
3. *Preziuso*, p.116.
4. *Ibid.*, p. 118.
5. *Schug*, p. 81.
6. John A. Schug, *A Padre Pio Profile* (hereafter *Profile*), Petersham, MA, 1987, p. 62.

Chapter 11. "l'Americana" Arrives
1. *Massa*, p. 20.
2. *Ibid.*
3. *Ruffin*, p. 214.
4. *Massa*, p. 21.
5. Geraldine Nolan, *A View of Padre Pio from Mary's House* (hereafter *Nolan*), San Giovanni Rotondo, 1993, p. 39.
6. *Massa*, p. 21.
7. *Gaudiose*, p. 44.
8. *Ibid.*
9. *Ibid.*, p. 45.
10. *Ibid.*
11. *Winowska*, p. 49.
12. *Gaudiose*, p. 47.
13. *Massa*, p. 25.
14. Paolo Scarano, *Gente*, September 25, 1997, p. 126.
15. *Ruffin*, p. 215.
16. *Gaudiose*, p. 52.

17. *Nolan*, p. 41.
18. *Gaudiose*, p. 46.
19. *Winowska*, p. 33.
20. *Massa*, p. 182.
21. *Nolan*, p. 52.
22. *Massa*, p. 27.
23. *Ibid.*, p. 28.
24. *Winowska*, p. 18.
25. *Gaudiose*, p. 50.
26. *Ibid.*, p. 53.
27. *Massa*, p. 38.

Chapter 12. Opposition and the First Suppression
1. *Ruffin*, p. 178.
2. *Allegri*, pp. 82-83.
3. *Preziuso*, p. 120.
4. *Ruffin*, p. 188.
5. *Ibid.*, p. 187.
6. *Preziuso*, p. 125.
7. *Ruffin*, p. 198.
8. *Ibid.*, p. 190.
9. *Ibid.*, p. 191.
10. *Ibid.*, p. 192.
11. *Ripabottoni*, p. 126.
12. *Saldutto*, pp. 154-155.
13. *Preziuso*, p. 127.
14. *Ripabottoni*, p. 254.
15. *Schug*, p. 99.
16. *Saldutto*, p. 172 (present author's translation).
17. *Ibid.*
18. *Ripabottoni*, p. 132.
19. *Preziuso*, p. 130.
20. *Ripabottoni*, p. 134.

Chapter 13. "l'Americana" as Collaborator
1. *Gaudiose*, p. 47.
2. *Ibid.*, p. 30.

3. *Guide*, p. 29.
4. Rev. Charles Mortimer Carty, *Padre Pio: The Stigmatist* (hereafter *Carty*), Rockford, IL, 1973, p. ix.
5. *Ibid.*
6. *Guide*, p. 29.
7. *Ruffin*, p. 216.
8. *Ibid.*, p. 217.
9. *Guide*, p. 30.
10. *Gaudiose*, p. 34.
11. *Ruffin*, p. 274.
12. *Ibid.*, p. 273.
13. www.pietrelcina.com/sacrafam. htm.
14. *Parente*, p. 89.
15. *Massa*, p. 227.
16. *Ruffin*, p. 225.
17. *Preziuso*, p. 137.
18. *Nolan*, p. 93.
19. *Massa*, p. 107.
20. *Ripabottoni*, p. 150.
21. *Preziuso*, p. 138.
22. *Ripabottoni*, p. 151.
23. *Nolan*, p. 95.
24. *Massa*, p. 230.
25. *Ibid.*, p. 138.

Chapter 14.
THE "IMPRISONMENT"

1. *Preziuso*, p. 140.
2. *Ripabottoni*, p. 161.
3. *Ruffin*, p. 230.
4. *Ripabottoni*, p. 165.
5. Cleonice Morcaldi, *La Mia Vita Vicino a Padre Pio: Diario Intimo Spirituale*, Rome, 1997.
6. *Ibid.*, p. 65 (present author's translation).
7. *Ibid.*

8. *Gaudiose*, p. 100.
9. *Ibid.*
10. *Ibid.*, p. 98.
11. *Ruffin*, p. 233.
12. *Ibid.*, p. 265.
13. *Gaudiose*, p. 99.
14. *Massa*, pp. 168-170.
15. *Schug*, p. 105.
16. *Gaudiose*, p. 100.
17. Cleonice Morcaldi, *Voce di Padre Pio*, Vol. XXXII, No. 3, 2001, p. 23, (present author's translation).
18. *Massa*, p. 232.
19. *Gaudiose*, p. 101.

Chapter 15.
MORE THAN A MYSTIC

1. Francesco Napolitano, *Padre Pio of Pietrelcina: Brief Biography* (hereafter *Napolitano*), San Giovanni Rotondo, 1979, p. 101.
2. Gherardo Leone, *Padre Pio and His Work* (hereafter *His Work*), San Giovanni Rotondo, 1986, p. 23.
3. *Ripabottoni*, p. 182.
4. *His Work*, p. 23.
5. *Ruffin*, p. 246.
6. *Preziuso*, p. 155.
7. *His Work*, p. 24.
8. *Ibid.*, p. 32.
9. *Ibid.*, p. 27.

Chapter 16. MARY PYLE
"INTERNED" AT PIETRELCINA

1. *Massa*, p. 34.
2. *Ibid.*, p. 36.
3. *Ibid.*, p. 37.

4. *Gaudiose*, p. 105.
5. Dorothy M. Gaudiose, *Prophet of the People: A Biography of Padre Pio*, New York, 1992, p. 140.
6. *Gaudiose*, p. 105.
7. *Massa*, p. 174.

Chapter 17. THE HOLY MAN ON THE MOUNTAIN

1. Information on Joe De Santis provided by Ray Ewen (see note 2 below).
2. Ray Ewen, phone interviews and correspondence beginning January 10, 2004.
3. *Ruffin*, p. 257.
4. Joseph Revelas, phone interviews and correspondence beginning February 4, 2004.
5. Fr. Paul Trinchard, *The Mass that Made Padre Pio*, Metairie, LA, 1997, p. 246.
6. Information on Bob Mohs provided by Joseph Revelas.

**Chapter 18.
"STRUCK" BY PADRE PIO**

1. Eugene McMahon, phone interviews and correspondence beginning January 13, 2004.
2. Anthony Afflitto, phone interviews and correspondence beginning January 5, 2004.
3. Carl Amato, phone interviews beginning January 12, 2004.
4. Pete Mier, phone interview January 9, 2004.
5. Joe Haines, phone interview and correspondence, beginning

January 6, 2004.
6. Robert Simmons, phone interview March 9, 2004.
7. Ed Karnes, phone interview May 10, 2004.
8. *Ruffin*, p. 264.
9. Fr. Leo Fanning, phone interviews beginning March 23, 2004.
10. *Ruffin*, p. 266.
11. *Ibid.*, p. 264.
12. *Ibid.*, p. 268.
13. Fr. Leo Fanning (see note 9).
14. Information on Fr. John McKenna provided by Charles Mandina, phone interviews and correspondence beginning December 30, 2003, and by Vince Crisci, email exchanges and phone interview beginning March 10, 2004.

**Chapter 19.
PADRE PIO "REMEMBRANCES"**

1. Information on Bob Coble provided by Alice Coble, email exchanges and correspondence beginning November 21, 2003.
2. Bob Coble, *The Voice of Padre Pio*, Vol. XXIII, No. 12, 1993, pp. 14-17.
3. Margie MacMillan, phone conversation February 20, 2004.
4. Bob Coble (editor), *Padre Pio: Remembrances*, Unpublished Manuscript.
5. Thom Peluso, email of April 20, 2004.
6. *Ruffin*, p. 270.

**Chapter 20. THREE AMERICAN
SPIRITUAL CHILDREN**
1. Mrs. Rita Peluso, phone interviews and correspondence beginning February 9, 2004.
2. Joseph Peluso Family, Copyright 2004, used by permission.
3. Phone interview with Joseph Peluso conducted by Fr. John Schug, July 2, 1993, made available courtesy of C. Bernard Ruffin.
4. *Ibid.*

**Chapter 22.
"RAY OF GOD'S LIGHT"**
1. Raymond Bunten, phone interview January 14, 2004. Most of his letter from the Coble manuscript is presented, with only minor editing.

**Chapter 23.
MORE VISITORS FROM THE 345TH**
1. Art Lucchesi, phone interviews and correspondence beginning January 15, 2004.
2. Ray Luichinger, phone interview February 20, 2004.
3. Dan Lemon, phone interview and correspondence beginning February 11, 2004.

**Chapter 24.
"THE ONLY PIECE OF HEAVEN
THAT I HAVE EVER KNOWN"**
1. Mario Avignone, phone interviews and correspondence, beginning March 11, 2004.

2. Mario Avignone, *Padre Pio: My Friend and Spiritual Father*, Unpublished Manuscript.

**Chapter 25. WILLIAM CARRIGAN
AND JOE PETERSON**
1. *Ruffin*, p. 258.
2. *Ibid.*, p. 259.
3. William M. Carrigan, "An Introduction to Padre Pio" (hereafter *Carrigan*), speech posted on www.padrepio.net.
4. *Ibid.*
5. *Ruffin*, p. 260.
6. Anne Wilson (editor), *Padre Pio of Pietrelcina: Walking in the Footsteps of Jesus Christ* (hereafter *Footsteps*), St. Paul, MN, 1993, pp. 5-10.
7. *Carrigan*, www.padrepio.net.
8. *Ruffin*, p. 267.
9. *Ibid.*, p. 292.
10. Fr. Ladis J. Cizik, Homily of Sunday, September 23, 2001, The National Blue Army Shrine of the Immaculate Heart of Mary, Washington, New Jersey, www.bluearmy.com
11. Joe Peterson, *Catholic Traveler* magazine (hereafter *Traveler*), Spring 1963, p. 52, (no longer published).
12. John McCaffery, *The Friar of San Giovanni: Tales of Padre Pio* (hereafter *McCaffery*), London, 1978, p. 98.
13. Dorothy Day, "On Pilgrimage—October 1963, *The Catholic Worker*, October 1963, pp. 3-8. This article (not copyrighted) is

available at www.catholic worker.org/dorothyday/.

14. *Traveler*, p. 51.
15. Bill Accousti, email exchanges and phone interviews, beginning April 24, 2004.

Chapter 26. THE FLYING MONK

1. Norman Lewis, *Naples '44*, New York, 1994, p. 110.
2. *Gaudiose*, pp. 109-110.
3. Piera Delfino Sessa, *Padre Pio da Pietrelcina*, Genova, 1950, p. 11.
4. *Parente*, p. 90.
5. Malachy Gerard Carroll, *Padre Pio*, Chicago, 1955, p. 39.
6. *McCaffery*, pp. 31-32.
7. *Massa*, pp. 195-196.
8. *Gaudiose*, pp. 109-110.
9. Paolo Scarano, *Gente*, October 24, 1994, p. 32.
10. Pascal Cataneo, *Padre Pio Gleanings* (hereafter *Gleanings*), Quebec, 1991, p. 99.
11. Renzo Allegri, *I Miracoli di Padre Pio* (hereafter *Miracoli*), Milan, 1993, pp. 110-111.
12. *Allegri*, p. 131.
13. *Carty*, pp. 23-24.
14. *Ruffin*, p. 250.
15. *Ibid.*
16. *Miracoli*, pp. 110-111.
17. *Ruffin*, p. 252.
18. *Footsteps*, p. 65.
19. *Gleanings*, p. 107.
20. Gaetano Pavone, phone interviews and correspondence beginning February 26, 2004.
21. Information on Bob Coble provided by Art Lucchesi, phone interviews and correspondence beginning January 15, 2004.

Chapter 27. POSTWAR, AND THE "WORK" OF PADRE PIO

1. Renato Luisi, *The Voice of Padre Pio*, Vol. VIII, No. 1, 1978, pp. 15-16.
2. *Ibid.*, p. 15.
3. *Nolan*, p. 106.
4. *Ruffin*, p. 271.
5. *Gaudiose*, p. 121.
6. Cleonice Morcaldi, *La Casa Sollievo della Sofferenza*, January-February 2004, Nos. 1 & 2, p. 14.
7. *Allegri*, p 196.
8. *Schug*, p. 222.
9. *Allegri*, p. 196.
10. *Ruffin*, p. 283.
11. *Preziuso*, p. 160.
12. *Gallagher*, p. 142.
13. *His Work*, p. 38.
14. *Allegri*, p. 197.
15. *Preziuso*, p. 162.
16. *Ibid.*, p. 164.
17. *His Work*, p. 151.
18. *Ibid.*, pp. 156-157.
19. *Ruffin*, p. 359.

Chapter 28. PADRE PIO PRAYER GROUPS

1. *Ripabottoni*, p. 198.
2. *Napolitano*, p. 149.
3. *D'Apolito*, p. 213.
4. Pope John Paul II, "Guard and Spread Padre Pio's Great Legacy," *l'Osservatore Romano*, Weekly English Language Edi-

tion, March 24, 2004, p. 9.
5. *His Work*, p. 49.
6. Riccardo Ruotolo, *The Prayer Groups of Padre Pio: Historical Notes, New Statute*, San Giovanni Rotondo, 1986, p. 41.
7. *Ibid.*, p. 51.
8. Fr. Francis Sariego, phone interviews beginning April 23, 2004.
9. Charles Mandina, phone interviews and correspondence beginning December 30, 2003.
10. *Ripabottoni*, p. 240.
11. Andrew Walther, *National Catholic Register*, September 15-21, 2002, p. 10.
12. Magneli Villanueva, email exchanges beginning April 16, 2004.
13. Mario Bruschi, phone interviews and correspondence beginning March 29, 2004.
14. Bro. Francis Mary Kalvelage, (editor), *Padre Pio: The Wonder Worker* (hereafter *Kalvelage*), New Bedford, MA, 1999, p. 199.
15. *Footsteps*, p. 60.

Chapter 29. THE LAST DECADE
1. *Preziuso*, p. 199.
2. Bill Accousti, phone interviews and email exchanges, beginning April 24, 2004.
3. *Ruffin*, p. 238.
4. *Allegri*, p. 216.
5. *Ruffin*, p. 354.
6. *Allegri*, p. 126.
7. *His Work*, p. 85.

8. *Allegri*, p. 218.
9. *Ruffin*, p. 354.
10. *Ibid.*, p. 353.
11. *Gallagher*, p. 173.
12. *Allegri*, pp. 218-219.
13. *Ibid.*, pp. 220-221
14. *Alimenti*, p. 156.
15. *Ruffin*, p. 357.
16. *His Work*, p. 89.
17. *Ruffin*, p. 358.
18. *Allegri*, p. 221.
19. *Preziuso*, p. 200.
20. *Allegri*, p. 223.
21. Carmelina Tamburrano, *La Casa Sollievo della Sofferenza*, January-February 2004, Nos. 1 & 2, p. 17.
22. *Allegri*, p. 225.
23. *Ibid.*, pp. 230-232.
24. *Ibid.*, p. 232.
25. *Ruffin*, p. 362.
26. *Napolitano*, p. 164.
27. *Ruffin*, pp. 361-362.
28. *Massa*, pp. 53-55.
29. *Gaudiose*, p. 172.
30. *Ibid.*, p. 178.
31. *Massa*, p. 52.
32. *Gaudiose*, p. 179.
33. *Massa*, p. 48.
34. *Ibid.*, p. 51.
35. *Ibid.*, p. 53.
36. *Ibid.* (A "lustra" is a five-year period.)
37. *Gaudiose*, p. 65.
38. *Massa*, pp. 205-206.
39. *Ibid.*, p. 56.
40. *Ibid.*, p. 57.
41. *Guide*, p. 49.

Chapter 30. FINAL WEEKEND . . .
JOY TURNED TO MOURNING
1. *Ruffin*, p. 371.
2. *Preziuso*, p. 206.
3. *D'Apolito*, p. 320.
4. *Schug*, p. 230.
5. *Allegri*, p. 243.
6. *Ibid.*
7. *D'Apolito*, pp. 321-322.
8. *Ibid.*, pp. 322-323.
9. *Napolitano*, p. 228.
10. *Allegri*, p. 245.
11. *Napolitano*, p. 232.
12. *Allegri*, p. 246.
13. *Ripabottoni*, p. 247.
14. *Gallagher*, p. 196.
15. *Schug*, p. 234.
16. *Ripabottoni*, p. 247.
17. *Ibid.*, pp. 248-249.
18. *Allegri*, p. 249.
19. *Ibid.*
20. *Preziuso*, p. 211.
21. *Napolitano*, p. 240.
22. *Preziuso*, p. 212.
23. *Ruffin*, p. 377.
24. *Allegri*, p. 253.
25. *His Work*, p. 98.
26. *Ripabottoni*, p. 253.
27. *Ibid.*, p. 254.
28. Andrea Tornielli, article in the Italian weekly, *Gente* (dateline San Giovanni Rotondo), June 27, 2002, pp. 21-25; the article is based on the book *Padre Pio, sulla soglia del Paradiso*, by Saverio Gaeta, Edizioni San Paolo, Cinisello Balsamo (MI), 2002.
29. *Ibid.*
30. *Ibid.*

Chapter 31. "BROTHER BILL."
1. *The Voice of Padre Pio*, Vol. XXX, No. 6, 2000, p. 23, (no author specified).
2. *Ibid.*
3. *Gallagher*, p. 200.
4. *Profile*, pp. 63-64.
5. *Ibid.*, p. 71.
6. *Ibid.*
7. *Ibid.*, pp. 72-73.
8. Jeanette Salerno, email exchanges beginning June 14, 2004.
9. Padre Paolo Cuvino, *The Voice of Padre Pio*, Vol. XXXI, No. 3, 2001, p.14.

Chapter 32.
TWO UNIQUE APOSTOLATES
1. Diane Allen, email exchanges and phone interviews beginning February 3, 2004.
2. Vincent Falco, phone interviews beginning January 23, 2004.
3. Liz Balmaseda, *The Miami Herald*, Sunday, June 23, 2002, p. 19B.

Chapter 33.
TWO MAJOR MINISTRIES
1. *Kalvelage*, p. 197.
2. Bro. Francis Mary, *Immaculata*, Fall 1973 special Padre Pio issue, p. 33.
3. *Ibid.*, p. 34.
4. Padre Pellegrino Funicelli, *The Voice of Padre Pio*, Vol. VIII, No. 1, 1978, p. 9.

Chapter 34.
RECENT DEVELOPMENTS

1. Paolo Scarano, *Gente*, October 24, 2002, pp. 70-74.
2. Pope John Paul II, "Guard and Spread Padre Pio's Great Legacy," *l'Osservatore Romano*, Weekly English Language Edition, March 24, 2004, p. 9.
3. Stefano Campanella, *Voce di Padre Pio*, Vol. XXXV, No. 5, May 2004, p. 49.
4. Mauro Sollazzo, *Magazine of Culture, Religious and Current Affairs*, Year 7, No. 1, Jan-Feb-Mar 2004, p. 2.

EPILOGUE
1. *Ruffin*, p. 248.

APPENDIX
1. Saverio Gaeta, *Padre Pio, sulla soglia del Paradiso* ["Padre Pio, at the Threshold of Paradise"] (Cinisello Balsamo (MI): Edizioni San Paolo), 2002.

Sources

Books

Acts of the First Congress of Studies on Padre Pio's Spirituality, (ed. by Fr. Gerardo Di Flumeri), San Giovanni Rotondo, Edizioni Padre Pio da Pietrelcina, 1978.

Alimenti, Dante, *Padre Pio*, Bergamo, Italy, VELAR, 1984.

Allegri, Renzo, *I Miracoli di Padre Pio*, Milan, Oscar Mondadori, 1993.

Allegri, Renzo, *Padre Pio: Man of Hope*, Ann Arbor, MI, Servant Publications, 2000.

Avignone, Mario, *Padre Pio: My Friend and Spiritual Father*, Unpublished Manuscript.

Cammilleri, Rino, *La Storia di Padre Pio*, Casale Monferrato, Edizione Piemme, 1995.

Carroll, Malachy Gerard, *Padre Pio*, Chicago, Henry Regnery Company, 1955.

Carty, Rev. Charles Mortimer, *Padre Pio: The Stigmatist*, Rockford, IL., TAN Books and Publishers, Inc., 1973.

Cataneo, Pascal, *Padre Pio Gleanings*, Sherbrooke, Quebec, Editions Paulines, 1991.

Coble, Bob (editor) *Padre Pio: Remembrances*, Unpublished Manuscript.

Cruz, Joan Carroll, *Mysteries, Marvels, Miracles—in the Lives of the Saints*, Rockford, IL, TAN Books and Publishers, Inc., 1997.

D'Apolito, Alberto, *Padre Pio of Pietrelcina: Memories, Experiences, Testimonials*, (trans. by Frank and Julia Ceravolo, Betsy Ann Spach), San Giovanni Rotondo, Editions: Padre Pio of Pietrelcina, 1986.

Douay-Rheims Bible, rpt. Rockford, IL, TAN Books and Publishers, Inc., 1989.

Gallagher, Jim, *Padre Pio: The Pierced Priest*, London, HarperCollins, 1995.

Gaudiose, Dorothy M., *Prophet of the People: A Biography of Padre Pio*, New York, Alba House, 1992.

Gaudiose, Dorothy M., *Mary's House. Mary Pyle: Under the Spiritual Guidance of Padre Pio*, New York, Alba House, 1993.

Ingoldsby, Mary F., *Padre Pio: His Life and Mission*, Dublin, Veritas Publications, 1988.

Kalvelage, Bro. Francis Mary (editor), *Padre Pio: The Wonder Worker*, New

Bedford, MA, Franciscan Friars of the Immaculate, 1999.

Leone, Gherardo, *Padre Pio and His Work*, San Giovanni Rotondo, Editions Casa Sollievo della Sofferenza, 1986.

Lewis, Norman, *Naples '44*, New York, Henry Holt, 1994.

Mandato, Graziella DeNunzio, *Padre Pio: Encounters with a Spiritual Daughter from Pietrelcina*, Sea Bright, NJ, Angelus Media Distribution Group, 2002.

Manelli, Stefano, *Padre Pio of Pietrelcina*, New Bedford, MA, Franciscans of the Immaculate, 1999.

Massa, Bonaventura, *Mary Pyle: She Lived Doing Good to All*, San Giovanni Rotondo, Our Lady of Grace Capuchin Friary, 1986.

McCaffery, John, *The Friar of San Giovanni: Tales of Padre Pio*, London, Darton, Longman & Todd, Ltd., 1978.

McGregor, Augustine, *Padre Pio: His Early Years*, (ed. by Fr. Alessio Parente), San Giovanni Rotondo, Editions: The Voice of Padre Pio, 1981.

Morcaldi, Cleonice, *La Mia Vita Vicino a Padre Pio: Diario Intimo Spirituale*, Rome, Edizione Dehoniane, 1997.

Napolitano, Francesco, *Padre Pio of Pietrelcina: Brief Biography*, (ed. by Fr. Alessio Parente), San Giovanni Rotondo, Edizioni Voce di Padre Pio, 1979.

Nolan, Geraldine, *A View of Padre Pio from Mary's House*, (ed. by Fr. Alessio Parente), San Giovanni Rotondo, Our Lady of Grace Capuchin Friary, 1993.

Padre Pio of Pietrelcina, *Letters, Vol. I: Correspondence with his Spiritual Directors (1910–1922)*, (ed. by Fr. Gerardo Di Flumeri), San Giovanni Rotondo, Editions: Voce di Padre Pio, 1980.

Padre Pio of Pietrelcina, *Letters, Vol. II: Correspondence with Raffaelina Cerase Noblewoman (1914–1915)*, (ed. by Fr. Gerardo Di Flumeri), San Giovanni Rotondo, Editions: Padre Pio da Pietrelcina, 1987.

Padre Pio of Pietrelcina, *Letters, Vol. III: Correspondence with His Spiritual Daughters (1915–1923)*, (ed. by Fr. Allesio Parente), San Giovanni Rotondo, Editions: Padre Pio da Pietrelcina, 1994.

Parente, Pascal P., *A City on a Mountain: Padre Pio of Pietrelcina*, St. Meinrad, IN, Grail Publications, 1956.

Preziuso, Gennaro, *The Life of Padre Pio: Between the Altar and the Confessional*, Alba House, New York, 2002.

Alessandro da Ripabottoni, *Padre Pio of Pietrelcina: Everybody's Cyrenean*, (ed. by Fr. Alessio Parente), San Giovanni Rotondo, Our Lady of Grace Capuchin Friary, 1987.

Alessandro da Ripabottoni, *Guide to Padre Pio's Pietrelcina*, (ed. by Fr.

Gerardo Di Flumeri), San Giovanni Rotondo, Editions: Padre Pio of Pietrelcina, 1987.

Robeck, Nesta De, *Padre Pio*, Milwaukee, Bruce Publishing, 1958.

Ruffin, Bernard, *Padre Pio: The True Story (Revised and Expanded)*, Huntington, IN, Our Sunday Visitor, 1991.

Ruotolo, Riccardo, *The Prayer Groups of Padre Pio: Historical Notes, New Statute*, San Giovanni Rotondo, Editions Casa Sollievo della Sofferenza, 1986.

Saldutto, Gerardo, *Un Tormentato Settennio (1918-1925) Nella Vita di Padre Pio da Pietrelcina*, San Giovanni Rotondo, Edizioni: Padre Pio da Pietrelcina, 1986.

Schug, John A., *A Padre Pio Profile*, Petersham, MA, St. Bede's Publications, 1987.

Schug, John A., *Padre Pio*, Chicago, Franciscan Herald Press, 1983.

Sessa, Piera Delfino, *Padre Pio da Pietrelcina*, Genova, Editrice Demos, 1950.

Trinchard, Fr. Paul, *The Mass that Made Padre Pio*, Metairie, LA, MAETA, 1997.

Wilson, Anne (editor), *Padre Pio of Pietrelcina: Walking in the Footsteps of Jesus Christ*, St. Paul, MN, Leaflet Missal Company, 1993.

Winowska, Maria, *The True Face of Padre Pio*, London, The Catholic Book Club, 1961.

Periodicals

Catholic Worker, The, New York, NY (published seven times a year; founded by Dorothy Day).

Gente: Settimanale di Attualita, Politica e Cultura, Milan, Italy, (Weekly Italian magazine of current events, politics, and culture).

Immaculata, monthly magazine formerly published by Franciscan Marytown Press, Kenosha, WI.

La Casa Sollievo della Sofferenza, Official Magazine of the Prayer Groups, San Giovanni Rotondo.

L'Osservatore Romano, Weekly English Language Edition, Vatican City.

Magazine of Culture, Religious and Current Affairs, Capuchin Friars, San Giovanni Rotondo.

Miami Herald, The, Miami FL. (Daily newspaper).

National Catholic Register, North Haven, CT. (Weekly Catholic newspaper).

Voce di Padre Pio, Piazzale "S. Maria delle Grazie," San Giovanni Rotondo

(Capuchin friars' Italian language monthly magazine).

Voice of Padre Pio, The, Piazzale "S. Maria delle Grazie," San Giovanni Rotondo (Capuchin friars' English language bi-monthly magazine).

Oral History

Accousti, Bill, email exchanges and phone interviews, beginning April 24, 2004.

Afflitto, Anthony, phone interviews and correspondence beginning January 5, 2004.

Allen, Diane, email exchanges and phone interviews, beginning February 3, 2004.

Amato, Carl, phone interviews beginning January 12, 2004.

Avignone, Mario, phone interviews and correspondence, beginning March 11, 2004.

Bruschi, Mario, phone interviews and correspondence beginning March 3, 2004.

Bunten, Raymond, phone interview January 14, 2004.

Coble, Alice, email exchanges and correspondence beginning November 21, 2003.

Crisci, Vince, email exchanges and phone interview beginning March 10, 2004.

De Bartoli, Susan, email exchanges and phone interviews beginning August 18, 2004.

Ewen, Ray, phone interviews and correspondence beginning January 10, 2004.

Falco, Vincent, phone interviews beginning January 23, 2004.

Fanning, Fr. Leo, phone interviews beginning March 23, 2004.

Haines, Joe, phone interview and correspondence beginning January 6, 2004.

Karnes, Edward, phone interview May 10, 2004.

Lemon, Dan, phone interview and correspondence beginning February 11, 2004.

Lucchesi, Art, phone interviews and correspondence beginning January 15, 2004.

Luichinger, Ray, phone interview February 20, 2004.

MacMillan, Margie, phone interview February 20, 2004.

Mandina, Charles, phone interviews and correspondence beginning December 30, 2003.

McMahon, Eugene, phone interviews and correspondence beginning January 13, 2004.

Mier, Pete, phone interview January 9, 2004.

Pavone, Gaetano, phone interviews and correspondence beginning February 26, 2004.

Peluso, Rita, phone interviews and correspondence beginning February 9, 2004.

Peluso, Thom, email exchanges and phone interviews beginning January 30, 2004.

Ruffin, Rev. C. Bernard, email exchanges and correspondence beginning March 24, 2004.

Salerno, Jeanette, email exchanges beginning June 14, 2004.

Revelas, Joseph, phone interviews and correspondence beginning February 4, 2004.

Sariego, Fr. Francis, phone interviews beginning April 23, 2004.

Simmons, Robert, phone interview March 9, 2004.

Villanueva, Magneli, email exchanges beginning April 16, 2004.

Winn, John and Janet, correspondence of March 2, 2004.

If you have enjoyed this book, consider making your next selection from among the following . . .

Prices subject to change.

Prices subject to change.

St. Teresa of Avila. *Forbes* 7.00
St. Ignatius Loyola. *Forbes* 7.00
St. Catherine of Siena. *Forbes* 7.00
The Agony of Jesus. *Padre Pio* 3.00
Sermons of the Curé of Ars. *Vianney* 15.00
St. Antony of the Desert. *St. Athanasius* 7.00
Is It a Saint's Name? *Fr. William Dunne* 3.00
St. Pius V—His Life, Times, Miracles. *Anderson* 7.00
Who Is Therese Neumann? *Fr. Charles Carty.* 3.50
Martyrs of the Coliseum. *Fr. O'Reilly.* 21.00
Way of the Cross. *St. Alphonsus Liguori* 1.50
Way of the Cross. *Franciscan version* 1.50
How Christ Said the First Mass. *Fr. Meagher* 21.00
Too Busy for God? Think Again! *D'Angelo* 7.00
St. Bernadette Soubirous. *Trochu* 21.00
Shroud of Turin. *Guerrera* 15.00
Treatise on the Love of God. 1 Vol. *St. Francis de Sales* 27.50
Confession Quizzes. *Radio Replies Press* 2.50
St. Philip Neri. *Fr. V. J. Matthews.* 7.50
St. Louise de Marillac. *Sr. Vincent Regnault* 7.50
The Old World and America. *Rev. Philip Furlong* 21.00
Prophecy for Today. *Edward Connor* 7.50
The Book of Infinite Love. *Mother de la Touche* 7.50
Chats with Converts. *Fr. M. D. Forrest.* 13.50
The Church Teaches. *Church Documents* 18.00
Conversation with Christ. *Peter T. Rohrbach* 12.50
Liberalism Is a Sin. *Sarda y Salvany* 9.00
Spiritual Legacy of Sr. Mary of the Trinity. *van den Broek* 13.00
The Creator and the Creature. *Fr. Frederick Faber* 17.50
Radio Replies. 3 Vols. *Frs. Rumble and Carty* 48.00
Convert's Catechism of Catholic Doctrine. *Fr. Geiermann* 5.00
Incarnation, Birth, Infancy of Jesus Christ. *St. Alphonsus* 13.50
Light and Peace. *Fr. R. P. Quadrupani* 8.00
Dogmatic Canons & Decrees of Trent, Vat. I. *Documents* 11.00
The Evolution Hoax Exposed. *A. N. Field* 9.00
The Priest, the Man of God. *St. Joseph Cafasso* 16.00
Blessed Sacrament. *Fr. Frederick Faber* 20.00
Christ Denied. *Fr. Paul Wickens* 3.50
New Regulations on Indulgences. *Fr. Winfrid Herbst* 3.00
A Tour of the Summa. *Msgr. Paul Glenn* 22.50
Spiritual Conferences. *Fr. Frederick Faber* 18.00
Latin Grammar. *Scanlon and Scanlon* 18.00
A Brief Life of Christ. *Fr. Rumble* 3.50
Marriage Quizzes. *Radio Replies Press* 2.50
True Church Quizzes. *Radio Replies Press* 2.50
The Secret of the Rosary. *St. Louis De Montfort* 5.00
Mary, Mother of the Church. *Church Documents* 5.00
The Sacred Heart and the Priesthood. *de la Touche* 10.00
Revelations of St. Bridget. *St. Bridget of Sweden* 4.50
Magnificent Prayers. *St. Bridget of Sweden* 2.00
The Happiness of Heaven. *Fr. J. Boudreau* 10.00
St. Catherine Labouré of the Miraculous Medal. *Dirvin* 16.50
The Glories of Mary. (Large ed.). *St. Alphonsus Liguori* 21.00

Prices subject to change.

Prices subject to change.

At your Bookdealer or direct from the Publisher.
Toll-Free 1-800-437-5876   **Fax 815-226-7770**
Tel. 815-226-7777   **www.tanbooks.com**

About the Author

A third Order (Secular) Franciscan, Frank Rega has long been an avid student of Padre Pio and St. Francis. He moderates a 350-member Internet St. Pio of Pietrelcina prayer and discussion group, and hosts a popular Padre Pio web site www.sanpadrepio.com. A Henry Rutgers Scholar and Phi Beta Kappa at Rutgers, Mr. Rega studied at Yale University's Institute of Human Relations on a Woodrow Wilson Fellowship. Most recently he was a software consultant for Compuware Corp., assigned to NASA and projects for the Department of Homeland Security.